The Political Economy of International Monetary Interdependence

The Political Economy of International Monetary Interdependence

Koichi Hamada

translated by
Charles Yuji Horioka
Chi-Hung Kwan

The MIT Press
Cambridge, Massachusetts
London, England

This book is an adapted translation of *Kokusai Kinyū no Seiji Keizaigaku*, Series of Quantitative Economics, no. 12 (Tokyo: Sōbunsha, 1982).

This book was set in Palatino by Asco Trade Typesetting Ltd., Hong Kong, and printed and bound by The Murray Printing Company in the United States of America.

Library of Congress Cataloging in Publication Data

Hamada, Koichi, 1936–
  The political economy of international monetary interdependence.

  Bibliography: p.
  Includes index.
  1. International finance.   2. Monetary policy.
I. Title.
HG3881.H266   1985   332'.042   85-8912
ISBN 0-262-08154-7

Contents

Preface

In a world where national economies have become more and more integrated, there is an urgent need to study the nature of interdependence among national economies. The nature of interdependence differs depending on whether the international monetary system is based on fixed exchange rates or on flexible exchange rates. Thus, the choice of an international monetary regime strongly influences the joint outcomes of the macroeconomic policies pursued by each country.

Two questions emerge when we consider the problem of the choice of an international monetary regime. First, how does the choice affect the nature of policy interdependence and the distribution of economic welfare among countries? Second, given the answer to the first question, what kind of international monetary regime will each country desire, and what kind of international monetary regime is likely to be realized?

I have been studying the politico-economic aspects of the choice of an international monetary regime and the interdependence of national monetary policies from these perspectives for more than ten years. This book integrates my articles on these subjects into a unified framework that is accessible to nontechnical readers.

In the first three chapters, I discuss the kinds of incentives participating countries face when deciding whether to agree on the adoption or alteration of a monetary regime. I will not be concerned so much with the question that already has been discussed extensively—the question of what is the ideal international monetary system—as with the question of what kinds of monetary regimes are more likely to be agreed on given the structure of the benefits and costs that those regimes confer on participating countries. In the second half of the book, I discuss how the nature of policy interdependence differs depending on the exchange rate regime. The linkages between national economies will be discussed not only in the context of extreme models of the Keynesian and monetarist types but also in the context of models in which inflation and unemployment coexist.

Throughout the book I appeal to the modern apparatus of economic theory. The concepts and frameworks of game theory, public economics, and oligopoly theory will be utilized extensively. These concepts and analytical methods will help us to understand the logical structure of the problem of interdependence.

In a world in which a few large nations have substantial influence, the recognition of mutual strategic interdependence is crucial. The analytical methods of oligopoly theory and game theory are effective for studying these situations. A system of flexible exchange rates has the merit of granting a higher degree of autonomy to the monetary authorities of participating countries as compared with a system of fixed exchange rates.

In the course of preparing this book, I have received support and assistance from many friends and colleagues. Makoto Sakurai of the Export-Import Bank of Japan kindly allowed me to incorporate a paper I wrote jointly with him into chapter 7. I would like to thank particularly Professor Ken-ichi Inada, editor of the Series of Quantitative Economics, and two anonymous referees for their helpful comments. Many other people have commented on various parts of the manuscript, and their help will be acknowledged at the beginning of each chapter. I am grateful to the Institute for Industrial Economics, the University of Tokyo, and the Tokyo Center for Economic Research for financial assistance. Finally, I thank Yūko Matsumoto and Yuriko Hiratsuka, who helped in preparing the manuscript, and Satoko Akita, who proofread the text. Mitsuo Koyama of the Sōbunsha Company edited the manuscript with great care and improved it substantially.

This book is dedicated to the late Professor Tsunehiko Watanabe. Tsunehiko Watanabe was not a specialist in international finance; however, he gave me stimulating criticism when I first presented some of the basic ideas developed in this book in a fragmentary, premature form at the Zushi Conference, organized by the Tokyo Center for Economic Research, in 1966. In the last conversation I had with him before his death, I told him of my plans to publish this book in the Series of Quantitative Economics, of which he was one of the enthusiastic editors. He always loved to talk to younger economists and to encourage our researches and experiments. I feel, still now, as if he were just about to appear beside my desk with his smiling, youthful face.

This is an adapted translation of my book *Kokusai Kinyū no Seiji Keizaigaku*, published by Sōbunsha in 1982. To this edition I have added a short postscript on recent developments in the field that seem to be attracting much attention.

I would like to express my sincere gratitude to the translators, Charles Yuji Horioka and Chi-Hung Kwan, who did a super job with speed and accuracy. I would also like to thank all my friends at Tokyo, Yale, MIT, LSE, and Chicago, where I have studied, visited, or taught. Particularly, I would like to express my gratitude to my teachers and advisers, to whom I owe much for my intellectual development in various stages of my study: Jagdish Bhagwati, Charles Kindleberger, Ryutaro Komiya, Franco Modigliani, Michio Morishima, Takashi Negishi, Yasuhiko Oishi, Edmund Phelps, Kazuo Sata, James Tobin, Robert Solow, Ryuichiro Tachi, and Hirofumi Uzawa.

With regard to the specific topic of this book, I am much indebted to Richard Cooper, who kindly helped me formulate my vague ideas into shape, and to Robert Aliber, who gave me chances to present my work to audiences at the Wingspread Conferences. I am also grateful to Rudiger Dornbusch, Jacob Frenkel, Marcus Miller, and Jeffrey Sachs for their encouragement in later stages. My thanks also go to Ryuhei Okumura, who pointed out errors in the Japanese edition, and to Tomoko Kashima, who typed the English manuscript so efficiently.

Last and by no means least, I would like to thank The MIT Press for the suggestion to prepare this English edition and for the excellent editing.

Koichi Hamada
June 1985

The Political Economy of
International Monetary
Interdependence

1

Political and Economic Aspects of International Monetary Relations

What is the ideal choice of an international monetary regime for the settlement of international transactions? This is a question of critical importance in a world economy in which flows of goods and services among countries are increasing constantly. Just as the levels of production and consumption activities, the distribution of income, and the rates of growth and inflation in a given country depend much on the nature and workings of that country's monetary regime, the levels of production and consumption activities and the rates of economic growth and inflation of the world economy, as well as the distribution of income between rich and poor countries, depend on the nature and workings of the international monetary system.

The domestic monetary system of a single country is ultimately based on national consensus and in many cases is the result of a long process of evolution. Seigniorage rights to issue money gradually became concentrated in the hands of a nation-state, while, at the same time, a national banking system gradually developed. By contrast, in the case of the international monetary system, political power is only partly concentrated, and because there exists no concentration of political power in the present world that is strong enough to be called a world government, the international monetary system is based directly and explicitly on a consensus among nations, albeit a consensus that reflects differences among nations in their relative bargaining power. When compared to the development process of domestic monetary systems, the prevailing stage of the international monetary system corresponds to the stage in which the consolidation of power had not yet been completed, many issuing banks coexisted, and many types of bank notes and coins circulated simultaneously. The situation may also be viewed as similar to the present state of international law, where power politics are often still explicit in resolving conflicts of interest among nations and where there still exist many treaties among nations that lack the power of enforcement.

There have been many proposals for the ideal international monetary regime, but most share a common shortcoming.[1] This shortcoming is that economists proposing an ideal regime discuss various desirable properties that would obtain if a particular regime were to be adopted but neglect to analyze the benefit-cost structure that affects the economic incentives of a country considering whether to join an agreement. In other words, they refrain from studying the political feasibility of their ideal plans. It is not sufficient to ask what the ideal international monetary system would be if feasibility considerations were disregarded. One should also ask what type of monetary regime is most likely to be adopted through negotiation in the light of the benefit-cost structure that each regime confers on the participating countries. This brings to mind one of Aesop's fables. Once the mice are able to put a bell on the cat, their problems would be solved. How to put the bell on the cat, however, remains the most difficult problem. One of the purposes of this book is to analyze the feasibility of international monetary reforms by clarifying the benefits and costs that accrue to each nation under alternative international monetary regimes.

The more integrated is the world economy through international trade and capital movements, the more interdependent become the effects of national economic policies. In the area of trade policy as well as in the interplay of macroeconomic policies, national policy authorities are compelled to act while taking account of the mutual interdependence of their economic policies. Moreover, the nature of this interdependence differs substantially depending on the nature of the international monetary regime. Another purpose of this book is to show that the interaction of economic policies, particularly monetary policies, takes different forms under alternative international regimes.

Let us start by clarifying two important concepts used in this book. "International monetary regime (or system)" refers to a set of rules, formal or informal, that governs the use of currencies in the settlement of international transactions such as trade and investment. As in the case of other economic institutions, the formation and development of an international monetary regime are based on an explicit or implicit consensus among the participants—in this case, nation-states. This book is designed to clarify the relationship between the rules of the international monetary system and the economic activities taking place under those rules.

Next, what is meant by "international interdependence"? The concept has at least three elements. The first element is the recognition that the world is closed as a whole and that Walras's Law holds for the world economy. The second element is that goods and assets of different countries are becoming closer substitutes for one another through the development of transportation and communications technology. The extreme examples of this are the purchasing-power-parity relationship in goods markets and perfect capital mobility in asset markets. Under such circumstances, as long as Japanese and American cars (for example) are homogeneous, their prices must be equal if converted into the same currency unit using the prevailing exchange rate. In fact, one of the merits of flexible exchange rates is that they block the link of substitutability among different national monies that exists under fixed exchange rates. The third element of interdependence is the small number of influential countries. Because the economic influence on the world economy of the United States, Germany, Japan, the European Community (EC), and the Organization of Petroleum Exporting Countries (OPEC) is quite strong, the authorities of these countries or groups of countries must take account of possible reactions from other major countries when formulating policy.

Brief History of the Postwar International Monetary System

The international monetary system has undergone several major changes during the postwar period. The Bretton Woods system (or the former IMF system) that endured for much of the postwar period was the result of cooperation among nations to prevent the undesirable consequences of the competitive devaluations that took place after World War I. It was a compromise between the Keynes plan of a "clearing union," representing the position of the British government, and the White plan, representing the position of the U.S. government. The compromise can be characterized as an adjustable peg system, but because the price of gold was fixed in terms of the dollar and because both gold and the dollar served as international currencies, it also retained certain characteristics of the gold exchange standard.

After the United States adopted a two-tier price system for gold in 1968, the international monetary system started losing its character as a gold standard and moved closer to a dollar standard. The critical date was August 1971, when President Nixon launched the New Economic Policy that destroyed the adjustable peg system root and branch. Thereafter, the floating exchange rate system came to be adopted by most developed countries. Except for a brief period between the end of 1971 and the beginning of 1973, when the Smithsonian system (a type of fixed exchange rate regime that allowed much wider margins of exchange rate fluctuations than the Bretton Woods system did) was in force, the international monetary system among developed countries has been dominated by a "managed float system." This series of major reforms resulting from the "Nixon shock" was based on unilateral action on the part of the United States designed to cope with its balance of payments crisis rather than on benefit-cost calculations by, or a consensus among, participating countries.

The fact that such reforms were inevitable suggests that the former IMF regime contained serious internal inconsistencies. First, while the credibility of the dollar was maintained by linking it to gold, the balance of payments deficits of the United States led to a decline in the credibility of the dollar, which in turn worsened the U.S. balance of payments. Thus there was an element of built-in instability in the system. Second, even after the link between gold and the dollar had been severed, the dollar standard could work well only if the United States assumed the role of maintaining world price stability. Once the United States abandoned this role and turned to the pursuit of policies directed at domestic objectives alone, the world economy was at the mercy of inflationary as well as deflationary pressures arising from U.S. monetary policies.

Efforts to restore international monetary stability and the operation of fixed exchange rates led to agreement on the formation of the Smithsonian system; however, this system lasted only briefly because it failed to cope with the rapidly changing international financial situation that was affected by external shocks such as the first oil crisis. Thereafter, the international monetary system transformed itself into a managed float system. Since 1973, despite the oil crisis and other disturbances, the world economy has func-tioned without any serious international monetary crises. Thus, it would be fair to say that the managed float system has worked despite its imperfections.

Method and Plan of the Book

In examinations of the politico-economic process of international agreement on the adoption and reform of international monetary regimes, the tradi-tional tools of economic analysis used in competitive theory are inadequate. Price theory, particularly the highly sophisticated theory of perfect competition, is based on the assumption that any individual economic agent has negligible influence on the market. When considering the international monetary problem, however, we notice the predominance of large countries such as the United States, West Germany, and Japan, a situation with strong implications for the process of negotiating a monetary regime as well as for the interplay of monetary policies under a given monetary regime. To cope with this situation, this book appeals to oligopoly theory and the powerful tool of game theory rather than to the theory of perfect competition.[2] My basic approach will be to apply these tools to an analysis of the impact of the rules of economic behavior on economic activity. In addition, I will make use of several useful tools from the field of public economics, such as Olson's theory of collective action and Buchanan's theory of clubs (Buchanan 1964).

Thus, this book represents an attempt to analyze the impact of rules of economic behavior on economic activity in the field of international monetary relations using the tools of economic theory. This amounts to studying the political process of adopting and reforming the international monetary system endogenously. There is growing recognition of the need to incorporate the political behavior of economic agents as endogenous variables in economic models of the domestic economy as well, as advocated by Buchanan (1971). I cannot support the drastic proposals advocated by the public choice school, such as the proposal that a balanced budget be guaranteed by law, but I find it meaningful in principle to view economic activities as social phenomena that should be studied in conjunction with the political process. In the field of international economics in particular, there is now a growing need to analyze the political aspect of agreeing on the rules of the game using an interdisciplinary approach that combines the tools of economics and political science inasmuch as the outcome of interactions among the macroeconomic policies of different countries depends crucially on the rules of the game that are formulated through the political process of international negotiation.

If we consider the relationship between rules and economic policies (or, more precisely, between the formation of rules and the interplay of economic policies among nations under a given set of rules), we can think of international monetary confrontations as gamelike situations with two distinct layers or stages. The first stage consists of the game of agreeing on a set of monetary rules—that is, of choosing or reforming an international monetary regime. In other words, it is a game of choosing the rules of the policy game that follows. The second stage consists of the game of policy interplays under a given set of monetary rules. In this game stage 1 and stage 2 are not necessarily played consecutively. Rather, they are often played simultaneously and are closely related to one another. For the purpose of analysis, however, it is helpful to distinguish between them.

In chapters 2 and 3, I concentrate on the first stage of the game and examine the process of negotiating the adoption or reform of the set of rules that defines an international monetary regime. In chapter 2, after clarifying the relationship between the first and second stages of the game, I examine the structure of the economic incentives faced by each country during the political process of agreeing on a set of monetary rules. I then show that the first stage of agreeing on a regime exhibits properties similar to the game of matching pennies in which both players gain when they choose the same side of the coin. It is a situation in which the ongoing set of rules persists until agreement is reached on reform.

In chapter 3, the politico-economic approach to analyzing the choice of an international monetary system will be applied to the problem of monetary unions or monetary integration, a typical example of which is monetary integration within the EC. In particular, the calculus of participation, an application of public economics to political processes, will be used to assist in the analysis of the problem of participation in a monetary union. The calculus of participation is based on the idea that the decision of whether to join a monetary union will depend on whether a given country can improve its level of economic welfare by joining. The benefits accruing to participating countries have the nature of public goods, while the costs have the nature of private goods. Moreover, the time profiles of the benefits and costs are different; the costs come first and the benefits later. For these reasons, monetary unions are difficult to achieve. If we review the historic experience of monetary centralization within individual nations and that of international monetary integration in the light of the calculus of participation as well as the theory of clubs, we find many interesting instances that indicate the difficulty of achieving a successful monetary union.

The remaining chapters are devoted to examining the second stage of the game of monetary confrontations: the game of policy interplays under a given set of rules. Chapter 4 examines the interdependence of monetary policies in the context of a Keynesian model that assumes a fixed price level and variable employment. Chapter 5 studies the interdependence of monetary policies in a monetarist model that takes the level of employment as given but allows the price level to be completely flexible. In both models the game of monetary policy interplays can be formulated in the form of an n-person non-zero-sum game. As is well known, there are many solution concepts to an n-person non-zero-sum game; however, solution concepts worth noting can be broadly classified into cooperative solutions that arise when countries cooperate and noncooperative solutions that arise when countries react more or less independently. Among the general requirements for cooperative solutions are the requirement that they be Pareto-optimal and that they represent situations more desirable than the initial situation for all participating countries. Noncooperative solutions include the Cournot-Nash equilibrium based on the passive behavior of all countries and the leadership equilibrium with a dominant country such as the United States acting as the leader. By comparing these alternative solution concepts, we obtain a number of interesting results. In chapter 5, for example, I show that if the increase in outside money such as gold or special drawing rights (SDRs) is larger (smaller) than the increase in total demand for international reserves by all countries, then the Cournot-Nash equilibrium as well as the leadership equilibrium will tend to be more inflationary (deflationary) than the cooperative outcome.

Put in terms of the concepts of public economics, the rate of world inflation is a public good (or public "bad") that is determined by the average rate of monetary growth of all countries. On the other hand, the balance of payments of a country is determined by the difference between the domestic rate of monetary growth and the average monetary growth rate of all countries. (In the two-country case, it depends on the difference between the monetary growth rates of the two countries.) Consider the case in which further inflation is undesirable for the world economy. Although each country recognizes that any increase in the world money supply would create the public bad of inflation, it may find it advantageous to raise its own monetary growth rate above those of other countries because by so doing it can attain a higher level of consumption, at least in the short run. This is analogous to the example of air pollution by automobiles. The more a driver uses his or her car, the more the driver benefits, but, at the same time, the more exhaust the automobile emits. Since the level of air pollution is determined by the total amount of exhaust emitted by all automobile users, there is a tendency for the air to be polluted more than is desired by society as a whole.

One of the drawbacks of the game-theoretic approach taken in most chapters of this book is that the analysis is limited to a static framework. At the end of chapter 5, however, I will experiment with a dynamic approach to the simple world money game by appealing to the technique of the differential game.

Neither the model in chapter 4 that assumes fixed price levels nor the model in chapter 5 that takes income and employment as exogenously given is sufficient to analyze the current state of the world economy (although they highlight some interesting aspects thereof), because we are living in a world in which inflation and unemployment coexist. In order to analyze simultaneous changes in price and employment levels, from chapter 6 on I examine the effects of monetary policy on economic fluctuations and the nature of the international transmission mechanism of business cycles in a model that incorporates the short-run and long-run Phillips curves. In chapter 6 I will present a monetary model that incorporates the Phillips curve and study its properties under alternative monetary systems. Under a fixed exchange rate system, both foreign inflation and changes in the terms of trade affect the domestic economy. On the other hand, under a flexible exchange rate system, while changes in the general price level abroad are absorbed through changes in the exchange rate, a deterioration in the terms of trade results in both unemployment and inflation (stagflation) in the domestic economy.

In chapter 7, this framework is extended to a two-country model. The two countries interact, first, directly through the effects of changes in money supply on the balance of payments, and, second, through the wage-price spiral accompanying changes in the terms of trade. The former link through the interaction of monetary policies operates only in the case of fixed exchange rates, while the second link through the terms of trade operates under both fixed and flexible exchange rates. While recession in one country tends to cause recession in the other under fixed rates, it tends to cause stagflation in the other under flexible rates. Moreover, the second link through the terms of trade becomes more important the lower is the elasticity of substitution between consumption goods. During the oil crises, the deterioration in the terms of trade of oil-importing countries was aggravated by exchange rate depreciation, as a result of which they suffered from serious cost-push inflation. The mechanism of this process seems to be well explained by the model developed in this chapter. The difference between the macroeconomic mechanisms under the fixed and flexible exchange rate systems stems mainly from the fact that, under fixed exchange rates, international reserves serve as a buffer, while under flexible exchange rates, exchange rates perform the adjusting function in the same way that other prices do. In the terminology of Hicks (1974), this difference corresponds to that between the mechanisms that characterize the "fix-price" economy and the "flex-price" economy.

The above policy-game approach is also applicable to the analysis of the managed float system, as we see in chapter 8. Intervention in the foreign exchange market has substantial effects on the intervening country, as well as on other countries. For example, a devaluation of the domestic currency implies an increase in the money supply of the rest of the world when measured in terms of domestic units, which results in strong inflationary effects as well as employment-creating effects on the domestic economy. On the other hand, for all other countries, a domestic devaluation implies a contraction of the money supply of the devaluing country measured in terms of their respective currency units, meaning that they face deflationary pressures instead. Accordingly, under the managed float system, a devaluation in a given country's exchange rate implies "beggar-thy-neighbor" effects.

This book, then, is an attempt to study international monetary confrontations, a topic that lies on the border between political science and international economics, using an interdisciplinary approach.

2 The Choice of International Monetary Regime

To reform the international monetary system is to change the rules of the world monetary game. Reformation therefore requires a consensus among the participating countries. Consequently, it is important to understand how the nature of a monetary regime (that is, the rules of the game) affects the operation of national economic policies. Under what circumstances is it feasible to replace one international monetary regime with another? How does the conduct of economic policy differ under different monetary regimes? And how do the resulting differences in macroeconomic policies affect economic variables such as employment levels and inflation rates in countries participating in a regime? Our analysis of the international monetary system would be incomplete without considering such questions.[1]

This chapter presents an economic analysis of the process of selecting an international monetary system. What would be the benefits and costs to participating countries if one international monetary regime were to be replaced by another? And, given this benefit-cost structure, would there be an incentive for each country to agree to a new monetary system or some kind of monetary reform? This chapter provides an economic or politico-economic analysis of these issues. First, however, it would be helpful to ask why these strategic or politico-economic aspects of international monetary relations have been neglected.

One reason is that traditional general equilibrium analysis is less powerful in a world in which individual agents have a non-negligible influence on the economy. It is probably this methodological limitation that has led economists to shy away from analyzing the strategic aspects of world monetary relations despite their importance owing to the presence of a number of large countries with substantial influence. Consequently, we have every reason to welcome the application of game theory to this area.

Incidentally, even the tools of game theory have been effective in analyzing the case in which the number of participants is so large that each participant has negligible influence. The highly elegant study of the core and its relationship to competitive equilibrium is a good example. However, if one's aim is to obtain new insights into economic reality through the use of game theory rather than merely to support or elaborate on the properties of existence and efficiency of competitive equilibrium that have been established by use of general equilibrium analysis, one must develop more apparatus suited to the analysis of situations in which interdependence exists among a small number of participants.

The second reason why the strategic aspects of international monetary relations have been neglected lies in the attitude of economists. Some economists, although they are potential representatives of the interests of a particular country or group, believe that they will sound more persuasive if they advocate a plan as if it were an ideal one drawn up with the general interest in mind than if they analyze the structure of the benefits and costs the plan confers on different countries.

A possible rebuttal to this argument is that both practitioners and economists must devote more energy to acquiring a better understanding of reality. In particular, economists must analyze the benefits and costs various reform proposals will confer on different countries and groups. In addition, they should try to correct the asymmetry of information between groups that are well informed of their own interests (for example, producers) and those that are less well informed (for example, consumers) and to correct the biases in the formation of economic policies that reflect such asymmetries of information.

Third, many economists feel more secure if they confine their attention to purely economic aspects of any issue. It is often argued that, since economists are laymen in political science, it would be dangerous if they were to become excessively involved with political considerations, and that too much concern with political feasibility would cause ideal plans to be discarded. This view is well expressed in the following concluding remarks in a textbook by Yeager (1968): "For at least two reasons, 'political impossibility' should not rule a proposal out of consideration. First, discussing how a proposed change is likely to work can be a useful pedagogical device. ... Secondly, 'political impossibility' is not an inherent operative property of an economic arrangement. It may be overcome. ... If an economist concerned with his reputation for practicality and reasonableness, makes amateur assessments of political feasibility and accordingly recommends policies other than those he truly considers best, he is shirking the responsibilities of the expert he claims to be."

I agree that economists should not abandon an ideal system just because

of the apparent political difficulty of achieving it, but I believe that economists, as social scientists, should not shy away from analyzing economic
variables relating to the feasibility of a proposal. In order to develop a
positive theory to explain negotiation processes and policy interplays in
addition to a normative theory to assist in the design of better international
monetary regimes, we need a theoretical framework with which to analyze
the benefit-cost structure of an interdependent world. Moreover, since few
political scientists are interested in or fully informed about international
monetary economics, if economists do not become involved there is a
danger of leaving this interdisciplinary field completely untouched.

International Monetary Regimes and National Interests

By a set of rules or an international monetary regime, I mean such systems as
the gold standard, the fixed exchange rate system (including the dollar
standard), the flexible exchange rate system, and the managed floating rate
system. Ideally the rules of the game should specify the set of players,
permissible strategies, and payoff functions corresponding to combinations
of strategies.

In some regimes the rules of the game are explicitly defined and well
understood. Under a fixed exchange rate regime, for example, the rule of the
game is that the monetary authorities of countries other than the reserve
currency country (formerly the United States) are assigned to intervene in
the foreign exchange market in order to keep exchange rates constant.
Under a purely flexible exchange rate regime the rule prohibits monetary
authorities from intervening in the exchange market. In these cases it is quite
clear what the rules of the game are and what policy interplays are possible
under the rules. In other cases the distinction is more subtle. Under a
managed float system, for example, the monetary authorities have some
latitude about how often and how much to intervene in the exchange
market, and hence the degree of intervention itself becomes a component of
their strategies.

To prepare for the game-theoretic or strategic approach that follows, let
us examine how different international monetary systems affect the interests
of different countries. Proposals for reforming the international monetary
system can be broadly classified into four categories: (1) the gold standard,
(2) the former IMF dollar standard, (3) the centralized issue of world money
by a world central bank, and (4) the flexible exchange rate system. There are
many variants of each of these systems, which may confer somewhat
different benefit-cost structures on each national economy; however, since

the purpose of this chapter is to clarify the fundamental nature of the conflicts of interest that arise when selecting an international monetary system, it will suffice to describe the basic institutional characteristics of these representative alternative systems.

The Gold Standard

A return to the gold standard implies restoring the rules of the old gold standard regime, under which the species flow mechanism is supposed to adjust the balance of payments. An outflow of gold, by shrinking the domestic money supply, lowers income and the price level, thus curtailing imports. On the other hand, an inflow of gold, by expanding the domestic money supply, raises income and the price level, thus promoting imports. In this way, balance of payments imbalances tend to be eliminated automatically.

A return to the gold standard implies the removal of national currencies such as the dollar and the pound sterling as international mediums of exchange. Gold thus becomes the only international currency, and this may help to check world inflation. Actually, however, the effectiveness of the gold standard as a check on world inflation would depend on the price level of gold in terms of national currencies, as well as on the extent to which currencies other than gold are eliminated as means of settling international transactions. It would therefore be difficult to predict quantitatively the strength of the inflation-curbing effect.

On the other hand, what is certain is that a return to the gold standard would increase the monetary demand for gold, which is quite apart from the industrial demand. As a result, the price of gold would rise, and thus adoption of the gold standard would benefit countries holding large stocks of gold, such as some European countries; gold-producing countries, such as South Africa; and the Soviet Union, which sells gold from time to time. Although the benefit to gold-holding countries would take the form of a once-and-for-all capital gain (or stock gain), the benefit to gold-producing countries would accrue as a recurrent income gain (or flow gain). In order to compare the income gain of gold-producing countries to the capital gain of gold-holding countries, the former would have to be capitalized by some discount rate. It is uncertain whether the United States would gain from an increase in gold price, because it holds a large stock of gold but at the same time issues the dollar, which is used as a reserve currency. Thus, when discussing the benefits and costs to the United States of returning to the gold standard, one needs to compare the U.S.'s capital gain resulting from the increase in gold price with the loss resulting from its giving up seigniorage rights.

The Former IMF Dollar Standard

The former IMF system operated as a gold exchange standard centering on gold and dollar reserves. It was at the same time a dollar standard, as the dollar, a liability of the U.S. Federal Reserve banks, was used as a means of settling international transactions. In the sense that the United States was the only country that had the right to issue international currency, it occupied a special position in the international monetary system.

The benefits deriving from the right of seigniorage can best be understood by imagining the benefits that accrue to an individual who is granted the right to issue money. If one's borrowing certificates were accepted unconditionally and circulated as money, one could then accumulate great wealth simply by paying the cost of printing money. Similarly, when a country finances its current account deficits by printing money, it gains, in principle, in the form of real transfers of purchasing power equal to the amount of its deficits. It could be argued that the current account deficits of the United States were indeed so financed.

More careful analysis of the situation, however, would show that the gain to the reserve currency country may not be as large as is usually imagined. Under the Bretton Woods system, the reserve currency country was required to hold a substantial stock of gold, and in addition the obligation to maintain the value of the reserve currency constrained the scope of its monetary policy. These represent costs to the reserve currency country that cannot be ignored.

Moreover, dollars that were supplied as foreign exchange reserves through current account deficits and long-term capital account deficits were usually held by non-Americans in the form of interest-bearing short-term securities on which the United States was required to pay interest. Accordingly, the seigniorage gain was limited to the difference between the rate of return on U.S. investment (at home or abroad) and the interest rate paid on liquid dollar assets. One may argue that, as long as commercial banks competed with one another, the United States did not earn any more profit under the dollar standard than what corresponds to a normal return for its services. Through borrowing on a short-term basis and lending on a long-term basis, the United States simply played the role of international financial intermediary or world banker.

There remains the possibility that creditor countries holding dollar assets might have suffered losses in the real purchasing power of their dollar-denominated assets when expansionary policy in the United States promoted world inflation. The United States probably did benefit from such an inflation tax. However, such a gain to the currency-issuing country would not exist if inflation were well anticipated and if inflationary expectations were fully reflected in nominal interest rates. Therefore, even when expanding expenditures in the reserve-currency country are accompanied by balance of payment deficits, as was the case during the Vietnam war, its gain from seigniorage would be large only if inflation were not fully reflected in the interest rates on the reserve assets held by non-reserve-currency countries.[2]

Centralized Money Issue by a World Central Bank

Of the two extreme types of international monetary systems, let us first consider the system under which an international organization issues an international currency, such as the SDRs of the IMF, that serves both as a means of payment in international transactions and as a reserve currency. Many proposals for an international currency to be issued by an international organization, such as the Keynes plan or the Triffin plan, aim at increasing international liquidity and, at the same time, avoiding the confidence problem associated with the use of national currencies as international currencies. Moreover, confining the right to issue international currencies to an international organization would cause the asymmetry between the reserve-currency country and non-reserve-currency countries to vanish. The only remaining problem would then be how to effect income or resource transfers from surplus countries to deficit countries when disequilibria arose in the balance of payments among nations. Such a system has the advantage of fully utilizing the public good nature of international currencies. At the same time, however, it retains the adjustment problems associated with the fixed exchange rate system.

   The proposal to set up substitution accounts in the IMF represents an attempt to replace the dollar with SDRs, but even if this plan succeeds, it will be a long time before the substitution accounts can function effectively as a world currency.

Flexible Exchange Rate System

Under a flexible exchange rate system, no country would be granted the exclusive right to issue international currency, and, because the balance of payments of individual countries would always be in equilibrium, the demand for international currencies by monetary authorities would be reduced to a minimum. As a result, conflicts of interest arising from the asymmetric distribution of seigniorage gains would be greatly mitigated. However, because there would still be private transactions demand for specific national currencies, such as the dollar, seigniorage gains would not vanish completely.

As long as the flexible exchange rate system operates in its pure form, it would allow countries to regain autonomy in the conduct of their monetary policies. Such a system would, of course, entail the cost of exchange risk and the inconvenience resulting from the absence of a world currency, but it would also guarantee individual countries a maximum degree of freedom in the conduct of their monetary policy and in that sense may be regarded as the regime that ensures the attainment of the maximin condition for each participating country.

At present, the prevailing international monetary system among the advanced countries is the system of "managed" or "controlled" float. By stressing exchange rate flexibility, this system has thus far worked well and has not precipitated any serious monetary crises despite the occurrence of at least two oil crises. Because the managed float system represents the status quo of the international monetary system at present, an understanding of the functioning of this system is essential when one is considering the possibility of, and the proposals for, international monetary reform.

Game-Theoretic Analysis of the Choice of International Monetary Regime

The choice of an international monetary regime can be regarded as a game, a so-called world money game, in which participating countries base their choice on benefit-cost considerations. When applying abstract game theory to an analysis of this problem, we must take account of two points.

The first concerns whether nations should be treated as the basic decision unit in the game. In many circumstances, it is difficult to define a uniform national interest. Although a nation is a political as well as an economic unit that participates in international negotiations, all individuals in a given nation do not necessarily share the same benefits and costs. For example, the interests of exporters often conflict with those of importers, and those of consumers conflict with those of producers. Although for convenience I treat nations as the basic decision unit in what follows, I would like to remind the reader that this is only a crude approximation of reality.

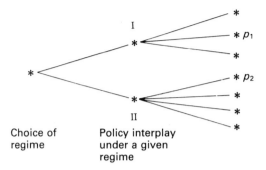

Figure 2.1
Game tree of the two-stage world money game.

Second, once nations are taken as the basic decision unit, the world money game can be regarded as a two-stage game, with the first stage being the game of agreeing on a set of monetary rules (that is, choosing an international monetary regime) and the second stage being the game of policy interplays under a given set of monetary rules. However, this does not mean that the two stages are played consecutively. In fact, they are often played simultaneously and are closely related to one other. For example, poor economic performance under a given set of rules will reveal their defects and lead to a change in the rules themselves. For convenience of analysis, however, it will be helpful to distinguish conceptually between the two stages.

If there exists a simple optimal combination of strategies in the second stage of the game, then the whole game can be reduced to a single-stage game by the principle of optimality. Consider a situation in which the dollar standard has been adopted as the result of a consensus among all countries. Suppose that the benefits and costs to both the United States and other countries of alternative combinations of economic policies, particularly monetary policies, under the dollar standard are known and that all countries know their optimal strategies under an alternative international monetary system, say the gold standard. Then, as long as these countries pursue their optimal policies, their ultimate payoffs will be determined as soon as they agree on the choice between the dollar standard and the gold standard.

Figure 2.1 represents this two-stage game in the form of a game tree. Suppose that p_1, the vector of payoffs for participants that will be realized by selecting the optimal combination of strategies under the first set of rules, and p_2, the vector of payoffs with the same property under the second set of rules, are known. Then the whole game can be reduced to the single-stage

Table 2.1
Payoff matrix of "battle of the sexes."

	Girl	
Boy	Fight	Ballet
Fight	(3, 1)	(0, 0)
Ballet	(0, 0)	(1, 3)

game of choosing between p_1 and p_2 by the principle of optimality. In other words, if the optimal combination of strategies to be played in the second stage is known to each participant, the ultimate payoffs will be determined as soon as the players agree on the choice of a regime. It is not an easy task to determine the optimal combination of strategies or the most reasonable outcome or which solution concepts of the game should be used in the second stage. For the moment, however, let us discuss the properties of the first stage of the game—that is, the game of selecting a regime under the assumption that the payoffs resulting from the combination of optimal policy interplays are given.[3]

An important characteristic of the first stage of the game is that the ongoing set of rules will prevail until an agreement on a change of rules is reached by all the participants, or at least by a considerable number of participants. This property gives this stage a payoff structure similar to what I will call the "battle of the sexes." The battle of the sexes is a game with a payoff structure implied by the following scenario: A boy and a girl each has a choice of an evening's entertainment, a prize fight or a ballet performance. The boy prefers the fight and the girl the ballet. However, if they reach no agreement, each stays alone at home. (The payoff matrix is as shown in table 2.1). Similarly, unless a new agreement for monetary reform is reached, the current system—the managed float system at the present moment—will continue. If we normalize the payoffs of the present system to (0, 0), the payoff matrix for adopting two alternative systems (say, a return to the gold standard and adoption of fixed exchange rates based on a dollar standard) could be illustrated as in table 2.2. Suppose that the gold standard is preferred by Europe and the dollar standard by the United States. Then we could assign values to the parameters such that $a < b$ and $c > d$. If $a, b, c,$ and d are positive, then this game of choosing a regime becomes analogous to the battle of the sexes. However, there is no assurance that $a, b, c,$ and d will all be positive, because it is not always the case that the payoffs from the new system will be better for all participants. Moreover, the probability of

Table 2.2
Payoff matrix of alternative monetary systems.

	Europe	
U.S.	Gold Standard	Dollar Standard
Gold Standard	(a, b)	$(0, 0)$
Dollar Standard	$(0, 0)$	(c, d)

negative values for these parameters becomes even higher if we take account of the adjustment costs that each country would incur when adapting to changes in the international monetary regime.

Let us summarize some of the properties of the battle of the sexes (Luce and Raiffa 1957, pp. 91–92). There are two equilibrium pairs in the sense of Nash, as indicated by the two diagonal pairs in table 2.1, since each strategy in one of the pairs is sustained unless the other changes his strategy. However, if combined differently, these strategies do not give equilibrium pairs in the sense of Nash. Moreover, the two equilibria on the diagonal yield different returns to the players. In the terminology of game theory, the two equilibria are neither interchangeable nor equivalent (Luce and Raiffa 1957, p. 106).

Mixed strategy combinations of the noncooperative form do not improve the outcome. Only preplay communication and coordination between the players will lead to the attainment of a solution on the diagonal. An equitable solution is obtained if they alternate between going to a fight and going to the ballet together or if they toss a coin to decide which type of entertainment to go to together (Luce and Raiffa 1957, p. 94).

From these observations, one can draw at least two implications concerning the first stage of selecting a monetary regime. First, in order for a new system to be adopted by a group of participants, the payoff structure must take the form of a genuine battle of the sexes. More precisely, at least one of the pairs (a, b) or (c, d) must be a pair of positive numbers. This could be achieved, of course, if an attractive plan were proposed. More realistically, however, this would be achieved only if the existing system showed serious defects that were well recognized by participating countries. The resultant deterioration in the payoffs of the ongoing regime would mean a relative increase in the payoffs of new regimes such as (a, b) and (c, d) because the origin $(0, 0)$ is used to express the status quo situation only as a normalizing device. Thus, an international economic crisis might well lead to fundamental changes in the international monetary regime. As Samuelson (1967, p. 699) puts it, "One does not have to be cynical, but merely realistic to guess that if fundamental changes are to come, they will come in the wake of some international crisis rather than as a result of predetermined planning and agreement."

Second, it can be concluded that a compromise combination or a hybrid regime is more likely to be agreed on than a pure form of one regime. A reasonable solution to the game of the battle of the sexes is a coordinated alternation between fight and ballet. It is difficult to conceive of a randomized solution to the problem of choosing a regime, but it is quite common to devise a system that combines the characteristics of pure regimes. The most notable example is the adjustable peg system in the Bretton Woods regime, which can be regarded as a convex combination of two pure regimes: fixed exchange rates and flexible exchange rates. Most of the time, the adjustable peg system is operated in a manner similar to the fixed rate system, but under circumstances of "fundamental disequilibrium" in the balance of payments, exchange rates become adjustable and hence the elements of a flexible rate system are brought in.[4]

It is not merely coincidence that the Bretton Woods system is described by Keynes as a hybrid of originally thoroughbred plans. Comparing plans to species of dogs, he observes that "the loss of the dog [his plan of a clearing union] we need not too much regret, though I still think that it was a more thoroughbred animal than what has now come out from a mixed marriage of ideas [the actually agreed upon International Monetary Fund]." However, he was also right in recognizing that "perhaps, as sometimes occurs, this dog of mixed origin is a sturdier and more serviceable animal and will prove not less loyal and faithful to the purposes for which it has been bred " (Keynes 1947, p. 369).

Appendix: Basic Concepts of Game Theory and Oligopoly Theory

For a thorough examination of game theory, see Suzuki 1959, Bacharach 1976, and the references contained in the Japanese edition of the latter. See Fellner 1949, Ōwase 1970, and Okuguchi 1971 for more detailed discussions of oligopoly theory.

Basic Concepts of Game Theory

A game consists of the following components: (1) two or more decision-making agents, called players, (2) the possible courses of action (strategies) open to each player, and (3) the payoff to each player, which depends on the strategies chosen by him and by the other players. A game (or the rules of a game) defines the possible strategies open to each player and specifies the payoff to each player when a particular combination of strategies is chosen.

A game can be represented in either extensive form or normal form (or in characteristic function form, which will not be considered here). In the extensive form, a game is represented as a game tree as shown in figure 2.1. A game tree is characterized by the presence of branches. At each branching point, the next step is determined either by the deliberate choice of a player or by chance. The payoff to each player is determined as the game progresses from the bottom to the top of the tree. (Figure 2.1 is not a true game tree because I have reduced the process of agreeing on a set of rules to a single branching point and the whole policy game under a given regime to another branching point.)

A strategy defines the courses of action of a player at all branching points at which a choice must be made. That is, a strategy is a conditional command that specifies the player's courses of action for all possible contingencies. Given the strategy of each player, the actual path taken along the game tree and the final outcome of the game are known. Therefore, the payoff to each player can be given as a function of the combinations of the players' strategies. Thus, a game can be formulated as follows (see Suzuki 1951, p. 32):

1. Given the set of possible strategies of each player, S_i ($i = 1, 2, \ldots, n$), and

2. given the set of payoffs to each player, F_i ($i = 1, 2, \ldots, n$), and

3. letting $S = S_1 \times S_2 \times \cdots \times S_n$ (the Cartesian product of S_i) and $F = F_1 \times F_2 \times \cdots \times F_n$ (the Cartesian product of F_i),

then a point s in S determines a point f in F through the function $f = f(s)$. This correspondence between S and F defines the rules of the game, which are known to all players. Such a formulation of a game in terms of the sets S and F and the relationship between them is known as the normal form. Tables 2.1 and 2.2 are simple examples of two-person ($n = 2$) games expressed in normal form, where each country can only choose between two strategies. Each of these strategies is called a pure strategy. On the other hand, a mixed strategy is a probability combination of the original pure strategies.

If the sum of the payoffs to all players of a game is always constant, then the game is called a constant-sum game. By transforming the payoff function, any constant-sum game can be formulated as an equivalent zero-sum game. A game in which the sum of the payoffs depends on the outcome of the game is called a non-constant-sum game or a non-zero-sum game.

In the case of a two-person zero-sum game, the gain of one player is the loss of the other player and there is no scope for cooperation. However, in the case of a non-zero-sum game, one may distinguish between a cooperative game in which the players cooperate in one form or another and a noncooperative game in which the players do not cooperate.

Among the normal-form non-zero-sum games used to examine conflicts of interest in society, the "prisoner's dilemma" attributed to Tucker is especially well known. It is a two-person non-zero-sum game with the following payoff structure. Consider a situation in which two partners in crime are captured and kept under custody in two separate cells. If both refuse to confess, both will be punished only lightly because of insufficient evidence. If both confess, both will be punished severely, but they will escape the severest punishment. However, if one of them confesses while the other does not, the one who confesses will be released for cooperating with the police, and the one who does not will receive the severest punishment (Luce and Raiffa 1957). The payoffs of alternative combinations of strategies are summarized as follows (the payoffs of prisoner 1 are shown on the left):

	Prisoner 2	
Prisoner 1	Don't confess	Confess
Don't confess	$(-1, -1)$	$(-10, 0)$
Confess	$(0, -10)$	$(-5, -5)$

In such a situation in which communication between players is completely blocked, it is highly probable that each player would prefer not to trust the other and confess. Similar cost-benefit structures are common in conflict situations such as oligopoly, trade wars, environmental protection, and the arms race.

Equilibrium and Solution Concepts

In a situation involving a conflict of interest, a participant may choose to maximize his minimum gain. That is, he seeks to minimize his loss (or expected loss). This postulate is called the principle of "maximin," and the corresponding strategy is called the maximin strategy. Von Neumann has shown that, for any two-person zero-sum game, if all players pursue mixed strategies, there will always exist an expected maximin payoff for one player and an expected minimax payoff for the other player that are equal to one other.

Generally, in a noncooperative game, a combination of player strategies is said to be an equilibrium point if no player has an incentive to make a unilateral change of strategy. That is, given the (expected) payoff functions f_i, an n-tuple of strategies $s^* = (s_1^*, \dots, s_n^*) \in S$ is an equilibrium point if, for all i,

$$f_i(s_1^*, \dots, s_{i-1}^*, s_i^*, s_{i+1}^*, \dots, s_n^*)$$
$$= \max_{s_i \in S_i} f_i(s_1^*, \dots, s_{i-1}^*, s_i, s_{i+1}^*, \dots, s_n^*).$$

Such an equilibrium point is called a Nash equilibrium, which is a generalization of the Cournot solution to the oligopoly problem. (The Nash equilibrium discussed here should be distinguished from the Nash solution in a cooperative game.)

There are also other important solution concepts such as the von Neumann–Morgenstern solution and the core solution. As a discussion of these solutions requires a knowledge of characteristic functions, they will not be considered in detail here. Instead we will take a brief look at the two-person cooperative game.

In a two-person cooperative game, a cooperative position that is agreeable to both players must satisfy the following conditions: (1) the combination of payoffs to the players must be Pareto-optimal, and (2) the payoff to each player must be no less than that obtained when, instead of cooperating, each independently pursues a noncooperative minimax strategy.

When generalized to the case of an n-person game, a third condition requires that the sum of the payoffs to any set of players must be no less than the sum of the payoffs that these players would obtain by forming a coalition. The set of payoff combinations satisfying all three conditions is called the core. This concept was first studied by Edgeworth (1881) and was subsequently refined by Aumann (1964), Scarf (1967), and others. It has been shown that when a market is formulated as a game, the core of the game converges to the market equilibrium as the number of participants increases.

Notes on Oligopoly Theory

Cournot (1838) analyzed the case of a duopoly consisting of two producers selling a homogeneous product by assuming that the two producers regard their respective levels of output as their strategies. His assumption concerning the behavior of the producers is that each chooses his own profit-maximizing level of output, taking the output level of the other producer as given. The correspondence between a producer's optimal level of output and the level of output of his rival is called his reaction function (reaction curve when shown graphically). An equilibrium is reached when each producer finds his prevailing level of output to be optimal given the output of his rival. This point is given by the intersection of the two producers' reaction curves and is called the Cournot solution. In a sense the Nash equilibrium is a generalization of the Cournot solution to the framework of game theory. Later, Bertrand (1883) showed that, if each producer takes the price (instead of the output level) of his rival as given, the Cournot solution is inherently unstable.

On the other hand, Stackelberg (1934) noted that a producer may be tempted to choose the optimal point along the reaction curve of his rival if he knows that his own output is always taken as given by his rival. The producer who acts passively along his own reaction curve is called the follower, and the one who optimizes along his rival's reaction curve is called the leader. The corresponding solution is called the Stackelberg leadership solution. Stackelberg showed, with the aid of a diagram that superimposes one set of indifference curves on the other, that equilibrium cannot be attained in a duopoly market if both producers attempt to act as the leader. However, if the technologies of the producers differ and each producer knows his rival's technology, there may be a natural assignment of one player to the role of leader and the other to the role of follower (Ono 1980).

Fellner (1949) has pointed out that, even in cases where there is no explicit coalition among firms because of various constraints, they may still seek to maximize joint profits implicitly. He thus argues that, in reality, outcomes similar to the cooperative solution in game theory may be the most plausible. (Telser 1972 and J. Friedman 1977 provide discussions of the leadership solution and joint-profit maximizing behavior, as well as of their relationship to game theory.)

3　On the Political Economy of Monetary Integration: A Public Economic Approach

One of the fundamental problems of international monetary relations is how and to what extent national economies should be incorporated into monetary unions. A main concern of the countries belonging to the EC is the progress of their monetary integration. For the world as a whole, the basic question is whether a subset of countries (or all nations) should unite into a single currency area with fixed exchange rates or whether each nation should remain an independent currency area with floating exchange rates.[1]

There has been considerable research on the benefits and costs of monetary integration (for example, Corden 1972, Ingram 1973, and Johnson and Swoboda 1973). However, this research has been concerned primarily with the global advantages and disadvantages of monetary integration. The impact of monetary integration on the participating countries has been examined less frequently. Only a few studies have analyzed the feasibility of monetary integration in the light of these advantages and disadvantages for each participating country.[2]

The purpose of this chapter is not to advocate an ideal plan for a monetary union or world monetary regime but rather to present a positive analysis of the politico-economic process of monetary integration and the formation of a new world monetary regime.[3] By analyzing the strategic positions of individual countries, we will attempt to answer the following questions: What kind of monetary integration do individual national actions based on national benefit and cost calculations lead to? Does the politically feasible monetary union tend to be larger or smaller than the monetary union of optimal size?

Recent developments in public economics have enabled economists to analyze the politico-economic aspects of economic conflicts. Progress in the application of price theory to institutional arrangements has made it possible to study the incentives to participate in joint actions. Olson (1965) has developed an analysis of collective action, but the analysis is of limited significance to cooperation in monetary integration because it assumes a predetermined membership. Buchanan (1964) has developed an economic theory of clubs that allows for variable size of membership. Although his analysis is directed mainly at the problem of efficiency rather than the political structure of conflict, it provides a useful tool for analyzing collective actions.

In the previous chapter, international monetary relations were characterized as a two-stage game. The first stage requires agreeing on a system or rule, and the second involves the interplay of economic policies under a given rule. The second stage is analogous to the prisoner's dilemma; the first is analogous to the battle of the sexes. This chapter concerns the first stage of agreeing on a rule, taking the case of monetary integration as an example.

The domestic monetary system of an individual country is based on national consensus and is the product of a long process in which the seigniorage rights to issue money gradually become concentrated in the hands of a nation-state simultaneously with the development of a banking system. By contrast, political power is only partly concentrated in the European Community and other monetary unions, and, since no world government exists, the world monetary regime is based directly and explicitly on a consensus among nations. This situation has an analogy in international law, where the power relationship is still often explicit in resolving conflicts of interest, whereas in domestic law it is mostly behind the veil of law and order.

Benefits and Costs of Monetary Integration

The term *monetary integration* or *monetary unification* encompasses varying degrees of integration. The following components should be distinguished:

1. The linking of national currencies with fixed parities accompanied by a narrowing or vanishing band without common reserves or a common central bank. This is what Corden (1972) called the pseudo-exchange rate union.

2. The coordination of economic policies, particularly monetary policies, to prevent disequilibria in the balance of payments.

3. Some clearing mechanism for disequilibria in the balance of payments using a common reserve asset. The asset chosen may be the currency of a member country, that of a nonmember such as the dollar (used by the European Community), a new accounting currency, SDRs, or gold.

4. Convertibility between currencies for capital transactions and for current transactions.

5. The establishment of public confidence in the irrevocable nature of the fixity of exchange parities. This confidence normally emerges only after a substantial transition period during which there is successful maintenance of the de facto fixity of exchange parities or after some kind of political unification.

6. Circulation of a common currency issued by a single central bank in the area of the monetary union. This leads to the complete exchange rate union.

At least one, and usually more than one, of these components exists in any monetary union. Monetary integration proceeds by adding new components to those already present.

The benefits and costs of the monetary union will differ depending on the degree of monetary integration. The main benefits from monetary integration include the following:[4]

1. The reduction or even disappearance of uncertainty concerning fluctuations in the exchange rates among national currencies of member nations. This benefit is prompted by component 1 but fully realized only after the emergence of component 5.

2. The economization of foreign exchange reserves for the countries as a whole (derived mainly from component 3).

3. The benefit arising from the shock-absorbing function of international reserves stressed by Laffer (1973) and Mundell (1973) (derived from component 1).

4. The increase in prestige deriving from the increased size of the monetary decision unit, either in the form of an increase in actual voting power in a monetary institution such as the IMF[5] or in the form of an increase in the satisfaction level of political leaders[6] in the participating countries. This benefit is normally derived from the increased coordination of economic policies (component 2).[7]

5. The saving of the cost of the mutual conversion of member currencies for trade and travel, which occurs fully only in the last stage of monetary integration.[8]

Most of these benefits show nonrivalry in consumption; enjoyment by one member does not reduce the enjoyment of other members. This jointness in consumption is one characteristic of public goods. At the same time, these benefits accrue mostly to participating member countries, except for spillover effects such as the reduced attention to relative exchange rates among member currencies by those in nonmember countries and the saving of the cost of currency exchange by tourists from nonmember countries.[9] Thus, most of the benefits exhibit nonrivalry, which is one characteristic of public goods, but they do not usually exhibit nonexclusion, which is another characteristic of public goods.

The most important of these benefits seem to be 1 and 5, which are closely associated with the functions of money as a unit of account, a medium of exchange, and a store of value. Thus, more basically, the public-good nature of the benefits of monetary unions stems from the nature of money. Money is a device that economizes on the information costs required for transactions and that allows one to procure a stable bundle of goods at lower cost, as emphasized by Brunner and Meltzer (1971). As with information generally, the use of money carries an intrinsic externality. Each individual chooses whether to hold money and how much, but the choice of an asset as money is a social choice. Once a monetary system is established, once an asset is chosen as its currency by a society, or once mutual confidence emerges in the use of a particular commodity or currency as the common currency, then the benefit from this public (implicit) consensus becomes a public good.

Turning to the costs of joining a monetary union, one such cost is that the monetary independence of national economies becomes limited, particularly when international capital mobility is high. Therefore the attainment of the nationally desired levels of unemployment and prices is sacrificed. The floating exchange rate system gives national economies the opportunity to follow a maximin strategy in the interplay of monetary policies. By joining a monetary union, a country gives up this maximin position and must adhere to the mutual consensus that results from policy coordination. Since countries differ in the position of their Phillips curves, in their rates of productivity growth, and in their preferences concerning the choice between unemployment and inflation, policy coordination often means that the participating countries will have to sacrifice attainment of their policy objectives.

In contrast to the benefits of monetary integration, which are mostly collective and international, the costs (the sacrifices made when a country joins a monetary union) are mostly national. This contrast between the benefits and costs of monetary integration is a crucial factor that makes it feasible to apply the calculus of participation to the problem of monetary integration.

Of course, as noted by Fleming (1971), the costs will also have a public-good character if the nonlinearity of the Phillips curve means that the aggregate tradeoff between inflation and unemployment is less favorable after a monetary union than before. The size of this negative effect of monetary integration is an empirical question, but we will assume in the following analysis that, as far as the costs are concerned, their private-good nature dominates their public-good nature.

The nature of the benefits and costs of monetary integration have several characteristics. First, the benefit-cost payoff to participating countries changes over time. Initially the costs of sacrificing domestic economic objectives and an independent monetary policy are large. As capital market integration proceeds, the financing of deficits becomes easier, so adjustment costs become smaller.

By contrast, the common benefits of monetary integration can be enjoyed only at a late stage. For example, the saving of the costs of currency conversion occurs only after a complete exchange rate union has been attained, and the benefits arising from the stability of exchange rates can be reaped only after confidence in the fixity of parities has been established. Therefore, the benefits can be attained only in the long run, and uncertainty remains whether they will actually be realized, whereas the costs of sacrificing an independent monetary policy are incurred with certainty at an early stage.

Second, although the costs are concrete (taking such forms as higher rates of inflation and increased unemployment), most of the benefits are vague and abstract. Of course, it is hard to neglect completely the benefits of having a single currency in a well-integrated economy. Suppose the United States were to be divided into two regions, each with its own monetary authority. The post-transition disadvantages of having two monetary systems provide a measure of the upper limit of the possible advantages of a complete monetary union.

Third, the openness of the participating country has an important influence on the magnitude of the benefits and costs it derives from monetary integration. If a country is open, with large import and export flows relative to domestic transactions, the costs of adjusting its GNP or employment level for balance of payments reasons will be small (McKinnon 1963). If the country is closed, however, the costs will be large. As for the benefits, the benefits arising from monetary integration and the attendant improvement in the trade environment—the benefit of greater stability and predictability of exchange rates and the saving of the costs of frequent currency conversion—will be larger the more open is the country. Here the degree of economic integration plays a crucial role because the more integrated are the international markets for goods and factors of production, the more open will countries tend to be. Thus, the integration of the markets for goods and factors of production strengthens the feasibility of monetary integration by increasing the benefits and decreasing the costs.

Calculus of Participation

Recently in the theory of participation, the tools of public economics have been applied to political science, providing the theoretical basis for associating group behavior with individual rationality. The application of tools developed in economics to politics requires caution, but recent developments in political science have shown that the application of economic analysis can clarify the political analysis of economic conflicts.

Before the calculus of participation approach can be applied, it is necessary to specify the decision unit (or player) in the international conflict game. The nation-state is the natural unit of decision making and will be adopted as the player in the game. However, it is difficult to think of a uniform "national interest." A country is indeed an economic as well as political unit and also a unit of international negotiation, but individuals in the same nation do not necessarily share common benefits and costs. The interests of exporters and importers differ, as do the interests of producers and consumers and those of the rich and the poor. Moreover, the interests of those lending and borrowing abroad may conflict with each other over the value of the exchange rate. It is necessary, therefore, to keep in mind the fact that regarding a nation as the decision unit is nothing but a first approximation.

The rational theory of participation (see, for example, Riker and Ordeshook 1973, chapter 3) indicates that an individual decision unit decides to participate in a collective action if the anticipated benefit is larger than the cost. The rational decision for a country contemplating membership in a monetary union is to join if the benefits from participation, such as those deriving from the use of a common currency, the reduction in uncertainty, and the increase in bargaining power as a group, are larger than the costs, such as the sacrifice of an independent monetary policy and the wider variation in the unemployment rate.

When the benefits of collective action exhibit a public-good character, however, the amount of collective action may be less than optimal, where optimality is judged by the Paretian standard. Olson showed this by applying the theory of public goods to collective action (Olson 1965; Olson and Zeckhauser 1966). Suppose there is a single public good whose benefits are commonly shared by participating agents. The rational decision by an individual agent is to equate the marginal private benefit from the public good to the marginal cost of supplying a unit of the public good. However, the optimal outcome from the point of view of society as a whole is to equate the marginal cost to the social benefit, which is the sum of the individual benefits. Thus, the supply of public goods may be less than optimal because the individual decision unit does not take account of the external effect on other decision units. Therefore, even when a consensus exists concerning the objective of a collective action, the amount produced may be too small. The interesting testable hypothesis about group behavior is that the behavior of a large group will be different from that of a small group; the shortfall in supply will be more likely the larger is the group because the free-rider problem intrinsic in the supply of public goods without the possibility of exclusion will be more acute if each member shares in the common benefit to only a small degree. A second hypothesis is that the decision unit that receives a relatively large proportion of the benefit of public goods will be likely to bear more than a proportional share of the cost. In other words if each participant behaves rationally according to the private benefit-cost calculation, a small decision unit can exploit a large one. (See the appendix to this chapter.)

The same argument can be applied to the analysis of public "bads" as well. If costs are incurred in preventing the generation of public bads, then there is a tendency to overproduce public bads, inasmuch as the marginal social harm of public bads is larger than their marginal private harm.

Olson's theory of collective action, interesting as it is, is subject to several criticisms. First, as pointed out by Wagner (1966) and developed in more detail by Frohlich, Oppenheimer, and Young (1971), the theory of collective action neglects the role of political entrepreneurship or leadership in integrating the individual benefits to a collective action. If an agent with political entrepreneurship can persuade the group of the effectiveness of collective action in spite of the apparent excess of individual cost over individual benefit, then the proper amount of collective goods may be supplied, with some leadership surplus being left over for that agent.

Second, the analysis assumes passive behavior on the part of each participant and accordingly neglects the leader-follower relationship analyzed in Stackelberg 1934. If a participant picks the most profitable point on the opponent's reaction curve, then he behaves as a leader and can enjoy the leadership or exploitation solution. (To avoid complications arising from the two uses of the word *leadership*, this case will be called *exploitation*, while leadership in the sense of political entrepreneurship will be called *political entrepreneurship*.)

Finally, Olson's analysis is limited by the assumption that the size of the collective group is given and that the collective benefit is not exclusionary. Under these assumptions, in a group with a given number of participants, the collective benefit will be enjoyed by each participant regardless of his willingness to pay.

An economic theory of clubs with variable size of group and with possible exclusion of nonmembers from enjoyment of the collective good has been developed by Buchanan (1964). According to his analysis, collective goods are supplied optimally provided that appropriate charges are imposed on the use of the service and provided that the services of the collective goods can be exclusively supplied to the member of the group. This approach has more relevance to monetary integration since the benefits of integration are public in that their enjoyment by a particular member does not diminish the enjoyment of others[10] but at the same time most of the benefits are enjoyed almost exclusively by the countries participating in the monetary union.[11] In short, there exists nonrivalry in the consumption of the services of a monetary union but not nonexclusiveness.

Another characteristic of participation in monetary unions is that the basic decision of whether to join the monetary union is discrete. This decision is made based on the terms of agreement concerning the process of monetary integration and the distribution of adjustment burdens. If we take account of such characteristics, the process of agreeing on monetary integration can be modeled as follows.

The decision of countries considering whether to participate is based on a comparison of the gains from joining a union with the costs and is an all-or-nothing decision as formulated in part II of the appendix to this chapter. The conclusion is straightforward: If there are externalities in increasing the size of membership, an individual nation's participation decision based on a rational calculation may lead to a smaller than optimal currency area even if the country is fully aware of the costs and benefits. The problem is that an individual nation's decision is based on a private benefit-cost calculation, while the public benefit to the group as a whole includes the gains to the countries that are already in the union.

Monetary Integration in Historical Perspective

Examples of monetary integration can be found in the formation process of nation-states. The experience of such countries as Germany, Italy, and Japan, which developed relatively late, is especially interesting because the process of monetary and currency unification in these countries meant uniting currencies issued by local provinces into a single national currency.[12] An analysis of this process may shed light on the interrelationship among the processes of political integration, economic integration, and monetary unification.

In Germany, economic unification was already in progress when the second Reich was founded in 1871. The *Zollverein* (customs union) led by Prussia represented a significant step toward economic unification because commerce among states relied on the use of foreign currencies. This required people to convert currencies amid frequent fluctuations in exchange rates. In order to alleviate this situation, attempts were made to fix the parities among local currencies. The southern states agreed to fix the parities among their currencies by the Munich Convention of 1837. This led to the Dresden Convention the following year, which established a fixed relationship between the thaler of the northern states and the florin of the southern states on the basis of the Cologne mark of fine silver. Prussia thus played the role of political entrepreneur in promoting economic as well as monetary integration (Stolper 1967; Henderson 1939).

There was, however, no common currency. When Germany became a nation-state in 1871, it was still divided into seven separate currency areas, based on silver. There were thirty-three banks of issue totally unconnected with one other and operating under different rules and regulations. When the new Reich was established, the states agreed on the relative values of their respective currencies. At the same time, the Reich established a unified currency on the gold standard. In 1871 the mark was adopted as the currency unit. Two years later, the gold standard was established by law; the use of silver was reduced to small coins. In 1875 the Prussian Bank, one of the thirty-three banks of issue, was reorganized as the Reichsbank, but not until 1935 was the right of issue concentrated in the Reichsbank (Stolper 1967).

In Italy, political unification led by the Kingdom of Sardinia came so suddenly in 1861 that neither economic nor monetary unification was planned prior to that date. Upon political unification, the tariffs of Sardinia were extended to the entire nation, creating a customs union. The monetary situation was chaotic; two different lira, that of Piedmont and that of Tuscany, the Austrian florin, the ducat of the Sicilies, and the scudo romano of the Papal States circulated simultaneously. To unify coinage, the Piedmont lira, based on the decimal system, was chosen as the standard currency; as a result, Piedmont played the role of political entrepreneur. In 1865, when Italy joined the Latin Monetary Union, the ratio of silver to gold was fixed at 15.5 to 1, although the existence of a large amount of irredeemable notes prevented Italy from completely joining the union.

The unification of paper currency was more difficult. Banks did not want to give up their seigniorage rights. The Sardinian National Bank grew far more rapidly than any other and absorbed two Tuscan banks of issue by merger to become the Bank of Italy in 1893. The Bank of Italy then became the de facto central bank and became a central bank de jure in 1926 (Clough 1964).

In Japan during the Tokugawa period, political power was highly concentrated in the central (Tokugawa) feudal government, and economic integration had also progressed considerably. It is true that agricultural labor was not allowed to migrate from one local district (Han) to another without permission. However, the trade of commodities between local districts by authorized merchants was allowed to take place almost completely free of customs barriers. The right to issue coins was monopolized by the central government, and the coinage system was on a bimetallic standard; three types of coin—gold, silver, and copper (later occasionally replaced by iron)—circulated, gold being currency by tail, silver currency by weight (later by tail), and copper for auxiliary use.

The right to issue notes for local circulation (Hansatsu) was left to the feudal lords of local provinces, subject to the authorization of the central government.[13] In 1661 the first feudal notes were issued. Local notes were issued mostly to ease the financial difficulty of local feudal lords and occasionally to provide a sufficient amount of currency as a medium of exchange during periods when deflationary coinage policies were being taken by the central government (Sakudō 1958). In 1871, 244 provinces were issuing nearly 1,700 kinds of local notes—probably the largest number of local issuing agents within the borders of an individual nation. The outstanding local notes amounted to more than 90 million Ryo, as compared to the outstanding coinage of 130 million Ryo (Yamaguchi 1966).

After the Meiji Restoration, the central government introduced the decimal system, and the yen became the new currency unit. From 1872 to 1879 the new government redeemed outstanding local notes. Newly established national banks were given the right to issue notes. After an inflationary period caused by the excessive issue of inconvertible bank notes and a subsequent deflation, the Bank of Japan was chartered as the sole issuing bank in 1899.

There were even several attempts at monetary integration across national borders in the nineteenth century. In 1857, K. L. von Bruck was instrumental in forming a monetary union to fix parities between the northern and southern states in the Zollverein and between them and the Austrian monetary system (Vienna Convention). He attempted to fix the exchange parities between the currencies of these areas based on the metric pound (Zollpfund) rather than attempting to create a single currency in all the Zollverein states and the Hapsburg Empire. His efforts did not succeed, however, because the Austrian government did not follow the agreement of

1857 but allowed the value of its paper currency to fluctuate; the monetary union came to an end with the Seven Week War. The provisions for fixed parities remained alive in the Zollverein, however, and paved the way for genuine currency unification in the new Reich.

The Latin Monetary Union was the most notable attempt at monetary unification in the nineteenth century (Saitō 1939; Willis 1901; Krämer 1971). It was formed when Belgium, Switzerland, and Italy adopted the bimetallic monetary standard that France had originated in 1803. Some joint circulation of currencies was already taking place before the union was formalized. The discovery of gold in Australia and California caused wide fluctuations in the parity between gold and silver, and the fluctuations became even more pronounced with the movement toward the gold standard in each country. Moreover, silver coins of lower quality minted in Italy and Switzerland were flowing into Belgium and France. In order to avoid confusion, Belgium took the initiative to create a union based on the French bimetallic standard in 1865.

The unit of denomination of the currencies of the member countries of the Latin Monetary Union—France, Belgium, Switzerland, and Italy—was adjusted to conform to the French franc. Each member could issue standard coins of 100, 50, 20, 10, and 5 francs in gold and 5 francs in silver; these coins were to circulate freely throughout the union. In addition, each member could mint subsidiary coins in limited amounts. The monetary authorities of the member countries were required to accept limited amounts of these coins in payment. The union was open to any country, but only Greece joined. Other countries, including Austria, Spain, Sweden, the Papal States, and the Balkan states, adopted the franc standard without joining the union.

The Latin Monetary Union was formed under the dominating influence of France in an attempt to sustain the bimetallic standard. In the 1870s, however, the movement toward the gold standard was a worldwide tide and was accompanied by the rapid depreciation of silver. This was probably the reason why many countries refrained from joining the union. The union was forced to depart from its bimetallic policy because the free coinage of silver in France and Belgium had induced a flood of silver inflows. The union limited the coinage of silver in 1874 and discontinued it in 1878, thus transforming bimetallism into a limping gold standard.

Another difficulty concerned the subsidiary currencies of Italy and Greece, both of which issued irredeemable paper money in addition to coining union subsidiary currency. When the paper money depreciated, the subsidiary currencies were exported. In 1878 the Italian subsidiary currency ceased to be legal tender in the other countries, and this provision was extended to Greek subsidiary currency in 1908. At the outbreak of World War I the member countries introduced a paper standard, and this led to the breakdown of the union. The union was formally dissolved in 1925 when Belgium withdrew.[14]

Another, and quite successful, monetary union was the Scandinavian Monetary Union (Nielsen 1933). In addition to the growing cultural ties among the Scandinavian nations, joint circulation of currencies was already occurring in several border regions. The union was established between Sweden and Denmark in 1873, and Norway joined in 1875. The krone was the common unit of denomination. At first, joint circulation was virtually limited to coins; in 1894, however, the note-issuing banks of Norway and Sweden agreed to accept one another's notes at par, and in 1900 Denmark joined this agreement. The banks of the member countries opened accounts for each other. Checks could be drawn on these accounts, but credit balances earned no interest. Monetary integration proceeded to the point where bank notes as well as token money circulated at par, checks could be liquidated at par, and the quotation of exchange rates was discontinued.

After 1905 the conditions governing the joint circulation of notes were modified to allow commissions to be charged when foreign notes were used. However, the joint circulation of bank notes continued successfully until World War I. With the outbreak of the war, the redemption of bank notes was suspended and the union ended.

These historical experiences provide several lessons. First, political integration invariably preceded complete monetary integration, while economic integration sometimes preceded and sometimes followed political integration. In Germany, the formation of a customs union preceded political integration. In Italy, political integration occurred before the free movement of goods and factors was achieved. In Japan, free trade had already been achieved when the Meiji government completely centralized political power, but the free movement of labor occurred only after the Meiji Restoration. In Germany some attempts at fixing the parities between local currencies were effective even without political integration, but they did not last long unless political integration consolidated the fixity of parities through currency unification (for a similar conclusion, see Krämer 1971).

Second, monetary unions in the form of exchange rate unions across national borders did not last long because the political integration needed to consolidate them did not occur. These unions were effective, at least in the short run, only if political leadership was provided by a dominant country, the number of members was few, and there was extensive economic integration.

Third, the existence of a metal money, or metal monies, was instrumental in maintaining confidence in the exchange rate union. The irredeemable paper money in Italy and Greece created difficulties for the Latin Monetary Union. On the other hand, adherence to the gold standard helped the Scandinavian Monetary Union.

These findings can be related to the calculus of participation. The benefits from monetary integration are similar to those from public goods, while the costs are directly borne by individual participants. Moreover, the benefits can be enjoyed only when strong confidence is attained in the fixed parities or when a single currency is circulated. Therefore, the metallic content of currencies was important to create confidence in the exchange rate union, and political integration was necessary to sustain that confidence for a long period.

Fourth, these historical experiences suggest the difficulty of keeping two kinds of money circulating at the same time. Gresham's Law was always at work: the currency of higher quality was either hoarded or exported, leading to an excess of the currency of lower quality in the union. Moreover, when there were two kinds of money, conflicts of interest often arose. In the Latin Monetary Union, for example, France had a vested interest in using silver as the standard currency; in Japan during the Tokugawa Period, a conflict over the metallic content of gold and silver coins arose between merchants around Tokyo where gold was more popular and those around Osaka where silver was more popular (Ōishi 1974).

Fifth, the cost to participating members of monetary unions in the nineteenth century involved the sacrifice of seigniorage, not the cost of policy adjustments. The costs associated with the underutilization of resources incurred in order to correct a disequilibrium in the balance of payments were hardly observed before the Great Depression (Guggenheim 1973, p. 97).

These historical experiences suggest that the relationship between economic and political factors depends on the formation and progress of monetary unification. They remind us of the long debate on the state or chartal theory of money (Ellis 1934, chapter 2), which states that money circulates because it is legal tender. This theory in its purest form is refuted by the effectiveness of Gresham's Law. At the same time, however, in such cases as Italy and the Zollverein, political leadership in the sense of entrepreneurship functioned as a catalyst in realizing the public-good character of money. It does not seem to be operationally meaningful to ask whether economic or political factors are primarily responsible for the emergence of a common currency. More analysis is needed to clarify the interaction between economic and political factors in the creation of a currency area.

Concluding Remarks

The foregoing politico-economic analysis of monetary integration and the historical sketches of examples of monetary integration during the last century provide several lessons for the current process of monetary integration in the EC and more generally for world monetary reform. It is difficult to achieve, and even more difficult to sustain, a monetary union without political unification. Unless the EC moves toward political integration, monetary integration will be difficult to achieve.

The benefits of monetary integration have the nature of public goods, not so much because of their nonexclusiveness as because of their nonrivalry in consumption. On the other hand, most of the costs of monetary integration have the nature of private goods (or bads); that is, each nation bears the costs directly and individually.

Another important characteristic of monetary integration, particularly that of the EC, is the difference in the time profile of benefits and costs. At present, and in the short run, the benefits seem mostly political: increased prestige and negotiating power due to the enlarged scale of the decision unit (Europe as a whole instead of each country individually). In other words, the benefits are abstract and political (or psychological) rather than concrete and economic. In the short run, the costs of joining a (pseudo) exchange rate union are concrete and definite. They are mostly economic except for the political or psychological loss from giving up monetary sovereignty. The loss to individual countries is mainly the sacrifice of the attainment of suitable employment and price levels.

The economic benefits from participating in a monetary union, if they exist, are realized only in the long run. They are attained only after the pseudo-exchange rate union becomes, or comes close to, a complete exchange rate union. The benefits of exchange rate stability are reaped only after public confidence in the irrevocable fixity of exchange rate emerges, and those of the saving of currency conversion costs are realized only after currency unification. The maintenance of public confidence is difficult without a metallic standard, and the attainment of currency unification is even harder in the absence of political integration.

Thus, many economists are dubious about the prospects for monetary integration in the EC. The immediate political effects from the increased prestige of Europe as a whole seem to be the main driving force behind the negotiations.

One analytical proposition we have obtained from the calculus of participation is that if the benefits from a joint action have the property of nonrivalry in consumption, then the isolated, individual, rational decision will make the realized size of the union smaller than optimal. This simple proposition requires several reservations if it is to be applied to the actual process of monetary integration in Europe.

First, the conclusion is reversed if the public-bad character of costs dominates the public-good character of benefits. In some situations the inclusion of an additional member may reduce the common benefits of monetary integration due to the nonlinearity of the Phillips curve (Fleming 1971). At the outset of monetary integration, this public-bad effect could be significant. However, in the later stages of monetary integration, as transaction and information costs are economized, the public-good character will come to dominate.

Second, the different time patterns of benefits and costs should be recognized. The tradeoff is not between actual costs and benefits but between the discounted values of the streams of expected future costs and benefits. The time preference and attitude toward risk of participating countries and their subjective evaluation of the future benefits of the monetary union play a crucial role.

Third, if side payments are feasible—for example, in the form of a concession in agricultural policies in favor of a new member—then mutual negotiations with a perfect understanding of the benefits and costs may lead to a union of optimal size.

Finally, the calculus of participation is applicable only on the assumption that the participants have correct information on the benefits and costs that accrue to them from a joint action. The question of the size of an actual union relative to the optimal size can be answered only if this assumption is satisfied. There are two difficulties. One is whether politicians are fully aware of the economic as well as political benefits and costs of monetary integration. The other is whether politicians represent a consensus of the preferences of the public—namely, some weighted average of the interests of the people.

To summarize, the benefits of irrevocably fixed exchange rates and the benefits of a unified currency are recognized. At the same time, however, we cannot neglect the fact that the benefits are attainable only in the long run, after public confidence is generated in the fixity of parities or after political integration progresses far enough to achieve currency unification. By contrast, the recent difficulty in the EC of maintaining the same exchange rates relative to the dollar dramatizes the substantial magnitude of the immediate economic losses arising from the sacrifice of short-run domestic objectives.

The recent formation of the European Monetary System (EMS) is more an attempt to stabilize exchange rates through coordinating economic policies, particularly monetary policies, than an attempt to fix exchange rates directly. No doubt, behind this development lies the desire for a common European currency, but the EMS represents a more practical approach than the original plan to create a unified currency for the EC. For reasons discussed above, however, it will be a long time before a unified currency for Europe can be realized.

The frame of reference developed in this chapter is also applicable to international monetary reform. The gold standard before World War I was a loose exchange rate union. The Tripartite Agreement concerning the formation of the IMF was an endeavor to regain the public benefits arising from the fixity of exchange rates. However, the recent breakdown of the Bretton Woods regime suggests that an exchange rate union without a unified world political authority is rather difficult. The costs are immediate; the benefits are uncertain and depend on such precarious factors as public confidence in the fixity of parities.

Suppose the world were united by an irrevocable currency union or even by a uniform currency. The public benefits from such a development would be quite large: the cost of information needed for exchanges would decline, people would be able to travel abroad without worrying about currency exchange. However, these gains would be realized only at the last moment, that is, only after people firmly believed in the fixity of exchange rates or only after worldwide political unification proceeded so that worldwide currency unification could be achieved. Yet the costs are immediate and concrete; the number of participants is too large; and the openness of many countries is insufficient to reduce the costs of sacrificing the effectiveness of demand-management policies. The Bretton Woods regime collapsed because of the immediate costs of policy adjustments. Moreover, the United States does not seem likely to recover in the near future the leadership position that it enjoyed during the last two decades. Therefore, a single currency area for the world as a whole is still only a dream.

Appendix: Analytical Formulation of the Calculus of Participation

I. Suppose there are N countries $(j = 1, 2, \ldots, N)$. Let C_j and X be the contribution of the jth country and the supply of the collective good, respectively. Let us assume that X is produced by the following production relationship:

$$X = F\left(\sum_{j=1}^{N} C_j \right), \qquad F' > 0, F'' < 0.$$

The satisfaction level of the jth participant is given by

$$U^j(X, C_j), \qquad U_1^j > 0, U_2^j < 0; U_{11}^j < 0, U_{22}^j < 0.$$

The analysis of Olson and Zeckhauser (1966) can then be reformulated as follows: The rational behavior of individual countries leads to

$$U_1^j F' + U_2^j \leqslant 0, \qquad C_j = 0 \text{ if strict inequality holds.} \tag{3A.1}$$

On the other hand, in order to obtain the Pareto-optimal configuration, we must maximize $\sum_{j=1}^{N} \beta^j U^j(X, C_j)$ where the β^j's are the Lagrange multipliers indicating the weight of evaluation, leading to

$$\sum_{j=1}^{N} \beta^j U_1^j F' + \beta^j U_2^j \leqslant 0, \qquad C_j = 0 \text{ if strict inequality holds.} \tag{3A.2}$$

Multiplying equation 3A.1 by β_j and summing with respect to j yields

$$\sum_{j=1}^{N} \beta^j U_1^j F' + \sum_{j=1}^{N} \beta^j U_2^j \leqslant 0. \tag{3A.3}$$

Since $U_{11}^j < 0$ and $F'' < 0$, the level of public good X corresponding to equation 3A.2 is larger than that corresponding to 3A.3. Therefore, we can see that production of the public good will be below the optimal level if each participant behaves according to individual rationality. It is also clear from equations 3A.2 and 3A.3 that the shortage of the collective good will be more serious in a group with many participants than in a group with few participants.

Moreover, if we assume in addition that the marginal rate of substitution between the collective good and individual sacrifice (i.e., $-U_1^j/U_2^j$) is smaller for a country whose relative size is smaller, then we can deduce from equation 3A.1 that a participant whose relative size is large must bear a disproportionate share of the burden. See Olson and Zeckhauser 1966 and Olson 1965.

II. In the above analysis, the size of the group is predetermined to be N. Here let us relax this assumption to allow for the possibility that a subgroup of countries creates a monetary union. Let I_j be the index of participation such that

$I_j = 1$ if the jth country is in the union

$\quad = 0$ if the jth country is not in the union.

Also define the set of j already participating in the union as J^+ such that

$J^+ = \{j/I_j = 1\}$.

Let $\lambda_j(\sum_{j=1}^{N} \lambda_j = 1)$ be the relative size of country j. Assume that the collective benefit is a function of the relative size of the monetary union. Let C_j be the cost to country j of joining the union. Then the rational choice for an individual country j outside the monetary union is given by the following rule:

$$\text{If} \quad U^j\left(F\left(\sum_{i \in \{J^+ + j\}} \lambda_i\right), C_j\right) > U^j(0,0), \quad \text{then join}$$

$$< U^j(0,0), \quad \text{then do not join.}$$

However, for the international community as a whole, the criterion for country j to join the union is

$$\sum_{i \in J^+} \beta^i \left\{ U^i\left(F\left(\sum_{i \in \{J^+ + j\}} \lambda_i\right), C_i\right) - U^i\left(F\left(\sum_{i \in J^+} \lambda_i\right), C_i\right) \right\}$$

$$+ \beta^j \left[U^j\left(F\left(\sum_{i \in \{J^+ + j\}} \lambda_i\right), C_j\right) - U^j(0,0) \right] > 0.$$

The term with the summation sign is positive if there exist external economies in the monetary union. Therefore, if the common benefits of a monetary union increase with size, the rational choices of individual countries will tend to lead to smaller monetary unions than optimal.

International Monetary Interdependence in a Keynesian Model

Thus far we have concentrated on the first stage of the world money game, the stage of choosing an international monetary regime. In the remainder of this book, we will turn to the second stage and examine the interplay of economic policies among countries when a particular monetary regime has been adopted as the outcome of the first stage of the game. Judging from the recent succession of international financial crises, it seems that the choice the world faces is not among several variants of the fixed exchange rate system, such as the gold standard or the adjustable peg, but among the fixed exchange rate system, the floating exchange rate system, and an appropriate combination of the two. We therefore focus on the interdependence of monetary policies under a system of fixed exchange rates and one of floating exchange rates. To prepare for the discussion, let us look at the literature concerning the coordination and conflicts of economic policies among national economies and see what problems remain.

Survey of Studies of Policy Interdependence

As early as the 1950s one can find, at least implicitly, substantial discussion about the consistency of national economic policies in a two-country model (Meade 1951, chapter 10). However, Meade is not so much concerned with international policy conflicts between two countries as with policy conflicts within each country. It is Cooper (1968) who puts forth the necessity of international cooperation directly and most persuasively. Taking as an example the Atlantic Community, which was under a fixed exchange rate regime, he points out that increasing interdependence complicates the successful pursuit of national objectives by way of three mechanisms.

First, increasing interdependence increases the number and magnitude of disturbances to which each country's balance of payments is subjected, and this directs national policy instruments toward the restoration of external balance. Second, increasing interdependence slows down the process by which policy authorities are able to attain domestic objectives. Finally, greater integration may lead a community of nations to engage in retaliatory actions, which leave all countries worse off than they need be. Therefore, Cooper argues, it is necessary for the Atlantic Community to engage at least partly in the joint determination of economic objectives and policies.

Thus the central problem of international economic cooperation is defined to be "how to keep the manifold benefits of extensive international inter-course free of crippling restrictions, while at the same time preserving a maximum degree of freedom for each nation to pursue its legitimate economic objectives" (Cooper 1968, p. 15). According to Cooper, as with marriage, the benefits of close international relations can be enjoyed only at the expense of giving up a certain amount of independence or autonomy. Here the main theme in the analysis of economic cooperation is clearly presented. In particular, the third factor mentioned above, that the independent pursuit of individual national policies may not lead to a desirable situation for the community as a whole, is the crucial reason for the need for cooperation in a highly integrated world economy.

Cooper also suggests that both the static and dynamic aspects of international cooperation should be considered. Even when all national objectives are consistent and there are a sufficient number of policy instruments with which to attain them, growing interdependence greatly slows down the process by which independently acting national authorities attain their economic objectives (the second factor above). Cooper distinguishes between policy coordination, where the gains are achieved from better mutual timing, and policy harmonization, which is based on static efficiency grounds. This dynamic aspect of coordination is developed further in Cooper 1969. By using a two-country Keynesian model with monetary and fiscal policies, Cooper calculates the values of the characteristic roots of the dynamic system of adjustment equations, assuming different degrees of interdependence. He finds that increasing interdependence reduces the absolute value of the dominant (negative) characteristic root and hence slows down the speed of adjustment of the system. The lack of coordination among policymakers delays the achievement of national objectives, such as full employment and target rates of growth, and, under fixed exchange rates, increases the need for international reserves. Most significantly, these delays in attaining targets and the need for reserves increase with the degree of economic interdependence among nations.

Given the problem of coordination as it is proposed here, one needs an analytical framework in order to analyze policy interactions among national economies. A series of illuminating models for this purpose has been developed by Mundell (1962, 1963, 1968). One of the common features of this variety of models is that they are general equilibrium models incorporating such monetary aspects as the stock of money and bonds. For the analysis of policy interdependence, two-country versions of these models are utilized.

There are several alternative approaches, which are not necessarily competing but often complementary, for analyzing policy interactions, coordination, and conflicts. The first and most natural approach is to advocate direct cooperation or joint actions among national policy authorities. Cooper's works are examples of what one might call the direct coordination approach. Later, when we examine economic cooperation under floating exchange rates, the proposal by McKinnon (1974) to create a tripartite agreement among the major countries of the world will be taken as one of the pleas for direct consultation and cooperation among national monetary authorities.

The second approach is the celebrated policy assignment approach, skillfully applied to international economics by Mundell. This approach, which is based on the general theory of economic policy of Tinbergen (1952), seeks to find the optimal assignment of targets to instruments of economic policy. Mundell advises that the achievement of desirable ends requires that each instrument be assigned to the market where it is relatively effective. Thus, this approach is also known as the principle of effective market classification.

In a generalized version of the two-country model, Swoboda and Dornbusch (1973) study the problem of global policy assignment and, in particular, that of reconciling national income targets in an interdependent world economy. They show that gearing monetary policies to the desired reserve distribution and fiscal policies to income targets constitutes a stable assignment of instruments to targets, while the reverse pairing leads to instability.

In fact, it is in the case of two (or more) countries in an integrated world economy that the principle of effective market classification really comes into its own (Niehans 1968), because in a national economy it is rather hard to find reasons why decentralized decision making among various branches of the government is needed, except perhaps for the sake of conserving on information flows between branches in the short run.

An international system is characterized by decentralized decision making almost by definition. The instruments of each country are assigned to its own targets. Since each country's policies usually have a comparative advantage with respect to its own targets, this assignment usually satisfies the requirement of effective market classification.

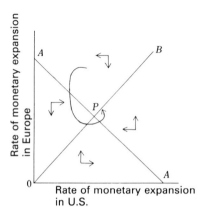

Figure 4.1

However, there are cases in which the international division of policy assignments does not necessarily coincide with the above "natural" assignments. As an example of the division of international policy assignments, Mundell (1971) advocates the following assignment of policies under the dollar standard: The United States adjusts its money supply to peg the price level for the world economy, and Europe (or the rest of the world) adjusts its money supply to maintain balance of payments equilibrium.

In figure 4.1, the rate of monetary expansion in country 1 (say, the United States) is measured along the horizontal axis and that of country 2 (Europe) along the vertical axis. The downward-sloping line AA indicates the rates of money growth in the two countries that would keep the international price level stable. The upward-sloping line OB shows the rates of money growth that would keep the balance of payments in each country in equilibrium. The downward slope of AA reflects the proposition that the world price level depends on the weighted average of the rate of monetary expansion in each country, while the positive slope of the OB schedule follows from the approximate dependence of the balance of payments on the difference between the money growth rates in the two countries.

Above line AA the world suffers from inflationary pressures; below it, from deflationary pressures. On the right side of line OB the balance of payments of the United States is in deficit; on the left it is in surplus. The policy assignment defined above (the assignment of the monetary policy of the United States to the price level target and that of Europe to the balance of payments target) will yield a stable result as indicated by the arrows; the reverse assignment will lead to instability.

A corollary of this assignment approach is what is called the "redundancy" problem (Mundell 1968, appendix to chapter 13). For the world as a whole, the sum of each country's balance of payments is equal to zero, or, more generally, to the increase in the amount of outside money in the international system (gold or SDRs). This is a direct consequence of the first element of interdependence. If there are n countries, only $(n - 1)$ of them can succeed in reaching their independent balance of payments targets; at least one of them must accept the position of acting as an international residual. In other words, interdependence necessarily imposes another constraint on national targets in order to render them consistent. Mundell argues that if each country has a distinct instrument with which to control its balance of payments, there is an additional degree of freedom. This redundant degree of freedom should be used to control the international price level according to Mundell (see also Cooper 1968 and Niehans 1968).

The strength of the assignment approach lies in its simplicity. One need be concerned only with the one-to-one correspondence between instruments and targets. The economy of information that results when this prescription is followed by policymakers is its advantage.

However, there are limitations to this approach that require it to be supplemented by alternative approaches. First, if one looks at the process of achieving economic targets, it is clear that a one-to-one pairing of instruments and targets is not sufficient because an optimal mix of economic policies of varying strengths is needed in order to achieve an efficient realization of conflicting goals. As a result, there is a need for another approach—the optimizing approach, developed by Niehans (1968). The first element is a social welfare function providing a ranking of the relevant bundles of target values. The second element is an efficient target frontier that specifies the maximum value of an objective that can be obtained for given values of the other objectives. The optimal combination of policy instruments is the one that maximizes the social welfare function within the feasible region of target combinations. Normally this point occurs at the point of tangency between the efficient target frontier and a social indifference curve.

The second limitation of the assignment approach, in particular when it is applied to the division of burdens in the international economy, is that it does not take into account the problem of whether there are sufficient incentives for national policy authorities to pursue the economic objective that should be assigned to them in order to achieve the best division of labor. In order for an international policy assignment to be sustainable by policy authorities, it is necessary that the policy assignment be "incentive compatible" in the sense that each country has an incentive to take the necessary actions if others are taking the necessary actions as well.

In Mundell's example of the dollar standard, incentives exist for Europe (or the rest of the world other than the United States) to adopt contractionary policies when its balance of payments is in deficit. But it is not always true that Europe has an incentive to adopt expansionary policies when its balance of payments is in surplus. Moreover, the United States does not necessarily have an incentive to play the role of benevolent world leader by adjusting its monetary or fiscal policies to keep the world price level constant.

Probably part of the reason why the Bretton Woods regime collapsed is that the rest of the world did not play the game symmetrically and the United States had to be concerned with domestic policy objectives other than world price stability (see also Niehans 1968, n. 22).

This second limitation leads to the necessity of adopting a strategic approach—that is, an approach based on the joint reactions and counterreactions of each participating country. This approach is most effectively implemented when one applies the theory of duopoly or oligopoly and some simple concepts of game theory to the problem.

As a matter of fact, further application of the optimizing approach to a two-country situation leads naturally to the strategic approach. As shown by Niehans (1968), once the optimizing approach is applied to a two-country model, each country's behavior depends on what it expects concerning the other's behavior. The remaining chapters represent an attempt to apply a strategic approach directly to the problem of international monetary interdependence.

The application of a strategic approach to international economics is not completely new. If we broaden our perspective to an area outside the scope of monetary or macroeconomic conflicts, we find that works by Scitovsky (1941), Johnson (1953), and Gorman (1958) on tariffs and retaliation are pioneering analyses of the interdependence and strategic nature of trade conflicts. The mutual taxation of foreign investment incomes can also be formulated as a game in which an agreement to avoid double taxation helps to achieve a contract curve situation (Hamada 1966). In the field of monetary relations only recently have the political or strategic aspects of confrontations concerning monetary policy and institution making begun to be treated explicitly in a theoretical framework.

It is just as hard, if not harder, to conduct a positive empirical analysis of policy interdependence as it is to test a hypothesis in duopoly or oligopoly theory incorporating conjectural variations on the behavior of others. In fact, the existing empirical literature is at most a verification of some of the theoretical propositions using two-country simulation models that are either constructed as hypothetical numerical examples or estimated with actual data.

In his analysis of the speed of adjustment in an interdependent economy, Cooper (1969) calculates the dominant characteristic roots corresponding to numerical models with varying degrees of interdependence. He also shows by way of simulations how income and reserve requirements vary with and without cooperation.

Using the linked American and Canadian econometric models, Helliwell and McRae (1977) study the effect of mutual responses of monetary policies on an initial fiscal disturbance in one country. The results of their simulation, which assumes that the same type of monetary policy is used in both countries, suggest that the effect of Canadian policies on the United States is larger and more cyclical if both countries follow the monetary policy of pegging interest rates than if they peg the money supply. In general, it is found that the nature of the transmission of economic disturbances takes different forms depending on the modus operandi of monetary policies adopted in the two countries.

A series of interesting studies on the role of sterilization policies has been conducted by De Grauwe (1975, 1977). By estimating the balance of payments equations for European countries and then experimenting with this system of equations, he finds that the systematic use of sterilization policies by two or more countries in an attempt to offset the monetary effects of balance of payments disequilibria is most likely to lead to explosive reserve flows and therefore to the breakdown of the system. Even when those policies do not lead to unstable reserve flows, their effectiveness is extremely limited. According to De Grauwe, because of the increased interdependence in the 1960s as compared to the 1950s, the use of sterilization policies should have created more acute policy conflicts during the second period.

Finally, Parkin (1977), in his study of the impact of monetary policy on world inflation and the balance of payments, shows that the main conclusion of the monetary approach to analyzing the balance of payments is approximately valid, and that the influence of productivity increase is also important. It is also noteworthy that a formula is derived for the rate of monetary expansion that is required for the attainment of price stability in the world economy (or in a monetary union).

One cannot deny that empirical analyses of macroeconomic coordination are still sparse, especially concerning policy reaction behavior. The importance of the studies mentioned here, however, should not be undervalued because, to the extent that they clarify the nature of interdependence in the current world economy, they are the steps required to provide a solid foundation for the empirical analysis of strategic policy interplay. Moreover, some of them (for example, the studies by De Grauwe and by Parkin) provide the rationale for the new type of monetary cooperation under the post-Smithsonian regime suggested by McKinnon.

Strategic Analysis of Policy Interactions in the Fixed Price Model

A variety of models may be used to analyze the interdependence of monetary policies under alternative monetary systems; however, to avoid complicating the analysis, I will base the discussion on the simplest macroeconomic models. The first model to be considered in this book is the textbook version of the Keynesian model that assumes fixed price levels but allows income and employment to adjust (Mundell 1968, chapters 16, 18; Niehans 1968). Recently, however, this model has been subjected to the criticism that it fails to capture the essence of Keynes's original idea.[1] Moreover, although this model may have some relevance to the case of fixed exchange rates, it may not be applicable to the case of flexible exchange rates, as daily fluctuations in the exchange rate may alter the relative price level between two countries.

At the other extreme is the so-called monetarist or quantity theory model that assumes fixed employment levels but flexible prices. In this model, real economic variables are determined by relative prices and the rational choice of economic agents. Monetary policy affects only financial variables such as the price level and the balance of payments and has no effect on income and employment. Whereas the former approach is concerned mainly with fluctuations in effective demand, the latter deals with long-run price trends and their relationship to the balance of payments.

The choice between these two extreme models depends primarily on one's interpretation of macroeconomic relations—namely, on whether one believes in the Phillips curve or in the natural rate of unemployment and on whether one views unemployment as frictional or structural. It is perhaps fair to say that the simple Keynesian model provides a good approximation of reality during periods of secular recession and that the monetarist model is useful for analyzing periods of chronic inflation. However, neither the Keynesian model nor the monetarist model alone seems to provide an adequate framework for analyzing the current state of the world economy in which unemployment and inflation coexist.

Recently the monetary approach has been introduced into analyses of the balance of payments with considerable success. This approach views the balance of payments as a relationship between a country's credits and debits on international account and the exchange rate as the relative price of two currencies and advocates that changes in these two variables be explained in terms of changes in the demand for, and the supply of, money. However, the monetary approach to the balance of payments should be distinguished from monetarism. The monetary approach is not so much an extension of the quantity theory to an open economy as an attempt to understand the balance of payments problem in a general equilibrium framework that takes Walras's Law into account (Komiya 1969). Thus, using the monetary approach does not necessarily entail adopting monetarist assumptions concerning the domestic economy. Indeed, from chapter 6 on I use the monetary approach to analyze a situation with unemployment.

In the remaining chapters the interdependence of monetary policies will be discussed in the following order. In the latter half of this chapter, the game of the interplay of monetary policies will be analyzed in a model that assumes fixed price levels. This will be followed in chapter 5 by an analysis of the interdependence of monetary policies under the assumptions of full employment and price flexibility. In many cases the extreme Keynesian and the extreme monetarist models provide only poor approximations of reality. To make up for this deficiency, a model incorporating the Phillips curve will be used from chapter 6 on to analyze how the macroeconomic mechanism differs under different monetary regimes. First we consider the small-country case in chapter 6, and then in chapter 7 we extend the analysis to the case in which two countries interact with each other.

In the remainder of this book, the main concern will be with the strategic aspects of the interdependence of national economic policies. Policy makers in each nation react to each other on the basis of some knowledge of the interdependence of their various policies. The strategic analysis here will appeal to the optimizing approach developed by Niehans rather than the fixed-target approach. Rather than counting the number of targets and policy instruments and assigning instruments to targets, we consider the tradeoff between targets along social indifference curves, as well as along the feasibility locus. Under the assumption that national economies try to use their monetary policies to optimize the combination of their objectives, we discuss what kind of overall outcome is most likely to occur as the result of the interdependence of monetary policies under alternative exchange-rate systems.

In some sense this analysis may be regarded as a generalization of Niehans's short-run analysis of two dependent economies under fixed exchange rates to the long-run growth process as well as to economies operating under flexible exchange rates. However, my treatment of the balance of payments is different. A surplus in the balance of payments is not always desirable. One of the recent findings from the analysis of seigniorage gains using the monetary approach is that a deficit in the balance of payments is desirable, at least from the consumers' standpoint, as long as a country can afford to continue the deficit. This is because a deficit in the balance of payments implies that the amount the country consumes and invests for future consumption, domestically or abroad, exceeds the amount it currently produces.

Of course, many central bankers prefer surpluses to deficit if the surpluses are not excessive, and this attitude is more likely to be reflected in actual economic policy. The outcome for the world economy depends crucially on the attitudes of the participating countries toward the balance of payments.

Monetary Interdependence under Fixed Exchange Rates

Let us think of the world economy as consisting of two economies linked by international trade and capital movements. We assume that the world capital market is competitive and that the same interest rate prevails in both countries.

In the simplest Keynesian model, the price level of each country is fixed and the income of each country is variable. We are interested chiefly in short-run fluctuations in national income and employment. The formal model used in the analysis is a variant of the two-country model developed by Mundell (1968).

The following notation will be used:

Y = real income,
I = investment,
S = saving,
B = balance of trade,
M = money supply,
D = demand for money,
R = international reserves,
r = real rate of interest,
q = foreign exchange rate (price of the home currency in terms of the foreign currency),
p = price level,
W = world reserves.

Variables with no superscript refer to the home country; those with an asterisk refer to the other country.

The commodity market is in equilibrium if the trade balance offsets the gap between saving and investment.[2]

$$I(r) + \overline{I} - S(Y) + B\left(Y, Y^*, \frac{qp}{p^*}\right) = 0, \tag{4.1}$$

where $\overline{I}$ indicates exogenous (government) spending. For the other country,

$$I^*(r^*) + \overline{I}^* - S^*(Y^*) - qB\left(Y, Y^*, \frac{qp}{p^*}\right) = 0. \tag{4.2}$$

The money market is in equilibrium if

$$\frac{M}{P} = L(r, Y), \tag{4.3}$$

and for the other country

$$\frac{M^*}{P^*} = L^*(r^*, Y^*). \tag{4.4}$$

The money supply is the sum of international reserves and the liabilities of the banking system:

$$M = D + R, \tag{4.5}$$

$$M^* = D^* + qR^*. \tag{4.6}$$

International reserves are assumed constant in the short run:

$$R + R^* = \overline{W}. \tag{4.7}$$

Moreover, in a Keynesian framework in which the price levels are fixed, nominal interest rates are equal to real interest rates, and by the assumption of perfect capital mobility, we have

$$r = r^*. \tag{4.8}$$

Also, by a suitable choice of units, we can put $p = p^* = 1$, and $q = 1$ under a system of fixed exchange rates. The equilibrium condition in the bond market is suppressed here because, by virtue of Walras's law, equilibrium in both money and commodity markets implies equilibrium in the bond market. Once a change in D or D^* occurs, capital moves to equate the rates of interest. But at the new equilibrium, net capital flows offset the trade balance, so that the amount of reserves remains constant.

Monetary policy in this system is viewed as an increase in the liabilities of the banking system, that is, an increase in D and D^*. It has been shown by Mundell that

$$\frac{\partial Y}{\partial D} > 0, \quad \frac{\partial Y^*}{\partial D} > 0, \quad \frac{\partial Y}{\partial D^*} > 0, \quad \frac{\partial Y^*}{\partial D^*} > 0. \tag{4.9}$$

Also, it is easy to see that

$$\frac{\partial R}{\partial D} < 0, \quad \frac{\partial R^*}{\partial D} > 0, \quad \frac{\partial R}{\partial D^*} > 0, \quad \frac{\partial R^*}{\partial D^*} < 0. \tag{4.10}$$

The choice open to the country under a system of fixed exchange rates is to adopt a suitable mix of monetary and fiscal policies to achieve the most desirable combination of targets—national income and the balance of payments, in the present example. Since we are primarily interested in the interaction of monetary policies, we assume that government spending is constant.

The country is assumed to have a preference ordering over various combinations of income levels and increases in reserves, following Niehans. Niehans assumes that a temporary surplus in the balance of payments is always desirable; however, for those countries that do not have a severe need for international reserves, and especially for those that can create international reserves by issuing debt to foreigners, the opposite may be true, as suggested in the discussion of seigniorage gains. A current account deficit implies that a country is consuming and investing in physical assets more than it currently produces. A deficit in the overall balance of payments implies that a country consumes and invests for future consumption, abroad as well as domestically, more than it currently produces.

We adopt the simplifying assumption here that the welfare of a country depends on its overall balance of payments at that moment. Thus, for any country, there must be a certain level of increase in international reserves beyond which any further increase implies a deterioration rather than an improvement in national welfare. Similarly, there must be a certain level of income beyond which further increases are not desirable because of inflation, although temporary increases in income may be possible.

There are problems with analyzing the risk of inflation in a model with fixed price levels, however, we will allow ourselves to assume that a temporary increase in national income above a certain level is not desirable for the country in question in order to illustrate the interdependence of monetary policies. We are justified in doing so because the interdependence of monetary polices continues to hold qualitatively even if the extreme

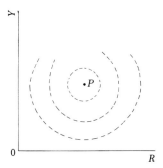

Figure 4.2
Y = real income; ΔR = increase in international reserves; P = optimal combination of Y and ΔR.

assumption of fixed prices is not made. The indifference curves are not drawn above the levels at which even temporary increases in real income are not possible. Thus the indifference curves do not look like the ordinary price theory textbook versions but rather have a saturation point or center.

Figure 4.2 depicts the government's indifference curves with respect to the level of national income and the international balance of payments. The center of these curves, that is, the saturation point or the optimal combination of income and increase in reserves, differs for various countries depending in part on their initial reserves. This point also depends on the eagerness of the country to attain full employment at the risk of inflation, on its position in the international financial system, and on the strength of restraints against losing international reserves. For a reserve currency country like the United States, the optimal increase in reserves may be negative because of its ability to increase the consumption level of its citizens by issuing its debt to other countries.[3]

Even within a country, judgments will differ on the best combination of income levels and increases in reserves. Thus, economists educated by Mundell, for example, will prefer a deficit, and the center of the circles will be near the vertical axis. Traditional bankers, on the other hand, will prefer a payments surplus, and the center will be relatively further to the right of the vertical axis. For those who prefer expansion, the center will be further above the horizontal axis, and for those who prefer economic stability, it will be nearer this axis.

Our main concern is the preference ordering of the monetary authority that has the power to determine monetary policy. This preference ordering is not absolutely fixed; its structure may change with economic education and past balance of payment experiences. Moreover, one country may find it

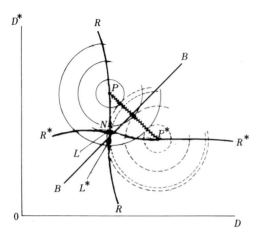

Figure 4.3
PP^* is contract curve; RR is country 1's reaction curve; R^*R^* is country 2's reaction curve; N is Nash equilibrium; L is leadership solution with country 1 as leader; L^* is leadership solution with country 2 as leader.

profitable to teach or persuade another country to change its preference ordering conerning the balance of payments.

If we assume that each country has a preference ordering and that there are only two countries, we can superimpose the Stackelberg diagram on the plane ordinated by the monetary policies of the two countries (figure 4.3). The abscissa indicates the money supply of the home country expressed in terms of the liabilities of the banking system D, and the ordinate indicates the money supply of the other country in terms of D^*.

Note that figures 4.2 and 4.3 have been drawn with different combinations of variables on the axes. As can be seen from equation 4.10, the balance of payments of country 1 deteriorates as D increases and improves as D^* increases. Furthermore, we can adopt the same approach as the one employed in the next chapter to analyze mathematically the monetary approach to the balance of payments to show that, as long as we ignore differences in the elasticities of money demand with respect to income and the interest rate, the balance of payments of the two countries to a large extent is determined by differences in their rates of monetary expansion. Therefore, the combinations of D and D^* that equilibrate the international balance of payments (of both countries) can be represented by the upward sloping BB curve in figure 4.3. The region to the right (left) of BB indicates a balance of payments surplus (deficit) for country 2 and a balance of payments deficit (surplus) for country 1. And from equation 4.9 we note that an increase in D in one country raises incomes in both countries. In figure 4.3 the indifference curves of the first country are drawn with solid lines and those of the second country with dotted lines. Since from equation 4.10 the region to the lower right of BB indicates a temporary deficit in the balance of payments for the first country, the indifference map of the first country is approximately an oblique mirror image of the indifference map shown in figure 4.2, while that of the second country is an oblique transposition.

Depending on the relative positions of the centers of the indifference curves—the relative positions that each country likes best—the policy interaction between the two countries will take different forms. Figure 4.3 depicts the case where neither country is satisfied with the initial level of reserves and both desire to accumulate more.

We proceed to analyze the strategic situation using figure 4.3. If we plot the locus of tangency between these two families of indifference curves, we obtain the contract curve PP^*—that is, the locus of Pareto-efficient points. A country situated on this contract curve cannot improve its satisfaction level without causing a deterioration in the satisfaction level of the other country. Thus, the cooperative solution of this interplay of monetary policies, or of this two-person game, will be some point on this contract curve. Needless to say, the first country prefers a situation close to P and the second a situation close to P^*. The relative bargaining strengths of the two countries will determine to which point on the contract curve cooperative action leads.

Reaction curves RR and R^*R^* are drawn in such a way that RR is the locus of the points where the indifference curves of the first country are tangent to a horizontal line and R^*R^* is the locus of the points where the indifference curves of the latter country are tangent to a vertical line. They indicate the optimal monetary policy of one country if it believes that the other country will keep its monetary policy constant. Thus the intersection of these reaction curves N is the point at which each country has no incentive to move away provided the other keeps its policy unchanged. Using game theory terminology, this is the Nash equilibrium. As Niehans pointed out, this intersection is generally not on the contract curve; the noncooperative solution is inferior to the cooperative solution.

The leadership solution is the best point on the opponent's reaction curve. If country 1 knows that country 2 will remain on its reaction curve, R^*R^*, country 1 will choose the money supply that will achieve L, the best point from country 1's standpoint on R^*R^*. Similarly we can find the leadership solution of country 2 as L^*.

In figure 4.3 where each country is assumed to prefer a temporary surplus in its balance of payments, which is the case analyzed by Niehans, the noncooperative solution will have a bias toward recession.[4] However, this conclusion depends on the relative positions of the centers of the two countries' indifference curves and may not always be valid. Several typical cases are depicted in figure 4.4. In the situation represented by figure 4.4a each country desires a deficit in its balance of payments. It is easy to see that the noncooperative solution N has an expansionary bias. In figure 4.4b, country 1 desires a deficit and country 2 desires a surplus but one smaller than the deficit preferred by country 1. This situation also leads to a noncooperative solution with an expansionary bias. Figure 4.4c represents the case in which both countries desire balance of payments equilibrium but each has a different preference concerning the level of income. In this case, the noncooperative solution will lie in the region where the more expansion-minded country ends up with a deficit in its balance of payments. The situation that prevailed immediately prior to President Nixon's adoption of the New Economic Policy in the summer of 1971 (the growing balance of payments surpluses of Japan and West Germany) may be interpreted in terms of case 4b. Here the U.S. corresponds to country 1, and Japan and West Germany correspond to country 2.

The textbook version of the Keynesian model that assumes fixed price levels is inadequate for the analysis of the transmission of inflation and stagflation across countries. Such topics will be taken up in the remaining chapters.

The economic significance of the above analysis can be summarized as follows. If two countries cooperate, they will reach a point on the contract curve whose position depends on their relative bargaining strengths. If they do not cooperate but passively respond to each other, they will reach the noncooperative (Nash) equilibrium, which is not on the Pareto-efficient contract curve. Moreover, if one country takes advantage of the fact that the other will remain on its reaction curve, the leadership solution will emerge, which is favorable to the leader and unfavorable to the follower. Whether noncooperative solutions lie on the inflationary or deflationary side of the contract curve depends on the attitudes of the two countries' toward their balance of payments.

This situation is quite similar to the prisoner's dilemma. If both parties cooperate, high payoffs to both result; if neither cooperates, low payoffs occur. But if one cooperates and the other does not, the payoff to the cooperating party is very low while that to the noncooperating party is very high.

This analysis of the fixed exchange rate system reveals the public-good character of monetary assets. If each country desires a surplus in its balance

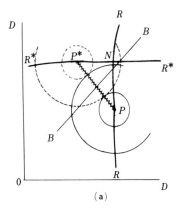

(a)

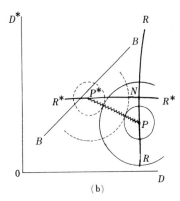

(b)

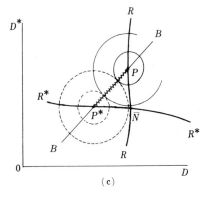

(c)

Figure 4.4

of payments, monetary expansion is a "public good" because each country prefers a higher rate of expansion of the total money supply but wants to expand its own money supply at a slower rate than that of other countries. On the other hand, if each country desires a deficit in its balance of payments, then monetary expansion becomes a "public bad" because each country wants to expand its own money supply at a higher rate than that of other countries but at the same time does not want the total money supply to expand too rapidly. In either case, the noncooperative solution is likely to result in an unfavorable situation with a scarcity of public goods or with a glut of public bads.

Thus far we have assumed two participating countries. If the number of countries increases, what modifications will be required? The formal structure is not hard to generalize. In the monetary model, for example, movements in the world price level will depend on the weighted average of rates of monetary expansion of all countries, while the balance of payments of a particular country will depend essentially on the difference between this average and its own rate of monetary expansion.

The analysis of strategic situations is more difficult. Small countries are more likely to behave passively, that is, to remain on their reaction curves. Thus, it might be easier for a large country to act as a leader. Another difference is that the contract curve solution may become more difficult to maintain because international agreement requires multilateral as well as bilateral agreement, and there is always the temptation for a country to become an outsider (Cooper 1968, pp. 172–173).

Various modifications to this argument are necessary if it is to be applied to more realistic situations. For example, the adjustable peg system differs from the fixed exchange rate system in allowing abrupt changes in parities. In the former system, the excessive accumulation of international reserves is undesirable not only because it implies the current sacrifice of consumption and investment but also because it involves the risk that the currency held as reserves might be devalued. Therefore, the shape of the indifference map becomes more sensitive to the cost of the accumulation of foreign currencies.

In the typical example of the prisoner's dilemma the two parties are unable to communicate with one other, but in the case of the interaction of monetary policies countries can communicate with one another by various means. One may therefore argue that the Cournot solution and the Stackelberg solution are irrelevant and that one should concentrate on the structure of cooperative solutions instead. However, even if one takes the optimistic view that negotiations will lead to outcomes close to a cooperative solution, an understanding of noncooperative solutions is still necessary inasmuch as there usually exist multiple cooperative solutions and the noncooperative solutions provide benchmarks for comparing the gains of these alternative cooperative solutions.

Moreover, the attainment of a cooperative solution becomes more and more difficult as the number of participants increases. The situation is further complicated by the fact that it is sometimes profitable for a country to conceal its preferences and to signal false information. The medium and speed of communication, as well as the level of mutual trust, will affect the performance of the world economy.

The creation of an international reserve asset such as SDRs can be utilized to move the noncooperative solution closer to the contract curve. If every country always desires to acquire more reserves, deflationary pressures will emerge in the world economy. The creation of an international asset will lead to the easing of deflationary pressures because a country can now obtain its desired reserves without running a balance of payments surplus. In terms of figure 4.3 the indifference maps of the two countries will move toward the central ray *BB*. Thus, the creation of international reserves by an international organization is meaningful, although there remains the problem of how to distribute such reserves.

Monetary Independence under Flexible Exchange Rates

Policy interactions under a system of floating exchange rates are now examined. Let us first consider the short-run problem of fluctuations in employment and effective demand, again using the Keynesian model. Monetary policy works differently under floating rates than under fixed exchange rates. Monetary expansion by one country increases its own income, but with capital mobility the income of the other country decreases rather than increasing. This result occurs because the monetary expansion and the decline in the interest rate induce an outflow of capital, as a result of which the exchange rate depreciates, causing recessionary effects on the other country. However, the other country can increase its own money supply to stimulate effective demand.

Formally, in the system of equations 4.1–4.8, R, R^*, and W can be equated to zero, meaning that the money supply of a country is equal to the liabilities of the banking system.

Letting q be variable, it can be shown that (Mundell 1968)

$$\frac{\partial Y}{\partial D} > 0, \quad \frac{\partial Y^*}{\partial D} < 0; \quad \frac{\partial Y}{\partial D^*} < 0, \quad \frac{\partial Y^*}{\partial D^*} > 0. \tag{4.11}$$

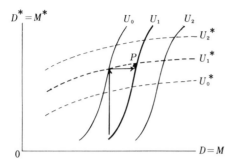

Figure 4.5
(U_1 and U_1^* are both optimal indifference curves and, at the same time, reaction curves.)

Also it is easy to see that

$$\frac{\partial r}{\partial D} < 0, \quad \frac{\partial r}{\partial D^*} < 0. \tag{4.12}$$

In this system there is no room for international transfers of purchasing power through payments deficits or surpluses. Such transfers could be effected through the acquisition of foreign currencies by private economic units for transactions or speculative purposes, but we cannot deal with that possibility here. Thus, the only major concern of each country is the level of income. Accordingly, the Stackelberg diagram becomes degenerate, as shown in figure 4.5. The upward-sloping curves are indifference curves, and the thick curve shows the optimal level of income. The upward slope of both families of curves reflects the fact that one country's monetary expansion depresses the other country's income level and necessitates monetary expansion in the other country in order to maintain the same income level.

In the absence of capital mobility, each country will determine its income level without reference to the monetary policy of the other country. In this special case, the indifference curves become straight lines: country 1's indifference curves are vertical while country 2's are horizontal. Therefore no strategic conflict arises.

Even if both families of curves are upward-sloping in a world with capital mobility, the reaction curves will coincide with the highest indifference curves provided that both countries are concerned solely with their income levels. In this general case, no serious strategic problem exists as far as the equilibrium solution is concerned. The intersection of reaction curves, namely the Nash equilibrium, coincides with the unique Pareto-optimal point. Thus, a system of floating exchange rates allows each country to pursue an independent monetary policy.

However, we should note the following interdependent aspects of monetary policies in the competitive world capital market. First, let us look at the adjustment process to the Nash equilibrium solution, which takes the form indicated by the arrows in figure 4.5. The time span during which this short-run analysis is applicable might be shorter than the time span during which the adjustment process takes place. That being so, a country's monetary expansion may cause a temporary reduction in the income level of the other country. Thus, with capital mobility, monetary expansion in one country may in the short run have a beggar-thy-neighbor effect on the rest of the world.

Second, a country cannot decide the interest rate by itself. From equation 4.12, the iso-interest curves could be superimposed as downward-sloping curves in figure 4.5. And if each country has a preference ordering concerning the combinations of interest rates and income levels, the situation shown in figures 4.3 and 4.4 can still occur under floating exchange rates. This aspect of interdependence is more sophisticated than that discussed under fixed exchange rates because there the rate of interest was not taken into account in the preference ordering. By relaxing the balance of payments constraint, the floating exchange rate system provides a country with more freedom to pursue other policy objectives.

Conclusions

A system of fixed exchange rates is more likely to bring about a confrontation of economic policies analogous to the prisoner's dilemma; the outcome of this conflicting situation depends on the degree of cooperation among countries. On the other hand, we have found that a system of floating exchange rates offers more independence and more room for monetary policies even though some conflict with respect to the real rate of interest may still exist. This suggests that even in the first stage of the game—that of agreeing on a particular system—the degree of mutual trust among countries affects the prospective payoffs. The two stages are linked by the degree of trust. If faith in the other country's economic policies is not strong enough, the system of floating exchange rates offers a safe (if not the best) strategy for guaranteeing a certain degree of independence. Thus, for a nation to adopt a flexible exchange rate by itself is something very close to the maximin strategy.

5   A Strategic Analysis of Monetary Interdependence: A Flexible Price Model

Under a system of fixed exchange rates, national monetary policies are closely interdependent. The same amount of monetary expansion in one country can have different effects on the domestic as well as the world economy depending on the monetary policies pursued by other countries in the system. Even in the case where, as at present, a system of floating exchange rates is partially adopted, the problem of the interdependence of monetary policies occurs within a monetary union if monetary integration has proceeded to such an extent that the exchange rates between the participating countries are fixed but the monetary authorities are not completely unified.

McKinnon (1974) has proposed a new tripartite agreement to maintain stable exchange rate relations among the United States, Germany, and Japan. As a precondition for such a proposal to be effective, we must know the strategic positions of the participating countries in such a monetary union within which exchange rates are to be more or less fixed. That is, we must ask what incentives countries are faced with when they decide on their monetary policies.

Most traditional approaches do not seem to pay sufficient attention to the interdependent nature of monetary policies. They either take the monetary policies of other countries as given or take the international cooperation of monetary policies for granted.

The monetary approach to the balance of payments suggests that a disequilibrium in the balance of payments can be understood as a monetary phenomenon. A surplus in the balance of payments appears when the demand for money of a nation exceeds the domestic supply of money; a deficit results when the domestic supply of money exceeds the demand for money. At the same time, this approach enables us to investigate formally the structure of interdependence of monetary policies. Johnson (1972a) has derived a set of instructive formulas relating the rate of inflation, the balance of payments, the rate of growth of international money, and the rate of credit expansion of the nations of the world. One can see in these formulas the two sources of interdependence: the world rate of inflation is the weighted average of the rates of domestic credit expansion, and disequilibrium in a country's balance of payments results from the deviation of its rate of credit expansion from the world average.

The purpose of this chapter is to study the interdependent and strategic nature of monetary policies by applying directly the monetary approach to the balance of payments. I set up a multicountry game situation where the monetary policy of each country is conducted in such a way as to maximize the objective function of its monetary authorities. Monetary policies are interdependent in the sense that the effect of a specific policy adopted by a country differs depending on the monetary policies pursued by other countries. Using this framework, we will consider how differences in national preferences concerning inflation and the balance of payments affect the realized outcome of the rate of world inflation. I will relate the findings to recent developments in the theory of public goods in political science (for example, Olson 1965).

Mundell (1972, chap. 16) addresses the question of the relationship between world inflation and the international balance of payments using a policy assignment approach. According to his analysis the reserve-currency country should be assigned the objective of price stability, while the other countries should be assigned the objective of equilibrating their balance of payments. Since countries may not have any incentive to follow such assignments, the analysis in this chapter will be carried out using the optimizing approach rather than the assignment approach.

The analysis of strategic interdependence that follows will be formulated in static terms, although the equilibrium relationships between growth rates will also be examined in a dynamic model. A more realistic analysis of the dynamic strategic structure would be very difficult. As an attempt in this direction, I will formulate the money game as a differential game in the appendix to this chapter.

Interplay of National Monetary Policies

Let us posit a world economy, or a subset thereof consisting of several countries, among which exchange rates are fixed. Assume that goods are mobile enough for the assumption of a common price level to be justified.[1] We will treat fiscal policies as fixed and focus on the interplay of monetary policies. We assume that the utility function of a nation's monetary authority depends on the rate of inflation and on the increase in its international reserves. More specifically, the monetary authority will be assumed to have a most desired rate of inflation (or deflation) and a most desired value of increase (or decrease) in foreign reserves. Usually, the lower the rate of inflation, the higher will be the level of national welfare; but if the rate of inflation falls below some specific value, a further reduction in inflation or a further increase in the rate of deflation may not be desirable.[2] Thus we will assume that there is a most desired rate of inflation or deflation for a nation that may differ from country to country. Similarly, an increase in the balance of payments surplus beyond a certain level may mean a reduction in consumption-investment opportunities for a nation. Thus, we will assume that there is a most preferred value for the increase or decrease in international reserves that may differ from country to country.

As is well known, discussions of the demand for international reserves are concerned mostly with the stock of reserves rather than the flow. At any time, however, movement to a desired level of stock can be expressed as a desired rate of change. We will interpret the most desired rate of change in international reserves that was introduced above in this sense for the time being.

Suppose there are n countries in the system. The exchange rates between these n currencies are assumed to be fixed at unity. Let D_i, R_i, and M_i denote, respectively, the money supply due to credit expansion by the monetary authority, international reserves, and the demand for money of the ith country. Then we have

$$D_i + R_i = M_i, \qquad i = 1, \ldots, n. \tag{5.1}$$

Here R_i is composed of gold, SDRs, and reserve currencies such as dollars.[3] The real demand for money is assumed to be a function of national income Q and the money rate of interest r.

$$\frac{M_i}{p} = L^i(Q_i, r_i), \tag{5.2}$$

where p is the common price level in the world, and

$$\frac{\partial L^i}{\partial Q_i} > 0, \quad \frac{\partial L^i}{\partial r_i} \leqq 0.$$

There are two alternative ways of formulating the monetary approach to the balance of payments. One is to use a discrete-time model and to allow lags in the process of balance of payments adjustment. Here the balance of payments is defined as the difference between the demand for and supply of money. The other way is to appeal to a continuous-time model and to describe the dynamic process as a moving equilibrium (Johnson 1972a). Here the demand for and supply of money are continuously adjusted to equilibrium by means of the flow of the balance of payments. In this chapter, where the primary concern is with dynamic changes in the rate of inflation rather than with dynamic changes in comparative statics, we will adopt the second approach and proceed in a continuous framework.

In order to focus on the strategic structure of the interplay of monetary policies, we will assume for simplicity that the effect of changes in interest rates on the demand for money can be neglected. If we differentiate equation 5.2 with respect to time, noting that $\partial L^i / \partial r_i = 0$ and dividing by M_i, we have

$$\frac{\dot{D}_i}{M_i} + \frac{\dot{R}_i}{M_i} = \frac{\dot{p}}{p} + \eta_i \frac{\dot{Q}_i}{Q_i}, \qquad i = 1, \ldots, n \tag{5.3}$$

where η_i denotes the income elasticity of demand for money,

$$\eta_i \equiv \frac{Q_i \partial L^i}{L^i \partial Q_i}.$$

Define the ratio of credit expansion to the demand for money in excess of the product of the growth rate of real national income and the income elasticity of demand for money as θ_i, and call it the rate of excess monetary expansion. That is,

$$\theta_i \equiv \frac{\dot{D}_i}{M_i} - \eta_i \frac{\dot{Q}_i}{Q_i}. \tag{5.4}$$

Here the growth rate of real national income is assumed to be given exogenously, and θ_i corresponds to the strategy of the ith country in the terminology of game theory.[4] Also define the balance of payments of country i normalized by its demand for money as z_i, that is,

$$z_i \equiv \frac{\dot{R}_i}{M_i}. \tag{5.5}$$

Then, by virtue of equations 5.4 and 5.5, equation 5.3 is reduced, by denoting the common rate of inflation $\dot{p}/p$ as π, to

$$z_i = \pi - \theta_i, \qquad i = 1, \ldots, n. \tag{5.6}$$

Let the total amount of international reserves in the world be R, so that

$$R = \sum_{i=1}^{n} R_i.$$

R_i consists of international reserves such as gold and SDRs. If country 1, say the United States, is the reserve-currency country, then R_i for the other countries (that is, for $i = 2, \ldots, n$) may include the liquid liabilities of the U.S. monetary system, so that R_1 may become negative. However, for the world as a whole, R consists of the international reserves that are outside of the system—namely, gold and SDRs.

Let the total amount of credit money and the total money demand of the system as a whole be R and M, respectively. Also let ω_i be the relative share of country i's money demand. That is,

$$\sum_{i=1}^{n} D_i \equiv D,$$

$$\sum_{i=1}^{n} M_i \equiv M,$$

and

$$\omega_i \equiv M_i/M, \quad \sum_{i=1}^{n} \omega_i = 1, \quad \omega_i > 0.$$

Define the ratio of the increase in international reserves (or outside money) to the total world money supply as

$$G_R \equiv \dot{R}/M.$$

By the definition of y_i and ω_i, we have

$$\sum_{i=1}^{n} \omega_i z_i = \sum_{i=1}^{n} \frac{M_i}{M} \frac{\dot{R}_i}{M_i} = \frac{\Sigma \dot{R}_i}{M} = \frac{\dot{R}}{M} \equiv G_R. \tag{5.7}$$

Therefore, multiplying (5.6) by ω_i and summing with respect to i, we obtain (noting that $\sum_{i=1}^{n} \omega_i = 1$)

$$\sum_{i=1}^{n} \omega_i z_i = \pi - \sum_{i=1}^{n} \omega_i \theta_i. \tag{5.8}$$

Finally, we have from equations 5.6 and 5.7 the following two basic equations, which are simplified representations of the monetary approach to the balance of payments:

$$\pi = \sum_{i=1}^{n} \omega_i \theta_i + G_R, \tag{5.9}$$

$$z_i = \pi - \theta_i, \quad i = 1, \ldots, n. \tag{5.10}$$

Equation 5.9 indicates that the rate of inflation in the world economy depends on the weighted average of the rates of excessive monetary expansion and the increase in international reserves. Equation 5.10 indicates that the balance of payments of a country depends on the difference between the weighted average of rates of excessive monetary expansion of all countries and its own rate of excessive monetary expansion. These two equations are essentially the same as the equations obtained by Johnson, except for some simplification of notation.[5]

Now let us turn to the objective function of the monetary authorities. The objective function of each monetary authority is assumed to depend on the common rate of price increase and on the balance of payments of the country. Let the utility function of the ith monetary authority be denoted by $u^i(\pi, z_i)$, where π is the rate of inflation common to all the countries and z_i is the ratio of the increase in international reserves to money demand in the ith country.

As explained above, $u^i(\pi, z_i)$ is assumed to be a strictly concave function of π and z_i and to have the following properties:

$$u_1^i = \frac{\partial u^i}{\partial \pi} \left\{ \begin{matrix} \geq \\ = \\ < \end{matrix} \right\} 0, \quad \text{according as } \pi \left\{ \begin{matrix} \leq \\ = \\ > \end{matrix} \right\} a_i \tag{5.11}$$

$$u_2^i = \frac{\partial u^i}{\partial z_i} \left\{ \begin{matrix} \geq \\ = \\ < \end{matrix} \right\} 0, \quad \text{according as } z_i \left\{ \begin{matrix} \leq \\ = \\ > \end{matrix} \right\} b_i. \tag{5.12}$$

Equations 5.11 and 5.12 indicate that country i has an ideal combination (bliss point) (a_i, b_i) of the rate of inflation and the rate of increase in international reserves. The value a_i can be negative for a country that prefers deflation; b_i can be negative for a country that prefers balance of payments deficits. Figure 5.1 indicates the indifference map for a country with a bliss point with $a_i > 0$ and $b_i < 0$. Indifference curves take circular shapes around the bliss point.

The game situation we have is thus the interplay of monetary policies (θ_i's) by the monetary authorities. The reaction curve for country i is obtained by maximizing $u^i(\pi, z_i)$ with respect to θ_i under the assumption that all other θ_j's ($j \neq i$) are given. Noting that

$$u^i(\pi, z_i) = u^i \left(G_R + \sum_{k=1}^{n} \omega_k \theta_k, G_R + \sum_{k=1}^{n} \omega_k \theta_k - \theta_i \right),$$

we obtain

$$\frac{\partial u^i}{\partial \theta_i} = \omega_i u_1^i + (\omega_i - 1) u_2^i = 0, \quad i = 1, \dots, n. \tag{5.13}$$

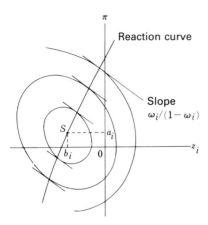

Figure 5.1

The maximization condition 5.13 can be rewritten as

$$-\frac{d\pi}{dz_i}\bigg|_{u^i \text{ const}} = \frac{u_2^i}{u_1^i} = \frac{\omega_i}{1-\omega_i}. \tag{5.14}$$

In words, the marginal rate of substitution between the rate of inflation and the growth rate of normalized international reserves must be equal to $\omega_i/(1-\omega_i)$, which is larger for a country with a larger relative size in the world economy. The reaction curve is the locus of points of tangency between indifference curves and lines with slope $\omega_i/(1-\omega_i)$. From figure 5.1, which shows the reaction curve, one can see that the smaller a country is, the flatter will be the tangency slope and the more will the reaction curve deviate from the horizontal line $\pi = a_i$ which indicates the preference of the ith country concerning the rate of inflation. The behavior of smaller countries has a relatively stronger impact on their own balance of payments than on the rate of worldwide inflation. The shape of the reaction curve is affected by the relative strengths of the two effects, which in turn depends on the size of the country. From equation 5.14, u_1^i and u_2^i have the same sign. Thus, $\pi > a_i$ implies $z_i > b_i$, and so forth. The country that desires a more stable price level should try to reduce the rate of inflation, sacrificing the target of balance of payments and incurring more surplus than is desirable. The exact point that a country actually chooses on the reaction curve depends on the behavior of the other countries. The Cournot solution is given by the intersection of the reaction curves (equation 5.13).

On the other hand, the Pareto-optimal configuration for the world economy is given by maximizing

$$\sum_{k=1}^{n} \beta_k u^k(\pi, z_k)$$

with respect to $\theta_i (i = 1, \ldots, n)$, where parameter β_k is the relative importance, or the index of bargaining power, of country k, normalized as

$$\sum_{k=1}^{n} \beta_k = 1, \qquad \beta_k > 0. \tag{5.15}$$

The first-order conditions for the Pareto-optimal configuration are

$$\sum_{k=1}^{n} \beta_k u_1^k \omega_i + \sum_{k=1}^{n} \beta_k u_2^k \omega_i - \beta_i u_2^i = 0, \qquad i = 1, \ldots, n. \tag{5.16}$$

The Pareto-optimal surface, on which a cooperative solution would lie, is obtained by varying the weight β_k subject to equation 5.15.[6]

Summing equations 5.9 with respect to i and noting that $\sum_{i=1}^{n} \omega_i = 1$, we obtain

$$\sum_{k=1}^{n} \beta_k u_1^k + \sum_{k=1}^{n} \beta_k u_2^k - \sum_{k=1}^{n} \beta_i u_2^i = 0$$

or

$$\sum_{k=1}^{n} \beta_k u_1^k = 0. \tag{5.17}$$

If the most desired rate of inflation for country k is attained, then $u_1^k = 0$. Thus, equation 5.17 indicates that the Pareto-optimal configuration is achieved if the weighted average of the marginal costs of inflation is equated to zero.[7]

On the other hand, summing equations 5.13 with respect to i, we obtain

$$\sum_{i=1}^{n} \omega_i u_1^i = \sum_{i=1}^{n} (1 - \omega_i) u_2^i. \tag{5.18}$$

Comparing equations 5.18 and 5.17, we can see that the Cournot solution does not generally lie on the Paretian configuration. When the right-hand side of equation 5.18 is positive, international reserves and credit expansion have the nature of public goods, giving a deflationary bias to the Cournot solution. When it is negative, international reserves and credit expansion have the nature of public bads, giving an inflationary bias to the Cournot solution. The reason is that in the case of public goods, each country welcomes a higher rate of increase in total money supply but tries to expand its own money supply at a slower rate than other countries. In the case of public bads, each country welcomes a lower rate of increase in total money supply but tries to expand its own money supply at a higher rate than other countries.

Suppose that the most desired rate of inflation is identical for every country. That is, $a_i = a$ for all i. (This includes the case where every country wants perfect price stability, $a_i = 0$ for all i.) Then the Paretian configuration is naturally $\pi = a$. Since π is common to every country, u_1^i will have the same sign for every i, and accordingly u_2^i will have the same sign for every i. More precisely, if the rate of inflation is larger than optimal $(\pi > a)$, then every country will get a larger increase in reserves than desired $(z_i - b_i > 0)$; if the rate of inflation is lower than optimal $(\pi < a)$, then every country will get a smaller increase in reserves than desired $(z_i - b_i < 0)$. In the case where $\pi > a$,

$$\sum_{i=1}^{n} \omega_i z_i - \sum_{i=1}^{n} \omega_i b_i > 0. \tag{5.19}$$

By equation 5.7,

$$G_R - \sum_{i=1}^{n} \omega_i b_i > 0. \tag{5.20}$$

It is easy to see that equation 5.20 implies $\pi > a$.

Thus, we can summarize: Suppose the most desired rate of inflation is identical for each country. Then the Cournot solution gives a rate of inflation higher (lower) than the most desired rate of inflation if and only if the relative increase in international reserves is larger (smaller) than the weighted average of desired increases in international reserves. In a situation with excessive expansion of world reserves, central banks defend themselves against reserve accumulation through expansion of domestic credit, thereby increasing world inflation.

Under the same assumption of identical a_i, let us consider the effect of increasing the number of countries. Suppose the nth country is split into two identical countries with identical preferences concerning the rate of inflation and the relative rate of increase of reserves so that $\bar{\omega}_n = \bar{\omega}_{n+1} = \bar{\omega}_n/2$ (the new weights being denoted by $\bar{\omega}_n$ and $\bar{\omega}_{n+1}$). Then, as indicated by equation 5.14, the reaction curves of these two split countries will deviate more from the Paretian line. Since the reaction curves of the first $(n-1)$ countries remain the same, the Cournot solution will diverge more from the most desired rate of inflation. In fact, with the same inflation rate and the same relative balance of payments, $(\pi; z_1, \ldots, \bar{z}_n, \bar{z}_{n+1})$, where $\bar{z}_n = \bar{z}_{n+1} = z_n$, will keep the left-hand side of equation 5.18 unchanged, but the absolute value of the right-hand side of equation 5.18 will be increased by the introduction of the new weight $\bar{\omega}_n = \bar{\omega}_{n+1} (= \omega_n/2)$. The equality of 5.18 can be restored only by increasing the divergence of π from the most desired rate of inflation a. Thus, splitting a country into two will make the Cournot solution diverge even more from the Paretian configuration.

The Stackelberg leadership solution can be defined in this n-country case as long as a single country, say country 1, behaves as the leader and the others as followers. The leader maximizes its own satisfaction level

$$u^1(\pi, z_1),$$

subject to the reaction curves of the others,

$$\omega_i u^i + (\omega_i - 1)u_2^i = 0, \qquad i = 2, \ldots, n.$$

The leadership solution also does not generally lie on the Paretian configuration. Whether the Cournot solution or the leadership solution deviates more from the Paretian surface cannot be determined unambiguously. This leadership solution is of special interest in the dollar standard system, where it is quite natural to regard the reserve country, the United States, as behaving also as the leader country. Since this situation is more relevant in the long-run context, we shall deal with the implications of the leadership solution later in this chapter.

So far we have neglected the effect of interest rates on the demand for money. If the rate of interest changes and if the interest elasticity of the demand for money is not negligible, then the analysis will have to be modified. To illustrate this, let us take the particular money demand function

$$\frac{M_i}{P_i} = e^{-\lambda r} Q_i^{\eta i},$$

which yields

$$\frac{\dot{M}_i}{M} = \pi - \lambda \dot{r} + \eta_i \frac{\dot{Q}_i}{Q_i}.$$

Suppose that the real rate of interest can be regarded as constant, being eventually determined by the time preference of the public. Then

$$\frac{\dot{M}_i}{M_i} = \pi - \lambda \dot{\pi}^e + \eta_i \frac{\dot{Q}_i}{Q_i}, \tag{5.21}$$

where π^e is the expected rate of inflation. With adaptive expectations,

$\dot{\pi}^e = \gamma(\pi - \pi^e)$, and hence

$$\frac{\dot{M}_i}{M_i} = (1 - \lambda\gamma)\pi + \lambda\gamma\pi^e + \eta_i\frac{\dot{Q}_i}{Q_i}. \tag{5.22}$$

From equations 5.21 and 5.22 we can estimate the direction of the effect of interest rates on the money demand function. When the rate of inflation is increasing, the expected rate of inflation will tend to rise, thus reducing the demand for money. This effect will make the reaction curve diverge more from the Paretian configuration on the inflationary side. On the other hand, when the rate of inflation is declining, the expectation of price decline is likely to occur, and this will increase the demand for money. This effect will cause the reaction curve to diverge more from the Paretian configuration on the deflationary side. Therefore, it is generally expected that the effect of interest rates will aggravate the divergence of the noncooperative solution from the cooperative solution but that the structure of conflict will remain unchanged. Accordingly, we will again neglect the effect of changes in the interest rate in the next two sections.

Illustrative Examples: Geometrical and Algebraic Analysis

In order to facilitate our understanding of the strategic structure of monetary interplay among countries that may have different sizes and different preferences, let us consider a geometrical analysis of some simple cases. At the same time, we will derive various solutions under a specific form of the utility function of the monetary authorities as a guide to the geometrical analysis. The form of the utility function is

$$u^i(\pi, z_i) = -\{(\pi - a_i)^2 + c(z_i - b_i)^2\}, \qquad i = 1, \dots, n \tag{5.23}$$

where c represents the relative weight of the balance of payments consideration as compared with the rate of inflation. The following analysis is valid even with different c_i's for different countries; the only change is the increased complexity of the formulas. This form of the utility function implies indifference curves that are ellipses with axes parallel to the (π, z_i) axes. This simplification of the form of the utility functions enables us to derive various solutions explicitly as functions of such parameters as a_i, b_i, ω_i, and c.

Let us begin the geometrical analysis with the two-country case ($n = 2$) in which the two countries are of equal size ($\omega_1 = \omega_2 = \frac{1}{2}$). Suppose that both countries want price stability ($a_1 = a_2 = 0$) and a balance of payments deficit ($b_1 < 0, b_2 < 0$). Also suppose that the increase in international

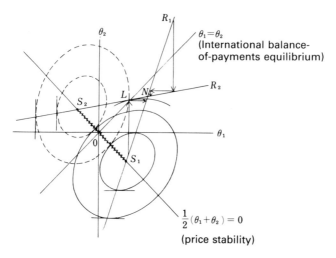

Figure 5.2

reserves is zero ($G_R = 0$). Then, from equations 5.9 and 5.10, which express the monetary approach, we obtain

$$\pi = \tfrac{1}{2}(\theta_1 + \theta_2),$$

$$z_1 = \tfrac{1}{2}(\theta_2 - \theta_1), \quad z_2 = \tfrac{1}{2}(\theta_1 - \theta_2).$$

In this simplest case, the rate of inflation is the average of the rates of excess monetary expansion, and the balance of payments is proportional to the difference of these rates.

The Stackelberg diagram is shown in figure 5.2; the x and y axes are the rates of excess monetary expansion, θ_1 and θ_2, respectively. The line $\theta_1 = \theta_2$ indicates the combination of monetary policies needed to maintain balance of payments equilibrium; $\theta_1 + \theta_2 = 0$ indicates the combination needed for price stability. The indifference curves of country 1 are drawn with solid lines and are, as shown in the last chapter, oblique mirror images of indifference curves in the (z_2, π) plane (see figure 5.1); the indifference curves of country 2 are drawn with dotted lines and are oblique transpositions of those in the (z_2, π) plane. In other words, the π axis in the (z_i, π) plane in figure 5.1 coincides with the line $\theta_1 = \theta_2$, while the z_i axis coincides with the line $\theta_1 + \theta_2 = 0$ with reversed direction for country 1 and with the same direction for country 2. The reaction curve of country 1 is the locus of points for which the tangency slope to the indifference curve of country 1 is horizontal— that is, the best points that country 1 can choose given the rate of excess monetary expansion in country 2, and similarly for the reaction curve of country 2. The Cournot solution N is the intersection of the two reaction curves. It is a stable solution, as the arrows in the figure indicate. The leadership solution L_1 with country 1 as the leader is the point where country 1's indifference curve is tangent to the reaction curve of country 2—that is, the best point for country 1 on the reaction curve of country 2. The leadership solution with country 2 as the leader is not depicted but can be defined in a symmetrical way. The Pareto-efficient frontier, or the contract curve, is the locus of the points of tangency between the two indifference curves and is the segment of $\omega_1\theta_1 + \omega_2\theta_2 = 0$ (or $\theta_1 + \theta_2 = 0$ in this case) between S_1 and S_2.

From figure 5.2, which represents the simplest case, we can see that neither the Cournot solution nor the leadership solution lies on the Paretian configuration (contract curve) and that both lie on the inflationary side of the Paretian configuration when b_1 and b_2 are negative. It is easy to see by constructing similar diagrams that if both b_i and b_2 were positive the Cournot solution and the leadership solution would lie on the deflationary side of the contract curve. If $b_1 + b_2 = 0$, then points S_1 and S_2 coincide, the contract curve shrinks to a single point, and the Cournot solution and the leadership solution coincide with the same point—namely, the Paretian point. We can do similar exercises by varying the values of a_1 and a_2.

Let us return to the case, depicted in figure 5.2, where b_1 and b_2 are negative and $a_1 = a_2 = 0$. Suppose, however, that there is an increase in international reserves. That is, suppose $G_R > 0$. Then the price stability line becomes $\frac{1}{2}(\theta_1 + \theta_2) + G_R = 0$, shifting itself in parallel fashion to the southwest. The locus showing equilibrium in the balance of payments for country 1 becomes $\frac{1}{2}(\theta_2 + \theta_1) + G_R = 0$ and that for country 2 becomes $\frac{1}{2}(\theta_2 - \theta_1) + G_R = 0$, shifting the equilibrium line of country 1 in parallel fashion to the southeast and that of country 2 to the northwest. Accordingly, the indifference map of country 1 moves to the south and that of country 2 to the west. Thus we obtain the Stackelberg diagram, as shown in figure 5.3. It can be seen that the divergence between the best points S_1 and S_2 is wider and that the Cournot as well as the leadership solutions lie further from the contract curve when compared to figure 5.2. However, in the case where both b_1 and b_2 are positive, the increase in G_R will reduce the distance between S_1 and S_2, moving the Cournot as well as the leadership solutions closer to the contract curve. In this case, an increase in international reserve assets contributes to improving the properties of the noncooperative solution.

Next we examine the effect of the relative size of a country. Starting again

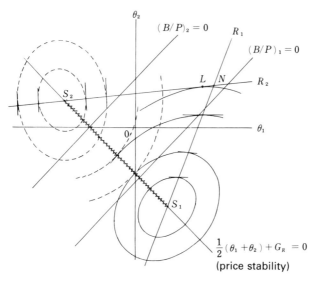

Figure 5.3

from figure 5.2 with $a_1 = a_2 = 0$, $b_1 < 0$, $b_2 < 0$, and $G_R = 0$, what happens to the diagram if ω_i is larger than $\frac{1}{2}$—that is, $\omega_1 > \frac{1}{2}$ and $\omega_2 < \frac{1}{2}$? The line indicating balance of payments equilibrium remains the same, but the price stability line becomes steeper. Indifference curves will accordingly become skewed. It can be seen that the reaction curve of the smaller country, country 2, deviates more from the Paretian configuration, as is shown in figure 5.4. Therefore, the smaller country can exploit the larger country as far as the Cournot solution is concerned (Olson 1965; Olson and Zeckhauser 1966).

Finally, let us consider the case with more than two countries. Suppose that the relative size of country 1 remains the same—that is, $\omega_1 = \frac{1}{2}$—but that country 2 is divided into two smaller, identical countries with identical preferences—that is, $\omega_2 = \omega_3 = \frac{1}{4}$. If these smaller countries behave passively and remain on their reaction curves, then they will behave identically. The slope of the reaction curve of the smaller countries is given by equation 5.14:

$$\frac{u_2^i}{u_1^i} = \frac{\frac{1}{4}}{1 - \frac{1}{4}} = \frac{1}{3}, \qquad i = 2, 3.$$

Thus, the slope of tangency becomes less steep and the reaction curves of the smaller countries deviate more from the Paretian line, as is shown in figure 5.5. This tendency becomes more acute if we divide country 2 into many

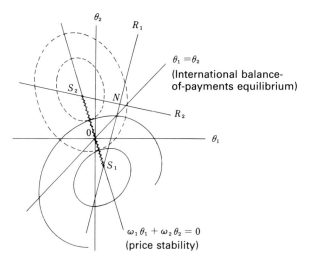

Figure 5.4

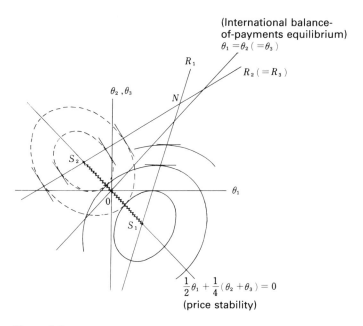

Figure 5.5

smaller identical countries. As Olson (1965) pointed out, the increase in the size of a group tends to work against the optimal supply of public goods.

The understanding of the geometrical analysis can be aided by considering the specific utility function 5.23 for the case in which $n = 2$. The reaction curves are obtained by solving

$$\frac{\partial u^i}{\partial \theta_i} = 0$$

or

$$\omega_i(\pi - a_i) = c(\omega_i - 1)(z_i - b_i) = 0, \qquad i = 1, 2, \ldots, n. \tag{5.24}$$

The Cournot solution is the intersection of the reaction curves. The values of π, z_1, and z_2 can be obtained by solving the system of simultaneous equations 5.24 and 5.7:

$$\sum_{i=1}^{n} \omega_i z_i = G_R.$$

Define a new weight $\bar{\omega}_1$ for country i as[8]

$$\bar{\omega}_i \equiv \frac{\omega_i^2}{1 - \omega_i} \bigg/ \sum_{i=1}^{n} \frac{\omega_i^2}{1 - \omega_i}, \qquad \bar{\omega} \equiv \sum_{i=1}^{n} \frac{\omega_i^2}{1 - \omega_i},$$

and the following weighted average:

$$\bar{a} \equiv \sum_{i=1}^{n} \bar{\omega}_i a_i, \qquad b \equiv \sum_{i=1}^{n} \omega_i b_i.$$

We can then obtain the formulas for the Cournot solution as

$$\pi = \bar{a} + \frac{c}{\bar{\omega}}(G_R - b) \tag{5.25}$$

and

$$z_i = b_i + \frac{\omega_i}{c(1 - \omega_i)}(\pi - a_i), \, i = 1, 2, \ldots, n. \tag{5.26}$$

From equation 5.25 we know that π equals the weighted average of a_i, the weight being the new weight $\bar{\omega}_i$, provided that G_R equals the simple weighted average of b_i. If the increase in international reserve assets falls short of the increase desired by the monetary authorities, there exists a deflationary bias in the Cournot solution; if the increase in international reserves exceeds the demand, there exists an inflationary bias in the Cournot solution.

The Pareto-optimal configuration, the cooperative solution, is obtained by maximizing

$$-\sum_{k=1}^{n} \beta_k \{(\pi - a_k)^2 + (z_k - b_k)^2\}, \qquad \sum_{k=1}^{n} \beta_k = 1, \quad \beta_k > 0$$

with respect to $\theta_i (i = 1, 2, \ldots, n)$. We obtain

$$-\sum_{k=1}^{n} \beta_k \{(\pi - a_k)\omega_i + c(\pi - \theta_k - b_k)(\omega_i - \delta_{ki})\} = 0,$$

$$i = 1, 2, \ldots, n$$

(5.27)

where δ_{ki} is the Kronecker delta such that $\delta_{ki} = 1$ if $k = i$ and $\delta_{ki} = 0$ if $k \neq i$.

Summing equation 5.27 with respect to i (see equation 5.17), we obtain

$$\sum_{k=1}^{n} \beta_k (\pi - a_k) = 0,$$

that is,

$$\pi = \sum_{k=1}^{n} \beta_k a_k = \hat{a}.$$

(5.28)

In other words, on the Paretian frontier, π should be equal to the weighted average of a_k, the weight β_k being the relative importance, or the index of bargaining power, of country k. Needless to say, $\bar{a}$ does not coincide with $\hat{a}$ unless all a_i are identical or $\beta_k = \bar{\omega}_i$ for all i. Comparing equations 5.25 and 5.28, we can see that the Cournot solution does not in general lie on the Paretian frontier.

Similarly, we can derive an explicit formula for the leadership solution with country 1 as the leader and country 2 as the follower. For the follower ($i = 2$), equation 5.24 is valid:

$$\omega_2 (\pi - a_2) + c(\omega_2 - 1)(z_2 - b_2) = 0.$$

(5.24')

On the other hand, from equation 5.7 we obtain

$$\omega_2 z_2 = G_R - \omega_1 z_1,$$

so that equation 5.24' is reduced to

$$\omega^* (\pi - a_2) - c(G_R - \omega_1 z_1 - \omega_2 b_2) = 0,$$

(5.29)

$$\omega^* \equiv \frac{\omega_2^2}{1 - \omega_2} = \frac{\omega_2^2}{\omega_1}.$$

Country 1, the leader, maximizes

$$-\{(\pi - a_1)^2 + c(z_1 - b_1)^2\}$$

subject to equation 5.29. By equating the marginal rate of substitution (MRS) of the isoquant of the objective function with the MRS of equation 5.29 between π and z_1, we obtain

$$\omega_1(\pi - a_1) - \omega^*(z_1 - b_1) = 0. \tag{5.30}$$

The leadership solution is derived explicitly by solving equations 5.29 and 5.30 simultaneously:

$$\pi = \frac{1}{\Delta}\{(c\omega_1{}^2 a_1 + \omega^{*2} a_2) + c\omega^*(G_R - b)\}, \tag{5.31}$$

$$z_1 = \frac{1}{\Delta}\{\omega_1\omega^*(a_2 - a_1) + c\omega_1(G_R - \omega_2 b_2) + \omega^{*2} b_1\}, \tag{5.32}$$

$$\Delta = c\omega_1{}^2 + \omega^{*2} > 0.$$

Whether the leadership solution deviates more from the Paretian frontier than the Cournot solution depends on the values of the parameters, particularly the value of c, as is seen by comparing equations 5.31 and 5.25.

The algebraic analysis in this section can easily be extended to the general n-country case. The formulas for the Cournot and Paretian solutions hold except for the index of summation, which now runs from 1 to n. The leadership solution is also obtained if all countries other than country 1 behave as followers. In that case the (aggregated) reaction curve along which the leader country, country 1, chooses the most favorable point can be written as (instead of equation 5.29)

$$\sum_{i=2}^{n} \frac{\omega_i{}^2}{1 - \omega_i}(\pi - a_i) - c\sum_{i=2}^{n} \omega_i(z_i - b_i) = 0,$$

or, noting equation 5.7, as

$$(\bar{\omega}^*\pi - \bar{a}^*) + c(\omega_1 z_1 + b^* - G_R) = 0, \tag{5.29'}$$

where

$$\omega_i^* \equiv \omega_i^2/(1 - \omega_i), \quad \bar{\omega}^* \equiv \sum_{i=2}^{n} \omega_i^*, \quad \bar{a}^* \equiv \sum_{i=2}^{n} \bar{\omega}_i^* a_i, \quad b^* \equiv \sum_{i=2}^{n} \omega_i b_i.$$

By equating the MRS of the isoquant of the objective function with the MRS of equation 5.29' between π and z_1, we obtain

$$\pi = \frac{1}{\Delta}\{(c\omega_1{}^2 a_1 + \bar{\omega}^* \bar{a}^*) + c\bar{\omega}^*(G_R - b_1)\},$$ (5.31′)

$$z_1 = \frac{1}{\Delta}\{\omega_1(\bar{a}^* - \bar{\omega}^* a_1 + cG_R) + (\bar{\omega}^{*2} b_1 - c\omega_1 b^*)\}.$$ (5.32′)

Thus, the qualitative characteristics of the leadership solution in the n-country case are the same as in the two-country case.

Long-Run Implications and the Role of the Reserve-Currency Country

So far this analysis has been carried out on the assumption that the utility functions of the monetary authorities are exogenously given. In particular, the value b_i, the most desired rate of change in international reserves, was assumed to be given. However, the demand for international reserves is usually formulated in the literature in terms of stock demand rather than flow demand (for example, Hamada and Ueda 1977). Thus, if we consider the dynamic process of adjusting the actual level of international reserves to the optimal level, b_i should be interpreted as a parameter, being dependent on the current level of the stock of reserves. To incorporate this dynamic aspect would require a more complex model with sophisticated analytical methods such as optimal control and the differential game. I make a preliminary attempt in this direction in the appendix of this chapter but here limit the examination to clarifying the nature of long-run situations where the b_i's can be assumed to be roughly equal to the desired rate of increase in international reserves and analyze the adjustment of the b_i's to the long-run state.

In the long run, the position of the reserve-currency country—the country whose currency is used as international reserves—becomes significant since in our formulation the reserve-currency country is the only country whose R_i can be negative. In the short run, $\dot{R}_i$ can be negative for any country, and accordingly b_i can be negative for any country that regards its current reserve holdings as excessive compared with the desired stock level. However, since R_i cannot be negative for a non-reserve-currency country, b_i for these countries cannot be negative in the long run.

In the long run where the desired stocks of international reserves are realized, let us suppose that the monetary authorities try to keep the ratio of international reserves to nominal national income constant. In other words, the monetary authorities want[9]

$$\frac{\dot{R}_i}{R_i} = \pi + \frac{\dot{Q}_i}{Q_i}$$

or

$$\frac{\dot{R}_i}{M_i} = \frac{R_i}{M_i}\left(\pi + \frac{\dot{Q}_i}{Q_i}\right).$$

Therefore, if we denote the optimal ratio of reserves to nominal income as μ_i, then, on the ideal path,

$$\frac{\dot{R}_i}{M_i} = \mu_i\left(\pi + \frac{\dot{Q}_i}{Q_i}\right), \quad \text{or} \quad z_i - \mu_i\pi = \mu_i\frac{\dot{Q}_i}{Q_i}.$$

We can see that, given the growth rate of real output, the monetary authorities of non-reserve-currency countries want to keep the normalized real change in reserves constant. Thus, in the long run, we can redefine the preference function of monetary authorities in terms of the rate of inflation π and the real change in reserves $(z_i - \mu_i\pi)$:

$$u^i(\pi, z_i - \mu_i\pi).$$

Here the b_i's can be regarded as positive constants equalizing $\mu_i\dot{Q}_i/Q_i$. Since $z_i = \pi - \theta_i$, the utility function can be rewritten as

$$u^i(\pi, (1 - \mu_i)\pi - \theta_i).$$

Formally, the same analysis applies to the reserve-currency country, except that b_i and μ_i can be negative. Because it is safe to assume that μ_i is less than unity, the analysis in the previous sections holds without any essential change except for the inclusion of μ_i. For example, instead of equation 5.13, the reaction functions can be written as

$$\frac{\partial u^i}{\partial \theta_i} = \omega_i u_1^i + \{(1 - \mu_i)\omega_i - 1\}u_2^i = 0.$$

The essential nature of policy interplay remains unchanged in the presence of the compensating term for capital losses (or gains) on international reserves.[10]

Thus we can essentially regard the analysis in the previous section as a description of the long-run situation. The only qualification is that only the reserve-currency country, say country 1, can have a negative b_i, and that the other countries should have positive b_i's in the long run. Therefore, the Stackelberg diagrams in the long run should be drawn with b_1 negative and the other b_i's positive. The lesson we obtained in the previous sections is that if

$$G_R - \sum_{i=1}^{n} \omega_i b_i > 0 \tag{5.20}$$

then world inflation is likely to occur for the case of identical a_i's. Suppose country 1, the reserve-currency country, has a negative b_i and the other countries have positive b_i's. Then the condition becomes

$$G_R + \omega_1 |b_1| > \sum_{i=2}^{n} \omega_i b_i.$$

Thus the Cournot solution will lie on the inflationary side if the (aggregated) desired increase in international reserves by the non-reserve-currency countries is more than matched by the creation of international reserves in the form of international money and the supply of money of the reserve-currency country.

The adjustment process from the short run to the long run can be visualized as in figure 5.2. Suppose that at the initial moment, country 2 has accumulated an excessive stock of reserves and is trying to decumulate it. Then b_2 as well as b_1 will be negative, leading to the Stackelberg diagram shown in figure 5.2. However, in the course of adjustment, the actual stock of reserves of country 2 will approach the desired level, and b_2 will become positive. The position of the Cournot solution in the long-run situation depends on the relative magnitudes of the absolute values of $\omega_1 b_1$ and $\omega_2 b_2$.

In the long run, it is quite likely that the only country that can behave as the leader is the reserve-currency country. Our analysis implies that, if the reserve-currency country keeps b_i negative with a large absolute value, then the noncooperative solution as well as the leadership solution will tend to be inflationary. In this respect, the failure of the dollar standard system can be regarded as largely due to the rule of the game that only the United States can have a large deficit—a negative b_i with a large absolute value—and that only it can behave as the leader. The system would have worked properly only if the United States behaved as a benevolent or paternalistic leader considering only the world rate of inflation rather than as a leader in the Stackelberg sense.

The example illustrated in figure 5.3 suggests the role of an international organization. If the international monetary organization sets the relative change in international money G_R equal to the (net) aggregated desired increase in international reserves, that is,

$$G_R = \sum_{i=1}^{n} \omega_i b_i,$$

then the noncooperative behavior of national monetary authorities will lead to attainment of the Paretian configuration because the Cournot, leadership, and Paretian solutions collapse into a single point. In the long run, G_R must

be positive, so optimization through the international monetary organization is workable as long as $\sum_{i=1}^{n} \omega_i b_i$ is non-negative. When the reserve
currency country desires so large a deficit that

$$\sum_{i=1}^{n} \omega_i b_i < 0,$$

or

$$-\omega_1 b_1 > \sum_{i=2}^{n} \omega_i b_i,$$

then the role of the international organization in inducing the noncooperative solution to converge to the Paretian solution is unworkable.

In the terminology of game theory, the international organization can,
under the favorable conditions mentioned above, change the payoff structure of the monetary game from a game akin to the prisoner's dilemma to a
game where the noncooperative solution coincides with the cooperative
solution. In fact the analysis is analogous to the approach in peace research in
political science that seeks a method for changing the payoff structures of the
prisoner's dilemma case for the better.

Concluding Remarks

The final outcome of monetary interdependence under a fixed exchange rate
system or in a subsystem of the world economy in which exchange rates are
fixed among the participating countries depends, as the examples in section
3 show, on the aggregated preferences of monetary authorities concerning
the rate of inflation and the balance of payments. If mutual cooperation is
possible, the divergence of various solutions from the cooperative solution
(the Paretian configuration) becomes less serious. Countries will cooperate to
achieve an outcome on the Paretian frontier. The only remaining problem,
which is potentially a difficult one politically, is how a particular country can
achieve a point on the Paretian surface that is relatively favorable to it—in
our context, how to achieve a Paretian solution with a higher value of β_i for
country i.

Cooperation is, however, not always possible. If it is not possible, in order
for any fixed exchange rate system to work successfully, the system must be
designed in such a way that the noncooperative solution—that is, the result
of individual rational behavior—will not be very far from the cooperative
solution. The analysis suggests at least two ways of achieving this objective.
One way is to manipulate the rate of increase in international reserve assets

to match the average preference of the monetary authorities for accumulating or decumulating reserves. The other is to devise a clearing system that shifts the preferences of monetary authorities concerning surpluses or deficits to suitable values.

Finally, let us consider the application of the analysis to a flexible exchange rate system. As was shown in the previous chapter, the conflict aspect is mostly eliminated under a system of flexible exchange rates. In the short run, conflicts over the level of interest rates may occur, and during the adjustment process, beggar-thy-neighbor policies may occur, but in the long run where the real rate of interest is determined by the time preferences of the participating nations, even the conflict over the rate of interest is unlikely to occur. However, under a managed-float system where intervention in the foreign exchange market is frequent, intervention policy plays a strategic role.

The fixed price model and the full employment model are only extreme abstractions of reality. We live in a world where both unemployment and inflation coexist. In order to add realism to the analysis, from the next chapter on we examine the interdependence of monetary policy in models that allow for the coexistence of unemployment and inflation.

Appendix: The World Money Game as a Differential Game

Some readers might feel that the analysis of policy interplays under fixed rates in this chapter is too static because monetary authorities should have preferences concerning the level of reserves rather than the change in reserves (the balance of payments). To formulate this conflict situation in a dynamic model generally requires the method of the differential game. This appendix presents a simple example to illustrate how the results obtained in the chapter could be extended to a dynamic context.

Consider the case of two countries of identical size ($\omega_1 = \omega_2 = \frac{1}{2}$). The symbol z denotes the level of international reserves of country 2. Thus, in terms of θ_1 and z_2 in the text, $\dot{z} = -z_1 = z_2$ ($\dot{z}$ being the time derivative of z). The basic differential equation of the system is then

$$\dot{z}(t) = (\theta_1(t) - \theta_2(t))/2. \tag{5A.1}$$

Also, we have

$$\pi(t) = (\theta_1(t) + \theta_2(t))/2. \tag{5A.2}$$

Country 1 is the reserve-currency country, and we will assume that it is concerned only with the rate of inflation π and the levels of consumption flows over time. Thus, the welfare function for each instant will be specified as

$$u^1(t) = -\pi(t)^2 + (c\dot{z}(t) - h\dot{z}(t)^2), \qquad c, h > 0. \tag{5A.3}$$

Underlying the welfare function 5A.3 is the assumption that increased consumption due to a balance of payments deficit confers marginal utility as long as $\dot{z}(t)$ is small but that marginal utility is decreasing. Country 1 maximizes the discounted utility integral (ρ being the rate of discount)

$$J^1 = \int_0^\infty \{-\pi(t)^2 + c\dot{z}(t) - h\dot{z}(t)^2\}e^{-\rho t}dt, \qquad \rho > 0 \tag{5A.4}$$

subject to the differential equation 5A.1 and an initial condition $z(0) = Z^0$.

Country 2, the non-reserve-currency country, is assumed to have the following instantaneous utility function because it needs some international reserves for trade transactions:

$$u^2(t) = -\pi(t)^2 + (-c\dot{z}(t) - h\dot{z}(t)^2) - m(z(t) - \bar{b})^2, \qquad m > 0. \tag{5A.5}$$

Here, for simplicity, the coefficients c and h are assumed to be identical with those of country 1. Since a balance of payments deficit of country 2—a negative value of $\dot{z}(t)$—corresponds to an increased flow of instantaneous consumption, the coefficient on $\dot{z}(t)$ is negative. Country 2 is assumed to have a loss function concerning the level of international reserves, which is proportional to the distance between the actual and most desired levels of reserves, the latter being denoted by $\bar{b}$. Thus, country 2 is assumed to maximize the utility integral:

$$J^2 = \int_0^\infty \{-\pi(t)^2 - c\dot{z}(t) - h\dot{z}(t)^2 - m(z(t) - \bar{b})^2\}e^{-\rho t}dt,$$

given the differential equation 5A.1 and an initial level of reserves $z(0) = z^0$.

Then this situation of policy interplays can readily be interpreted as a differential game. In fact, because of the simplified structure of this non-zero-sum differential game, one can easily obtain the Nash solution.

One can distinguish two types of Nash solutions to a differential game: the open-loop solution in which each player is assumed to neglect the possibility that the other player's strategy may depend on the values of the state variables—here, on the value of $z(t)$—and the closed-loop solution in which each player takes account of the dependence of the other player's path on the state variable.

Formally, the Nash solution $\hat{\theta}_1(t)$, $\hat{\theta}_2(t)$ of the open-loop type is defined such that, for any (piecewise continuous) feasible control $\theta_1(t)$ and $\theta_2(t)$ (see Simaan and Takayama 1974),

$$J^1(\hat{\theta}_1(t), \hat{\theta}_2(t)) \geqq J^1(\theta_1(t), \hat{\theta}_2(t)),$$

$$J^2(\hat{\theta}_1(t), \hat{\theta}_2(t)) \geqq J^2(\hat{\theta}_1(t), \theta_2(t)).$$

The Nash solution $\hat{\theta}_1(t, z(t))$, $\hat{\theta}_2(t, z(t))$ of the closed-loop type is defined as the paths satisfying, for any (piecewise continuous) feasible control $\theta_1(t, z(t))$ and $\theta_2(t, z(t))$,

$$J^1(\hat{\theta}_1(t, z(t)), \hat{\theta}_2(t, z(t))) \geqq J^1(\theta_1(t, z(t)), \hat{\theta}_2(t, z(t))),$$

$$J^2(\hat{\theta}_1(t, z(t)), \hat{\theta}_2(t, z(t))) \geqq J^2(\hat{\theta}_1(t, z(t)), \theta_2(t, z(t))).$$

Here we will examine the property of the simple solution—the Nash solution of the open-loop type—using a variational approach (Berkovitz 1971; Simaan and Takayama 1974). The Hamiltonians for the two countries are (omitting time notations)

$$H^1 = -\pi^2 + c\dot{z} - h\dot{z}^2,$$

$$H^2 = -\pi^2 - c\dot{z} - h\dot{z}^2 - m(z - \overline{b})^2 + \lambda(\theta_1 - \theta_2)/2,$$

where $\pi = (\theta_1 + \theta_2)/2$, $\dot{z} = (\theta_1 - \theta_2)/2$, and $\lambda(\equiv \lambda(t))$ is an auxiliary variable that can be interpreted as the undiscounted shadow value attached to the level of reserves for country 2. The open-loop Nash solution is given by the solution satisfying the following conditions in addition to equation 5A.1: for country 1

$$\frac{\partial H^1}{\partial \theta_1} = -\frac{\theta_1 + \theta_2}{2} + \frac{c}{2} - \frac{h}{2}(\theta_1 - \theta_2) = 0; \tag{5A.6}$$

for country 2

$$\frac{\partial H^2}{\partial \theta_2} = -\frac{\theta_1 + \theta_2}{2} + \frac{c}{2} + \frac{h}{2}(\theta_1 - \theta_2) - \frac{\lambda}{2} = 0, \tag{5A.7}$$

$$\lambda - \rho\lambda = \frac{\partial H^2}{\partial z} = 2m(z - \overline{b}), \tag{5A.8}$$

$$\lim_{t \to \infty} \lambda e^{-\rho t} = 0. \tag{5A.9}$$

By simple substitution, one can obtain the following pair of differential equations in terms of z and λ:

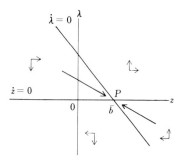

Figure 5A.1

$$\dot{z} = \lambda/4h, \tag{5A.10}$$

$$\dot{\lambda} = 2m(z - \overline{b}) + \rho\lambda. \tag{5A.11}$$

By the use of a phase diagram that is familiar to economists, the optimal trajectory of π is found to be the stable branches of the saddle point, because no other paths satisfy the transversality condition 5A.9 (figure 5A.1). It is easy to show that at the equilibrium P the rate of inflation is positive;

$$\pi = (\theta_1 + \theta_2)/2 = c/2 > 0. \tag{5A.12}$$

Thus, the open-loop Nash solution converges to an inflationary solution as long as the marginal utility of increasing consumption by running a balance of payments deficit is positive. The characteristic equation of 5A.10 and 5A.11 is

$$(\rho - y)y + m/(2h) = 0,$$

and the characteristic root corresponding to the stable branches is

$$y = \rho/2 - \tfrac{1}{2}\sqrt{\rho^2 + 2\,(m/h)}.$$

Thus, it is easy to show that an increase in m/h will speed up the process of convergence.

Next let us consider the Paretian or von Neumann solution resulting from coordinated behavior by the two monetary authorities. Suppose they cooperate to maximize $\beta J^1 + (1 - \beta)J^2$, where β is the weight of country 1's bargaining power. Then the problem is reduced to a usual variational problem in which the Hamiltonian is expressed as

$$H = -\pi^2 + (2\beta - 1)c\dot{z} - h\dot{z}^2 - (1 - \beta)m(z - \overline{b})^2 + \lambda(\theta_1 - \theta_2)/2.$$

Thus one gets the optimal conditions:

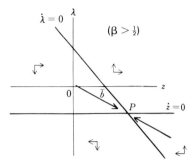

Figure 5A.2

$$\frac{\partial H}{\partial \theta_1} = -\frac{\theta_1 + \theta_2}{2} + \frac{2\beta - 1}{2}c - \frac{\theta_1 - \theta_2}{2}h + \frac{\lambda}{2} = 0, \tag{5A.13}$$

$$\frac{\partial H}{\partial \theta_2} = -\frac{\theta_1 + \theta_2}{2} + \frac{2\beta - 1}{2}c - \frac{\theta_1 - \theta_2}{2}h - \frac{\lambda}{2} = 0, \tag{5A.14}$$

$$\dot{\lambda} - \rho\lambda = -\frac{\partial H}{\partial z} = 2(1 - \beta)m(z - \bar{b}), \tag{5A.15}$$

$$\lim_{t \to \infty} \lambda e^{-\rho t} = 0. \tag{5A.16}$$

It is easy to see that along any path satisfying equations 5A.13 and 5A.14

$$\pi = (\theta_1 + \theta_2)/2 = 0. \tag{5A.17}$$

Thus, the trajectory of the von Neumann solution gives price stability throughout the adjustment process. The optimal path is the stable branches of the following differential equations (figure 5A.2):

$$\dot{z} = \frac{1}{2h}\lambda + \frac{2\beta - 1}{2h}c \tag{5A.18}$$

$$\dot{\lambda} = 2(1 - \beta)m(z - \bar{b}) + \rho\lambda. \tag{5A.19}$$

It may be slightly more realistic to assume that u^2 has the following form because a higher level of reserves than the required level $\bar{b}$ may do no harm and because the benefits from the possible decumulation of reserves are already reflected in the consumption increase term:

$$u^2 = -\pi(t)^2 + (-c\dot{z}(t) - h\dot{z}(t)^2) - m(z(t) - \bar{b})^2 \quad \text{if } z(t) \leqslant \bar{b}$$

$$= -\pi(t)^2 + (-c\dot{z}(t) - h\dot{z}(t)^2) \quad \text{if } z(t) > \bar{b}. \tag{5A.5'}$$

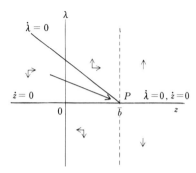

Figure 5A.3

The resulting pair of differential equations for the Nash solution can be written

$$\left.\begin{array}{l} \dot{z} = \lambda/4h, \\ \dot{\lambda} = 2m(z - \bar{b}) - \rho\lambda \end{array}\right\} \quad \text{if } z(t) \leqslant \bar{b}$$

$$\left.\begin{array}{l} \dot{z} = 0, \\ \dot{\lambda} = \rho\lambda \end{array}\right\} \quad \text{if } z(t) > \bar{b}.$$

In this example the equilibrium point P is not just one point but is extended to a line segment on the horizontal axis from $z = \bar{b}$. The qualitative characteristics will not be any different from the discussion in the main body of this chapter. (The triangular area to the southeast of P and containing the stable branch in figure 5A.1 is compressed to a single line segment. See figure 5A.3.)

There remain many unresolved questions. For example, what are the effects of including the balance of payments objective for country 1, of asymmetrical utility functions, or of relative country side? What are the properties of the closed-loop solution or the Stackelberg solution? These questions furnish topics for further research.

The foregoing dynamic analysis suggests, however, that the results obtained in the static formulation are quite likely to be generalizable to a dynamic situation. For example, the finding that if the rules of the game are not properly set, the noncooperative interplay of monetary policies would result in a situation outside the von Neumann solution frontier would not be altered.

Exchange Rate Regimes and the Effect of Changes in the Terms of Trade

In the real world, both the price level and income are variable, and inflation and unemployment usually coexist, so in this chapter we employ a more realistic model than those used thus far to analyze how the tradeoffs between inflation and unemployment of nations are related internationally and how the monetary policies of nations affect one another under the alternative systems of fixed and flexible exchange rates.

Since the adoption of flexible exchange rates (or, more precisely, of the managed float) by many developed countries, the question of differences in macroeconomic mechanisms between fixed and flexible exchange rate regimes has become a subject of practical concern. There are many un-answered questions concerning the differences between the two exchange rate regimes. For example, how do the effects of a general price rise in international markets on the domestic economy differ under the two regimes? How do the effects of a deterioration (or improvement) in the terms of trade on the domestic economy differ under the two regimes? Can the flexible exchange rate regime insulate the domestic economy from all types of economic disturbances from abroad?

To answer these questions in a model that allows for the simultaneous existence of inflation and unemployment would be quite complicated. In this chapter, by way of preparation for such an analysis in the next chapter, we first consider the relationship between inflation and unemployment in a small-country model that takes the terms of trade and international prices as exogenously given.

Because the focus is on a single country, this chapter is somewhat of a digression from the topic of the interdependence of monetary policies that constitutes the central theme of this work. It is included because a prelimi-nary analysis of a one-country model may help to acquaint readers with concepts used in analyzing the interdependence between two countries. Furthermore, the model in this chapter has important implications for the conduct of domestic monetary policy when there is a sharp change in the terms of trade, as happened during the two oil crises.

Consider a small economy for which the international prices of traded goods are exogenously determined. Then under fixed exchange rates the country can neither pursue an independent monetary policy nor choose its price level as long as the exchange rate is not altered. On the other hand, under flexible exchange rates one is tempted to believe that a country can pursue an independent monetary policy and achieve the price level of its own choice. If world inflation proceeds in such a way that the general international price level rises without any change in the terms of trade, a small country can achieve, under certain conditions, the rate of inflation of its own choice through monetary policy. If, however, world inflation is accompanied by a change in the terms of trade between the exportables and importables of a small country, then a deterioration in the terms of trade will not only exert inflationary pressure but also cause a reduction in employment in the country. Therefore, an understanding of the effects of changes in the terms of trade on the domestic economy is of utmost importance, especially since the international transmission of inflation accompanying the oil crises has become a serious problem confronting the world economy.

Other questions examined in this chapter concern the role of nontraded goods and the effects of money illusion and price expectations in an open economy. In his discussion of optimal currency areas, McKinnon (1963) has pointed out the importance of nontraded goods and of money illusion in wage formation as criteria for the effectiveness of flexible exchange rates. In addition, the role of money illusion is significant in the case of devaluation in developing countries (Cooper 1971). It is still an open question, however, whether the flexible exchange rate system is workable in a very open economy without any money illusion. It would also be interesting to see how the existence of nontraded goods alters the relationship between the world price level and the domestic price level.

In order to answer these questions, we will construct a dynamic model allowing for fluctuations in both prices and employment. Most of the works that compare the mechanisms of fixed and flexible exchange rates, including the previous two chapters, assume either price flexibility with full employment or unemployment with a fixed domestic price level. In his pioneering attempt, Gordon (1977) considered simultaneous fluctuations in prices as well as employment. He pointed out that the two approaches—the domestic Phillips curve approach and the international monetary approach to balance of payments—supplement each other in explaining the inflationary process of an underemployed open economy. I follow Gordon's lead and try to integrate the domestic Phillips curve approach and the international monetary approach into a unified model of an open economy. The short-run and long-run Phillips curves are introduced, and the wage-price spiral is combined with the impact of price expectations.

In order to focus on the short-run interrelationship of absolute prices, relative prices, and employment, I adopt several simplifying assumptions. For example, capital and other factors of production will be assumed to be constant, and capital accumulation will be assumed to be negligible. Also, it is assumed that the only financial asset in the country is domestic money and that the demand for money takes such a form that the consumption velocity of money depends only on the expected rate of inflation.

Under these assumptions, one can contrast clearly the nature of both inflation and unemployment under fixed and flexible exchange rates. In short, the conclusions here support the general view concerning the alternative exchange rate systems that monetary shocks can be easily absorbed or insulated under a flexible exchange rate regime but that real shocks (such as a change in relative prices) cannot be absorbed and are transmitted even under a flexible exchange rate regime. This analysis will lead to an understanding of the process of imported inflation that occurred after the oil crisis in many countries, some of which had adopted floating exchange rates.

The Basic Framework

Let us consider an economy that produces a single commodity, which is also exportable, and imports another commodity, the import good. Suppose that this economy occupies a small portion of the world market so that the small-country assumption concerning international prices of traded goods is justified. In other words, the international relative price of the export and import goods can be regarded as exogenously given to this country. The domestic price of the export good and that of the import good are p_1 and p_2, respectively. The international price of the export good and that of the import good are denoted by p_1^* and p_2^*, respectively. If one denotes the exchange rate—the price of foreign currency in terms of the domestic currency—as q, then one can write

$$p_1 = q p_1^*, \tag{6.1}$$

$$p_2 = q p_2^*. \tag{6.2}$$

Under a system of fixed exchange rates, q is a constant, subject possibly to once-for-all changes in case of devaluation or revaluation; under a system of flexible exchange rates, q is an endogenous variable that depends on the domestic and international economic situations.

Let X_1 be the level of production of the domestic (export) good. We will assume that the factors of production other than labor are fixed in this framework. We will also assume that X_1 is produced according to the production function

$$X_1 = N_1^{\beta_1}, \qquad 0 < \beta_1 < 1 \tag{6.3}$$

where N_1 indicates the amount of labor employed.[1] Labor is employed until its marginal value product is equated to the money wage rate w, that is,

$$w = p_1 \beta_1 N_1^{\beta_1 - 1}. \tag{6.4}$$

Let C_1 and C_2 be the consumption of domestic goods and import goods, respectively. Let us assume that the proportion of total expenditure to be spent on the domestic good is constant; that is,

$$p_1 C_1 = \alpha_1 (p_1 C_1 + p_2 C_2),$$

or

$$(1 - \alpha_1) p_1 C_1 = \alpha_1 p_2 C_2. \tag{6.5}$$

Total expenditure is, in turn, assumed to depend on the money balance:

$$p_1 C_1 + p_2 C_2 = v(\pi) M, \tag{6.6}$$

where M is the total money balance in the national economy and v is the consumption velocity, which may depend on expectations concerning the rate of price rise π.

Equation 6.6 can also be regarded as the hoarding function. In fact, equations 6.5 and 6.6 are consistent with the consumption and hoarding behavior derived by Dornbusch and Mussa (1975), as is shown in the appendix to this chapter.

The price index is assumed to take the dynamic form

$$\hat{p} = \alpha_1 \hat{p}_1 + \alpha_2 \hat{p}_2, \qquad \alpha_1 + \alpha_2 = 1. \tag{6.7}$$

This price index corresponds to the deflater in the indirect utility function, which can be derived from the Cobb-Douglas or log-additive utility function that implies the consumption behavior expressed in equation 6.5 (see appendix 6A).

Expectations concerning the general price level are assumed to be formed by a process of adaptive expectations. The expected rate of inflation π is generated by the differential equation

$$\dot{\pi} = \gamma(\hat{p} - \pi), \tag{6.8}$$

where $\gamma > 0$ is a constant indicating the speed of adjustment.

We are well aware of the limitations of the adaptive formulation of expectations formation that have been seriously raised by adherents of the rational expectations hypothesis. However, as B. Friedman (1979) has correctly pointed out, in the real world where information is imperfect and hence can be obtained only through a learning process, the expectations of rational economic agents can at best be formed adaptively. Moreover, the observed pattern of business cycles does not necessarily contradict the implications of macroeconomic models that incorporate the short-run and long-run Phillips curves linked through adaptively formed inflation expectations. Thus, the adaptive expectations hypothesis is still applicable to real world problems, and we will regard expectations as being formed adaptively throughout the remainder of this book.[2]

Given the expected rate of inflation π, the short-run Phillips curve can be written as

$$\hat{w} = \phi(N_1) + \lambda\pi, \quad 0 \leqq \lambda \leqq 1, \quad \phi'(N_1) > 0, \tag{6.9}$$

where λ is an indicator of the degree of money illusion. If λ equals unity, there is no money illusion, and the long-run Phillips curve becomes vertical, crossing the horizontal coordinate at the value $\bar{N}_1$ that satisfies $\phi(\bar{N}_1) = 0$. If λ is less than unity—that is, if there is some degree of money illusion—the economy retains the long-run tradeoff between inflation and unemployment to a certain extent.

Since there are no financial assets other than money, the balance of payments B of this economy equals the negative of net absorption—that is, income minus expenditure:

$$B = p_1 X_1 - (p_1 C_1 + p_2 C_2).$$

The balance of payments is also equal to the excess demand for money. Therefore, one can write

$$\dot{M} - \dot{M}^S = p_1 X_1 - (p_1 C_1 + p_2 C_2) \tag{6.10}$$

where $\dot{M}^S$ is the supply of money created by transfer payments.

We have now introduced all the components of our economic model of a small open economy. There are ten equations in the system. Ten variables $N_1, X_1, C_1, C_2, w, \pi, p, p_1, p_2,$ and M are always endogenous, $p_1^*, p_2^*,$ and $\dot{M}^S$ are always exogenous. Under flexible exchange rates, q is also an endogenous variable, and we have an additional equation:

$$\dot{M} - \dot{M}^S = 0. \tag{6.11}$$

Under fixed exchange rates, q is an exogenous variable, and we do not have equation 6.11.

By differentiating equations 6.1–6.4 logarithmically, we obtain the following relationships among the rates of increase in prices, employment and production:

$$\hat{p}_1 = \hat{q} + \hat{p}_1^*, \tag{6.1'}$$

$$\hat{p}_2 = \hat{q} + \hat{p}_2^*, \tag{6.2'}$$

$$\hat{X}_1 = \beta_1 \hat{N}_1, \tag{6.3'}$$

$$\hat{w} = \hat{p}_1 - (1 - \beta_1)\hat{N}_1. \tag{6.4'}$$

Substituting equation 6.4′ into 6.9, we obtain

$$\hat{N} = \frac{1}{1 - \beta_1}\{\hat{p}_1 - \phi(N_1) - \lambda\pi\}. \tag{6.12}$$

From equations 6.7 and 6.8, we obtain

$$\dot{\pi} = \gamma(\alpha_1\hat{p}_1 + \alpha_2\hat{p}_2 - \pi). \tag{6.13}$$

Equations 6.12 and 6.13 form a system of simultaneous differential equations in terms of N_1 and π that summarize the monetary mechanisms of an open economy under fixed as well as flexible exchange rates. Let us examine the properties of the system under each regime in turn.

Fixed Exchange Rates

Under a fixed exchange rate regime, the exchange rate is fixed, that is, $\hat{q} = 0$, and, accordingly, $\hat{p}_1 = \hat{p}_1^*$ and $\hat{p}_2 = \hat{p}_2^*$. If we define $y \equiv \log N_1$ and $\psi(y) \equiv \phi(N_1) = \phi(e^y)$, the basic differential equations 6.12 and 6.13 can be reduced to

$$\dot{y} = \frac{1}{1 - \beta_1}\{\hat{p}_1^* - \psi(y) - \lambda\pi\} \tag{6.14}$$

and

$$\dot{\pi} = \gamma\{\hat{p}_1^* + \alpha_2(\hat{p}_2^* - \hat{p}_1^*) - \pi\}, \tag{6.15}$$

from which we can see the properties of the monetary mechanism under fixed exchange rates.

Let us start from the equilibrium values of y and π, which we will denote by $\bar{\pi}$ and $\bar{y}$. By assuming $\dot{\pi} = \dot{y} = 0$, we can obtain the equilibrium values of π and y or $\hat{p}$ and y:

$$(\hat{p} =) \bar{\pi} = \hat{p}_1^* + \alpha_2(\hat{p}_2^* - \hat{p}_1^*)$$

$$= (1 - \alpha_2)\hat{p}_1^* + \alpha_2\hat{p}_2^*, \tag{6.16}$$

$$\psi(\bar{y}) = (1 - \lambda)\hat{p}_1^* - \lambda\alpha_2(\hat{p}_2^* - \hat{p}_1^*). \tag{6.17}$$

From equation 6.16 we can observe that a small country cannot determine its own equilibrium rate of inflation or deflation. The rate of increase in export prices and that in import prices completely determine the equilibrium rate of inflation of this small economy.

From equation 6.17, one can easily see that if $\lambda = 1$—that is, in the complete absence of money illusion—

$$\psi(\bar{y}) = -\alpha_2(\hat{p}_2^* - \hat{p}_1^*). \tag{6.18}$$

Equation 6.18 shows that if the rates of price increase of the export good and the import good are identical, then the equilibrium level of employment of this economy will correspond to the natural rate of unemployment of a closed economy, which is indicated by the relation $\psi(\bar{y}) = 0$ or $\phi(\bar{N}_1) = 0$. Even in the absence of money illusion ($\lambda = 1$), however, if the terms of trade are deteriorating continuously—that is, if $\hat{p}_1^* - \hat{p}_2^* < 0$—then equation 6.18 shows that $\psi(\bar{y})$ can be negative. Formally,

$$\frac{\partial \bar{y}}{\partial(\hat{p}_1^* - \hat{p}_2^*)} = \frac{\alpha_2}{\psi'} > 0. \tag{6.19}$$

The economy cannot attain the equilibrium level of employment corresponding to the natural rate of unemployment. A continuous deterioration in the terms of trade can cause an increase in unemployment in equilibrium.[3]

If some money illusion remains and λ is less than unity, then overall inflation abroad without any change in the terms of trade such that $\hat{p}_1^* = \hat{p}_2^* > 0$ can cause an improvement in the equilibrium level of employment, as indicated by equation 6.17.

Next let us turn to the process of adjustment to the equilibrium levels of π and y. It is easy to see that the system of equations 6.14 and 6.15 is locally stable.[4] In figure 6.1, the graph of $\dot{y} = 0$ is given as a downward-sloping, turned-over Phillips curve relation; the graph of $\dot{\pi} = 0$ is a horizontal line. Suppose $\hat{p}_1^*$ and $\hat{p}_2^*$ rise simultaneously at the same rate so that the terms of trade remain constant. Then, in the absence of money illusion ($\lambda = 1$), both curves will shift upward as indicated by the dotted lines, and the new

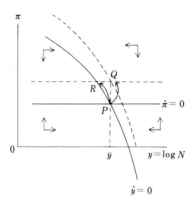

Figure 6.1

equilibrium will lie directly above P as indicated by Q in figure 6.1. (Q will be to the northeast of P if $\lambda < 1$.) The economy will start moving from P to Q as indicated by the arrow. In the absence of money illusion, the economy will enjoy a boom in employment but eventually will return to the same level of employment with a higher rate of inflation that is equal to $\hat{p}_1^* \; (= \hat{p}_2^*)$.

Next consider the effects of a deterioration in the terms of trade. Suppose the rate of increase in the export price $\hat{p}_1^*$ remains the same, but the rate of increase in the import price $\hat{p}_2^*$ increases. Then it is clear from equation 6.14 that the $\dot{y} = 0$ curve will remain the same but clear from equation 6.15 that the $\dot{\pi} = 0$ curve will shift upward, and the equilibrium will move from P to R. In other words, stagflation with an increase in both the rate of inflation and unemployment will develop. The reader can do a similar exercise for the case where $\hat{p}_2^*$ is constant but $\hat{p}_1^*$ is falling. The result is a reduction in employment and a falling rate of inflation in this economy. Thus, we can summarize as follows: Under the fixed exchange rate regime, a small country cannot choose its own rate of inflation. In the absence of money illusion, a general rise in the international price level without changes in the terms of trade keeps the equilibrium level of employment constant; continuous deterioration in the terms of trade reduces the equilibrium level of employment.

Flexible Exchange Rates

Under a system of flexible exchange rates, the exchange rate as well as the domestic prices of the export and import goods become endogenous variables; however, we have an additional condition (6.11), so that the amount of money becomes an exogenous variable. Let θ be the rate of increase in the supply of money that is determined by the monetary authority. That is, $(\dot{M} =)\dot{M}^S = \theta M$. From equations 6.11 and 6.10, we obtain

$$p_1 X_1 = p_1 C_1 + p_2 C_2. \tag{6.20}$$

Substituting equation 6.20 into 6.5, we have

$$p_1 X_1 = v(\pi)M. \tag{6.21}$$

If we approximate $v(\pi)$ by $v(\pi) = ae^{\varepsilon\pi}$ and differentiate equation 6.21 logarithmically, we obtain

$$\hat{p}_1 + \hat{X}_1 = \varepsilon\dot{\pi} + \theta, \tag{6.22}$$

or, by virtue of equation 6.3',

$$\hat{p}_1 = \theta + \varepsilon\dot{\pi} - \beta_1 \hat{N}_1. \tag{6.23}$$

From equations 6.1' and 6.2', we know that

$$\hat{p}_2 = \hat{p}_1 + (\hat{p}_2^* - \hat{p}_1^*). \tag{6.24}$$

If we substitute 6.23 and 6.24 into 6.12 and 6.13, we have

$$\hat{N}_1 = \theta + \varepsilon\dot{\pi} - \phi(N_1) - \lambda\pi, \tag{6.25}$$

$$\dot{\pi} = \gamma\{\theta + \varepsilon\dot{\pi} - \beta_1 \hat{N}_1 + \alpha_2(\hat{p}_2^* - \hat{p}_1^*) - \pi\}. \tag{6.26}$$

In terms of $y = \log N_1$, and $\psi(y) \equiv \phi(e^y)$, we have, after some rearrangement of terms, a system of differential equations:

$$\dot{y} = \varepsilon\dot{\pi} + \theta - \psi(y) - \lambda\pi, \tag{6.25'}$$

$$\dot{\pi} = \frac{\gamma}{1 - \varepsilon\gamma}\{-\beta_1\dot{y} + \theta + \alpha_2(\hat{p}_2^* - \hat{p}_1^*) - \pi\}. \tag{6.26'}$$

Equilibrium values are given by

$$\psi(\bar{y}) = (1 - \lambda)\theta - \lambda\alpha_2(\hat{p}_2^* - \hat{p}_1^*), \tag{6.27}$$

$$\bar{\pi} = \theta + \alpha_2(\hat{p}_2^* - \hat{p}_1^*). \tag{6.28}$$

From equations 6.27 and 6.28, we can see that, in contrast to the case of fixed exchange rates, a country can affect its equilibrium rate of inflation by changing the rate of increase of the money supply θ and that it can affect its equilibrium rate of employment as long as there is a degree of money illusion ($\lambda < 1$). From equations 6.27 and 6.28, we can also see that simultaneous increases in $\hat{p}_2^*$ and $\hat{p}_1^*$ without any change in the terms of trade (that is, with continued equality between $\hat{p}_1^*$ and $\hat{p}_2^*$) do not affect the equilibrium values of y and π at all. Moreover, the system of dynamic equations 6.25' and 6.26' remains unchanged in response to a simultaneous increase in international prices without any change in relative prices. Thus, regardless of the existence of money illusion, simultaneous increases in the international prices of the export and import goods without any change in the terms of trade leave the domestic economy unaffected under flexible exchange rates. Changes in the exchange rate can completely absorb the general rise in price levels.

On the other hand, suppose that the terms of trade are deteriorating in such a way that $\hat{p}_2^* - \hat{p}_1^* > 0$. Then, as can easily be shown,

$$\frac{\partial \bar{\pi}}{\partial(\hat{p}_2^* - \hat{p}_1^*)} = \alpha_2, \tag{6.29}$$

$$\frac{\partial \bar{y}}{\partial(\hat{p}_2^* - \hat{p}_1^*)} = -\frac{\alpha_2 \lambda}{\psi'} < 0. \tag{6.30}$$

The equilibrium rate of expected inflation (and, accordingly, the actual rate of inflation in equilibrium) will increase, and the equilibrium level of employment will decrease. Thus, even under flexible exchange rates, a small country cannot insulate itself from the effect of changing relative prices abroad. It is interesting to note that a fall in the price of the export good, with the price of the import goods remaining constant, will cause an increase in the domestic rate of inflation and a reduction in unemployment. Thus, under a regime of flexible exchange rates, any continuous deterioration in the terms of trade, even in the form of falling export prices, will cause stagflationary pressures on the domestic economy. Under fixed exchange rates, by contrast, a fall in the price of the export good, with the price of the import good remaining constant, will cause not only a reduction in employment but also a reduction in the rate of domestic inflation.

Thus, the same rate of increase in the money supply will cause different rates of inflation depending on the trend of the terms of trade. This result may seem strange, but reflection will tell us that the result is natural because real income or real consumption possibilities are continuously decreasing whenever the terms of trade are continuously deteriorating.

By solving equations 6.25' and 6.26' in terms of $\dot{y}$ and $\dot{\pi}$, we have

$$\dot{y} = \frac{1}{\Delta}\{\theta + \varepsilon\gamma\alpha_2(\hat{p}_2^* - \hat{p}_1^*) - (1 - \gamma_2\varepsilon)\psi(y)$$

$$- [\lambda(1 - \gamma\varepsilon) + \gamma\varepsilon]\pi\}, \tag{6.25''}$$

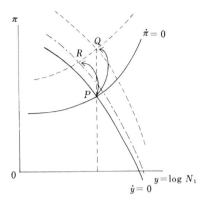

Figure 6.2

$$\dot{\pi} = \frac{\gamma}{\Delta}\{(1 - \beta)\theta + \alpha_2(\hat{p}_2^* - \hat{p}_1^*) + \beta\psi(y) - (1 - \beta\lambda)\pi\}, \qquad (6.26'')$$

$$\Delta \equiv 1 - \gamma\varepsilon(1 - \beta).$$

The system is stable if $1 - \varepsilon\gamma > 0$.[5] The process of adjustment to the equilibrium is illustrated in figure 6.2. The $\dot{y} = 0$ locus is a downward-sloping curve as in the case of fixed exchange rates. The $\dot{\pi} = 0$ locus is an upward-sloping curve. Suppose that $1 - \varepsilon\gamma > 0$. Then if y is to the left (right) of the $\dot{y} = 0$ locus, y is increasing (decreasing); if π is below (above) the curve $\dot{\pi} = 0$, π is increasing (decreasing).

An increase in the rate of increase of the money supply θ will shift both curves upward. In the absence of money illusion ($\lambda = 1$), it will shift them by the same distance so that the new equilibrium Q lies directly above P. In the presence of money illusion ($\lambda < 1$), Q will lie to the northeast of P. If $\lambda = 1$, the increase in θ will exert no influence on the equilibrium value of employment $\bar{y}$ but will induce a temporary boom as indicated by the arrow from P to Q in figure 6.2.

A general rise in the international price level without any change in the terms of trade ($\hat{p}_1^* = \hat{p}_2^*$) will affect neither curve and accordingly will affect neither y nor π. However, a continuous deterioration in the terms of trade ($\hat{p}_1^* < \hat{p}_2^*$) will shift both curves upward but will shift the $\dot{\pi} = 0$ locus more than the $\dot{y} = 0$ locus.[6] Therefore the new equilibrium R will be situated to the northwest of P, and the adjustment path will follow the course indicated by the arrow from P to R in figure 6.2.

So far we have been concerned with a chronic or continuous worsening of the terms of trade, but the effects of a once-and-for-all change in the terms of

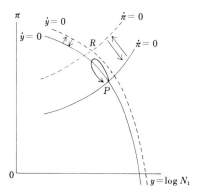

Figure 6.3

trade can be studied as well. Suppose that a once-and-for-all deterioration in the terms of trade takes place. This process can be approximated by a sharp rise in $(\hat{p}_2^* - \hat{p}_1^*)$ for a short period of time, followed by a return of $(\hat{p}_2^* - \hat{p}_1^*)$ to zero. In our framework, this process implies that the curves in figure 6.3 shift upward to the dotted curves temporarily and then return to their initial positions. The eventual equilibrium point remains at P, but the dynamic paths of y and π roughly follow the paths indicated by the arrows in figure 6.3. Thus, even a once-and-for-all deterioration in the terms of trade can exert a stagflationary effect in the short run.

The Role of Nontraded Goods under Flexible Exchange Rates

Nontraded goods play an important role in an open economy (Dornbusch 1973; Komiya 1966). The introduction of nontraded goods into our model would, in general, complicate the analysis considerably, particularly in the case of fixed exchange rates. However, under flexible exchange rates and under our assumption that the share of spending on each good is constant, we can easily analyze the effect of nontraded goods.

Let us denote the output of nontraded goods by X_0 and employment in that sector by N_0. The production function and the demand for labor in the nontraded-goods sector will be written as

$$X_0 = N_0^{\beta_0}, \qquad 0 < \beta_0 < 1 \tag{6.31}$$

$$w = p_0 \beta_0 N_0^{\beta_0 - 1}, \tag{6.32}$$

where p_0 is the price of nontraded goods and w is the common wage rate for the export and nontraded-goods sectors. Expenditure on each commodity is given by

$$p_0 C_0 = \alpha_0 (p_0 C_0 + p_1 C_1 + p_2 C_2), \tag{6.33}$$

$$p_1 C_1 = \alpha_1 (p_0 C_0 + p_1 C_1 + p_2 C_2), \tag{6.34}$$

and the price index by

$$\hat{p} = \alpha_0 \hat{p}_0 + \alpha_1 \hat{p}_1 + \alpha_2 \hat{p}_2, \qquad \sum_{i=0}^{2} \alpha_i = 1. \tag{6.35}$$

Total spending is determined by

$$p_0 C_0 + p_1 C_1 + p_2 C_2 = v(\pi)M. \tag{6.36}$$

Equilibrium in the nontraded-goods sector requires that

$$X_0 = C_0. \tag{6.37}$$

Let N be total employment,

$$N = N_0 + N_1, \tag{6.38}$$

and let the short-run Phillips curve be expressed as

$$\hat{w} = \phi(N) + \lambda \pi, \qquad 0 \le \lambda \le 1, \qquad \phi'(N) > 0. \tag{6.39}$$

Under flexible exchange rates, income equals expenditure:

$$p_0 X_0 + p_1 X_1 = p_0 C_0 + p_1 C_1 + p_2 C_2. \tag{6.40}$$

Equations 6.31–6.40 and 6.1–6.5 constitute the model of a small open economy with nontraded goods under flexible exchange rates. In this case we can again reduce the whole system to a pair of differential equations.

From equations 6.33, 6.36, and 6.37,

$$p_0 X_0 = p_0 C_0 = \alpha_0 v(\pi)M. \tag{6.41}$$

Differentiating equation 6.41 logarithmically, we obtain

$$\hat{p}_0 + \hat{X}_0 = \varepsilon \hat{\pi} + \theta. \tag{6.42}$$

From equations 6.40 and 6.41, we have

$$p_1 X_1 = p_1 C_1 + p_2 C_2 = (\alpha_1 + \alpha_2) v(\pi)M,$$

which yields

$$\hat{p}_1 + \hat{X}_1 = \varepsilon \hat{\pi} + \theta. \tag{6.43}$$

From equations 6.42 and 6.43, we have

$$\hat{p}_0 + \hat{X}_0 = \hat{p}_1 + \hat{X}_1. \tag{6.44}$$

On the other hand, from wage equations 6.32 and 6.4 we have

$$\hat{p}_0 + (\beta_0 - 1)\hat{N}_0 = \hat{p}_1 + (\beta_1 - 1)\hat{N}_1,$$

$$\hat{p}_0 + \hat{X}_0 - \hat{N}_0 = \hat{p}_1 + \hat{X}_1 - \hat{N}_1. \tag{6.45}$$

Therefore, comparing equations 6.44 and 6.45 and noting equation 6.38, we obtain

$$\hat{N}_0 = \hat{N}_1 = \hat{N}. \tag{6.46}$$

Accordingly, we can reduce the system to one of differential equations in terms of N and π. From equations 6.42, 6.43, and 6.46,

$$\hat{p}_0 = \varepsilon\dot{\pi} + \theta - \beta_0\hat{N}, \tag{6.47}$$

$$\hat{p}_1 = \varepsilon\dot{\pi} + \theta - \beta_1\hat{N}, \tag{6.48}$$

and, as before,

$$\hat{p}_2 = \hat{p}_1 + (\hat{p}_2^* - \hat{p}_1^*). \tag{6.49}$$

From equations 6.48 and 6.4,

$$\hat{w} = \hat{p}_1 + (\beta_1 - 1)\hat{N}.$$

$$= \varepsilon\dot{\pi} + \theta - \hat{N}. \tag{6.50}$$

Substituting 6.50 into 6.39, and substituting 6.47, 6.48, and 6.49 into 6.35, and again 6.35 into 6.8, we obtain

$$\hat{N} = \theta + \varepsilon\dot{\pi} - \phi(N) - \lambda\pi, \tag{6.51}$$

$$\dot{\pi} = \gamma\{\theta + \varepsilon\dot{\pi} - (\alpha_0\beta_0 + (\alpha_1 + \alpha_2)\beta_1)\hat{N} + \alpha_2(\hat{p}_2^* - \hat{p}_1^*) - \pi\}. \tag{6.52}$$

Comparing the system of equations 6.51 and 6.52 with that of 6.25 and 6.26, we can see that both systems have identical qualitative properties. Thus, even in the presence of nontraded goods, the effects of monetary expansion, of overall increases in the international price level, and of a deterioration in the terms of trade under flexible exchange rates can be analyzed in precisely the same way as in the absence of nontraded goods. In addition, equation 6.46 indicates that, under flexible exchange rates and under our assumption of a constant relative share of expenditures on each commodity, employment in the traded goods sector and employment in the nontraded-goods sector move in synchronized fashion.

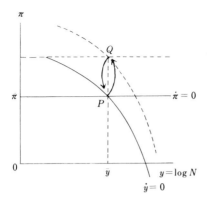

Figure 6.4

Implications of the Analysis

The analysis can be applied to various problems concerning inflation and unemployment in an open economy. The first application concerns the effectiveness of devaluation in a small country. Cooper (1971) analyzed this problem with respect to money illusion and the terms of trade. In our model a once-and-for-all devaluation can be approximated as a sudden and temporary increase in $\hat{q}$ or as a sudden and temporary increase in $\hat{p}_1$ and $\hat{p}_2$, maintaining the equality between $\hat{p}_1$ and $\hat{p}_2$, followed by the return of $\hat{q}$ or $\hat{p}_1$ and $\hat{p}_2$ to their initial values. As shown in figure 6.4, which illustrates equations 6.14 and 6.15 for the case without any money illusion ($\lambda = 1$), both the $\dot{y} = 0$ and $\dot{\pi} = 0$ loci shift upward in such a way that they intersect at Q instead of P. Soon thereafter, they return to their initial positions so that they intersect each other again at P. The dynamic path is roughly as indicated by the arrows. As suggested by Cooper, the increase in employment from devaluation is likely to be obtained only if there is some element of money illusion ($\lambda < 1$), which will lead to Q being situated to the northeast of P. Even in the presence of money illusion, however, a once-and-for-all change in the exchange rate will not enable a small economy to enjoy the fruits of increased employment for long as long as $\hat{p}_1^*$ and $\hat{p}_2^*$ remain constant after the devaluation because the adjustment path will eventually return to its initial position.

The second application concerns optimal currency areas. McKinnon (1963) introduced a useful criterion concerning the openness of a country, which it can use when deciding whether it should join other countries in forming a larger currency area or form a currency area by itself. The present analysis suggests that if dependence on imports is higher—that is, if α_2 is large—then even a flexible exchange rate system cannot insulate the country from the effects of a deterioration in the terms of trade. However, it also suggests that even if the economy is very open—even if α_0 is small—insulation from general price trends is still possible under a flexible exchange rate regime. In addition the analysis indicates that the existence of money illusion is not a necessary condition for the effectiveness of a flexible exchange rate system even though it is a condition for the effectiveness of a once-and-for-all devaluation.

Finally, one may also derive policy implications from this model for an economy experiencing supply shocks such as Japan did during the two oil crises. In the present framework, a supply shock can be interpreted as a once-and-for-all or step-by-step deterioration in the terms of trade. Under a flexible exchange rate system, as long as the stance of monetary policy remains unchanged, the economy will follow a path from P to R and then back to the original position, as shown in figure 6.3. However, it is more likely that in the face of stagflationary pressures induced by a deterioration in the terms of trade, the monetary authority will choose to respond in one of the following two ways: first, to minimize the adjustment in the employment level, the monetary authority may choose to raise the rate of monetary growth, or second, it may be willing to accept a higher rate of unemployment in order to achieve a stable price level. In terms of figure 6.3, the former policy attempts to keep the adjustment path to the right by moving R further upward (further to the northeast when $\lambda < 1$), while the latter seeks to achieve an adjustment path close to the horizontal axis by moving R downward (to the southwest if $\lambda < 1$). Which policy is more desirable depends, among other things, on whether there is a degree of money illusion. When there is some money illusion ($\lambda < 1$), the first policy may be desirable since it moves R upward to the right. The final choice ultimately depends on the country's preference with respect to price stability and lower unemployment.

In addition, we can derive the following policy conclusions from the above analysis. First, although it might be desirable to reduce the monetary growth rate temporarily in order to cope with a supply shock, such a reduction should not be permanent, since, in the absence of further deterioration in the terms of trade, it would result in deflationary pressures. Second, as we have seen in the case of flexible exchange rates, the same rate of monetary growth is more inflationary in the case where the terms of trade are deteriorating continuously than in the case where the terms of trade remain constant. Thus, in order to maintain price stability, the money supply should be increased at a slower rate in the former than in the latter case. This may provide one reason why the monetary policy of Japan has performed relatively well since the second oil crisis.

The analysis has limitations. The results depend on a number of simplifying assumptions, although some of these assumptions can be relaxed without changing the qualitative nature of the conclusions. For example, the constancy of α_1 and α_2 in the price index equation can be relaxed. Suppose that the substitution of other goods for import goods is difficult. Then the relative value content of import goods in the market basket will rise when p_2^* is rising faster than p_1^*. Accordingly, the unfavourable effect of deteriorating terms of trade will be aggravated when the economy consumes a fixed physical quantity of import goods rather than a fixed value. However, the other assumptions such as the neglect of capital accumulation and of financial assets other than money contributed to the clarified picture presented and at the same time leave room for a modification of the policy conclusions derived from this analysis.

This chapter has compared the macroeconomic mechanism of a small, open economy under the fixed and flexible exchange rate regimes. The analysis supports the general view that a flexible exchange rate regime is effective in insulating monetary shocks from abroad but not real shocks such as changes in relative prices. It is true that the neglect of discipline by monetary authorities was a major cause for the worldwide inflation that followed the oil crisis. At the same time, however, the analysis suggests that, even under a flexible exchange rate regime, an endogenous mechanism may be embedded in the world economy through which a deterioration in the terms of trade triggers stagflation in an open economy.

Appendix: The Microeconomic Foundations of Money Hoarding and Spending Behavior

In the model described in this chapter, equation 6.6, which relates total expenditures to money holdings, is of fundamental importance. Moreover, we need to ascertain that the model has been formulated consistently with the underlying budget constraints being properly respected. The purpose of this appendix is to provide a stronger theoretical foundation for the model by formulating the microeconomic behavior of economic agents.

Individual Behavior

Let $u(C_1, C_2)$ be a homothetic function of consumption flows C_1 and C_2, and let $U(u, M/p)$ be a homothetic individual utility function that depends on consumption and the services from real balances of money. Consider the following intertemporal optimization problem. Maximize the utility integral

$$\int_0^\infty U(u(C_1, C_2), M/p)e^{-\rho t}dt, \tag{6A.1}$$

given the initial stock of money M_0 and subject to the budget constraint

$$p_1 C_1 + p_2 C_2 + \dot{M} = Y + T. \tag{6A.2}$$

Here ρ is the rate of time preference, and Y and T are, respectively, nominal earned income and nominal transfer payments. It would be quite natural to take the implicit price index appearing in the indirect utility function derived from $u(C_1, C_2)$ as the general price level p.

Define the indirect utility function as

$$\bar{u}(E, p_1, p_2) = \left\{ \max_{C_1, C_2} u(C_1, C_2), \text{ subject to } p_1 C_1 + p_2 C_2 = E \right\},$$

where E is the level of nominal expenditures. Then it can be shown (Ohyama 1976) that if $u(C_1, C_2)$ is homothetic, $\bar{u}$ can be expressed as

$$\bar{u}(E, p_1, p_2) = \bar{u}(E/p),$$

where $p = f(p_1, p_2)$ is a linear homogeneous function of p_1 and p_2. By adopting this price index as the price index used to deflate real money balances, we can write

$$U(u(C_1, C_2), M/p) = U(\bar{u}(E/p), M/p)$$

$$= V(E/p, M/p)$$

$$= V(c, m),$$

where c and m are, respectively, real expenditures and real money balances.

Now let us write the budget constraint 6A.2 in terms of real expenditures c and real balances m. From 6A.2,

$$\frac{p_1 C_1 + p_2 C_2}{p} + \frac{\dot{M}}{p} = \frac{Y}{p} + \frac{T}{p},$$

or

$$\frac{p_1 C_1 + p_2 C_2}{p} + \frac{d}{dt}\left(\frac{M}{p}\right) + \frac{\dot{p}}{p} \cdot \frac{M}{p} = \frac{Y}{p} + \frac{T}{p};$$

that is,

$$c + \dot{m} + \pi m = y + \tau. \tag{6A.3}$$

Here y and τ are, respectively, real earned income and real transfers. I substituted the expected rate of inflation π for $\dot{p}/p$ because the budget constraints 6A.2 and 6A.3 are the constraints imagined by each individual based on his expectation concerning future price increases.

The original optimization problem can now be decomposed into the following two problems (see Ohyama 1976):

1. Maximize $\int_0^\infty V(c, m)e^{-\rho t}dt$ with respect to c and m, given m_0 and subject to equation 6A.3.
2. Maximize $U(C_1, C_2)$ with respect to C_1 and C_2, subject to $p_1 C_1 + p_2 C_2 = pc$.

Problem 1 has already been solved by Dornbusch and Mussa (1975). In particular, when $V(c,m)$ is homogeneous of degree 1, the real expenditure function can be written as

$$c = vm, \tag{6A.4}$$

where v is the consumption velocity of money. v is determined by the relationship

$$g(v) = g(c/m) = \pi + \rho, \tag{6A.5}$$

where $g(c/m)$ is defined, in the light of the assumption of homotheticity, by

$$g(c/m) = \frac{\partial V}{\partial m} \Big/ \frac{\partial V}{\partial c} = -\frac{dc}{dm}\Big|_{V = \text{const}}$$

It can be seen, by following the procedure taken by Dornbusch and Mussa, that $g(c/m)$ is an increasing function of c/m and that $v = c/m$ is an increasing function of $\pi + \rho$. Regarding ρ as constant, we adopt a special form of v—$v = a_0 e^{\varepsilon\pi}$—in the text.

The planned accumulation of real money balances can now be writen as

$$\dot{m} = y + \tau - c - \pi m = (y + \tau - vm) - \pi m. \tag{6A.6}$$

However, since the expected rate of inflation may diverge from the actual rate, we will assume that the actual ex post accumulation of real balances is

$$\dot{m} = (y + \tau - vm) - \hat{p}m. \tag{6A.7}$$

In particular, if $u(C_1, C_2)$ is of Cobb-Douglas form, then

$$u(C_1, C_2) = C_1^\alpha C_2^{1-\alpha},$$

and the expenditure function of equations 6.5 and 6.6 can be derived.

Aggregative Constraints

So far we have analyzed the behavior of the representative individual, given his initial money balances, income transfers, and prices. For the economy as a whole, the following aggregative constraints must be satisfied, depending on the exchange rate regime.

Flexible Exchange Rates
Under a flexible exchange rate regime, $\dot{M} = \theta M$, and, for the economy as a whole, $T = \theta M$. (Note that this cannot be assumed in the individual case, because it is unlikely that an individual will expect that he can receive more transfer payments if he holds more money balances). Therefore, from equation 6A.2, it follows that

$$E = p_1 C_1 + p_2 C_2 = Y. \tag{6A.8}$$

Thus, equation 6.20 is justified.
    From equation 6A.4, we obtain

$$\frac{p_1 C_1 + p_2 C_2}{p} = v(\pi)\frac{M}{p},$$

or

$$p_1 C_1 + p_2 C_2 = v(\pi)M,$$

which is equation 6.6.

Fixed Exchange Rates
Under a fixed exchange rate regime, equation 6A.4 (and, accordingly, equation 6.6) still holds. However, equation 6A.8 is no longer true. Although $T = \theta M$, the actual increase in the money supply is determined by

$$\dot{M} = (Y - E) + \theta M$$

$$= (Y - vM) + \theta M$$

$$= \text{Balance of payments} + \text{Domestic credit expansion.} \tag{6A.9}$$

In fact,

$$Y - pc = \text{Balance on current account} \tag{6A.10}$$

is the basic equation of the absorption approach, while equation 6A.9 is that of the monetary approach to the balance of payments. Equation 6.10 shows that the two approaches are equivalent.

Incidentally, the increase in real money balances can be written as

$$\dot{m} = (y - vm) + \theta m - \hat{p}m$$

$$= y - (v + \hat{p} - \theta)m. \qquad (6A.11)$$

From equation 6A.11 it can be seen that for real money balances to be stable under constant income y, we need $v + \hat{p} > \theta$ ($\hat{p} = \hat{p}^*$ under fixed exchange rates). For both the balance of payments and real money balances to be stable, θ must be equal to $\hat{p}$; that is, the rate of monetary expansion must be equal to the international rate of inflation. Also, if $\theta < \hat{p}$, then a chronic surplus in the balance of payments accompanies stable real balances; if $\theta > \hat{p}$, a chronic deficit results.

7　The International Transmission of Stagflation under Fixed and Flexible Exchange Rates

It is often maintained that under flexible exchange rates a country can pursue its monetary policy independent of the monetary policies of other countries, and also that under flexible exchange rates economic disturbances originating in other countries are absorbed by changes in exchange rates so that they do not have any adverse effects on the national economy. In a two-country model of unemployment, Laursen and Metzler (1950) have demonstrated that the insulation effect can be more than 100 percent in the presence of nonproportional Keynesian consumption functions. Mundell (1968) has shown in his discussion of the policy mix that an expansionary monetary policy taken by one country may have a deflationary impact on the other country through a change in the exchange rate in the presence of capital mobility. In other words, as we have seen in chapter 4, an expansionary monetary policy in one country exerts a contractionary impact on the other.

According to these views, economic fluctuations in various countries should in some sense be more desynchronized under flexible exchange rates than under fixed exchange rates. However, if we look at the world's experience with the floating exchange rate regime since the adoption of the New Economic Policy in August 1971, and especially since the oil crisis, we still observe a high degree of synchronization in fluctuations in unemployment and price levels among many countries of the world. This phenomenon is partly a reflection of the fact that the current float system is not a pure type of flexible exchange rate system but rather a highly managed float that is a mixture of flexible and fixed exchange rates. At the same time, there may be some mechanism operating even under a purely flexible exchange rate regime that gives rise to synchronized economic fluctuations.

This chapter examines the transmission of economic fluctuations between two countries under the alternative systems of fixed and flexible exchange rates. It is an attempt to extend the small-country model developed in the last chapter to a two-country setting. We will examine the following channels of transmission. The first is monetary interdependence under a fixed exchange rate system, and it is also present in the model in chapter 5 that allows for the existence of unemployment. In this chapter we add a second channel consisting of changes in the terms of trade and the wage-price spiral. Suppose that an exogenous decline in employment and accordingly a decline in output occurs in a foreign country. Then the relative price of the foreign product will increase and the terms of trade of the home country will deteriorate, causing an unfavorable shift in the wage-price relationship and triggering stagflation in the home country.

We thus develop a two-country model that, like the small-country model, embodies short-run and long-run Phillips curves connected by adaptive price expectations. Each country is assumed to be specialized in the production of a single commodity. We also assume that money is the only financial asset in each country and that the demand for money is proportional to national expenditure. The two countries trade with each other, and their consumers consume both commodities. We also assume that the elasticity of substitution in consumption between the two commodities is constant and identical for the two countries. Under these assumptions we can easily compare the nature of economic interdependence (or independence) between two open economies under fixed and flexible exchange rates.

Under fixed exchange rates there are two channels of interdependence. One channel is monetary interdependence through the balance of payments. When a monetary authority supplies more money than is demanded domestically, the balance of payments goes into deficit, causing international reserves (and accordingly the money supply of the other country) to increase. This channel of monetary interdependence has been discussed in some detail in chapters 4 and 5. In the following model incorporating Phillips curves, there is another channel of interdependence: through the effect of changes in the terms of trade on wage formation. If the output of a country declines, a deterioration in the terms of trade of the other country may result, exerting an unfavorable influence on the price-wage relationship in the other country.

Under flexible exchange rates, on the other hand, the first channel of monetary interdependence is blocked. A country can independently determine its own money supply. Even under flexible rates, however, the second channel through the wage-price spiral is still effective. If the output of a country declines, stagflationary pressures on the other country will result. For example, a reduction in the rate of increase of the money supply will have a recessionary effect on an economy, at least in the short run. Therefore, even though monetary interdependence is blocked under flexible exchange rates, a short-run recession will be transmitted through this second channel of the wage-price spiral. However, whereas recession in one country is likely to be transmitted to the other country as recession under fixed exchange rates, under flexible exchange rates, recession in one country is likely to be transmitted to the other as stagflation.

There have been a few attempts recently to incorporate the Phillips curve relationship into a two-country model of economic fluctuations. Brito and Richardson (1975) analyze the interaction of Phillips curves in a Keynesian framework in which monetary influences are suppressed by the assumption that the monetary authorities maintain an invariant interest-rate target. Ethier (1976) studies the implications of Phillips curves under alternative assumptions, such as that the monetary authorities peg both exchange rates and interest rates or that they try to maintain desired levels of employment. In both of these works the analysis centers on dynamic behavior around stationary equilibria where price levels are constant.[1]

In contrast to these studies, we are mainly concerned with the interaction of monetary policies that fix the rates of monetary expansion and with the nature of economic fluctuations around moving equilibria where price levels and exchange rates are changing at a constant rate. Moreover, the principal purpose of this chapter is to clarify how the economic performance of national economies is affected by differences in exchange rate regimes—that is, by differences in the rules of the game in the international economy.

The contrast to be obtained depends on our simplifying assumptions. In particular, the neglect of bonds as financial assets or the neglect of capital movements may overemphasize the contrast between the two regimes. My conjecture is that allowance for capital movements would make the contrast less sharp because individuals can acquire foreign bonds as a substitute for foreign money even under flexible exchange rates. The effect of capital movements and the evaluation of the relative strength of the synchronizing wage-price channel versus the desynchronizing channel discussed by Mundell in the presence of capital mobility represent topics for further research.

A Two-Country Framework

Suppose that there are two countries in the world that trade with each other. Each is completely specialized in the production of one product. In order to focus attention on fluctuations in employment and prices, we will assume that capital and factors of production other than labor are kept constant and that net capital accumulation is negligible.

Country 1 produces commodity 1, denoted by X_1; country 2 produces commodity 2, denoted by X_2^*. Asterisks denote variables relating to country 2. The production functions of X_1 and X_2^* are assumed to be of the following simple type:[2]

$$X_1 = N^\beta, \tag{7.1a}$$

$$X_2^* = N^{*\beta}, \tag{7.1b}$$

$$0 < \beta < 1$$

where N and N^* are, respectively, labor employed in country 1 and country 2.

The demand for labor is given by the marginal principle, so that

$$w = p_1 \frac{\partial X_1}{\partial N} = p_1 \beta N^{\beta-1}, \tag{7.2a}$$

$$w^* = p_2^* \frac{\partial X_2^*}{\partial N^*} = p_2^* \beta N^{*\beta-1}, \tag{7.2b}$$

where w and w^* indicate money wages in the two countries. p_1 indicates the price of commodity 1 in country 1; p_2^* indicates the price of commodity 2 in country 2.

International trade is conducted in a competitive market without transaction costs, so that

$$p_1 = q p_1^*, \tag{7.3a}$$

$$p_2 = q p_2^*, \tag{7.3b}$$

where q is the exchange rate (in terms of the currency of country 1). Needless to say, p_2 is the price of commodity 2 in country 1, and p_1^* is the price of commodity 1 in country 2.

Next we introduce assumptions concerning consumption behavior. Let us assume for simplicity that individuals in each country spend a constant fraction of their expenditures on commodity 1; that is,

$$p_1 C_1 = \alpha(p_1 C_1 + p_2 C_2), \tag{7.4a}$$

$$p_1^* C_1^* = \alpha(p_1^* C_1^* + p_2^* C_2^*), \tag{7.4b}$$

$$0 < \alpha < 1$$

where C_1 and C_2 indicate consumption flows of commodities 1 and 2 in country 1, and C_1^* and C_2^* indicate those in country 2.

This assumption implies a utility function, defined on consumption flows, of the Cobb-Douglas or log-additive type. For example, the benefit derived by a representative consumer in country 1 from consuming C_1 and C_2 can be represented by

$$u = \alpha \log C_1 + (1 - \alpha) \log C_2,$$

and so forth.

Therefore, the indirect utility function corresponding to the above utility function can be written as

$$\bar{u} = \log E - \{\alpha \log p_1 + (1 - \alpha) \log p_2\},$$

where E is total expenditures. Therefore, the proper price indices p and p^* for consumers in the two countries can be written as

$$p = p_1{}^\alpha p_2{}^{1-\alpha},$$

$$p^* = p_1^{*\alpha} p_2^{*1-\alpha},$$

or, in terms of the rates of price increase,

$$\hat{p} = \alpha \hat{p}_1 + (1 - \alpha) \hat{p}_2, \tag{7.5a}$$

$$\hat{p}^* = \alpha \hat{p}_1^* + (1 - \alpha) \hat{p}_2^*, \tag{7.5b}$$

where a caret indicates the rate of increase—that is, $\hat{p} \equiv \dot{p}/p$. The implications of formulating consumption behavior as in equations 7.4 are clearly seen by rewriting those equations as

$$(1 - \alpha) p_1 C_1 = \alpha p_2 C_2,$$

$$(1 - \alpha) p_1^* C_1^* = \alpha p_2^* C_2^*.$$

By differentiating the above equations logarithmically, we obtain

$$\hat{p}_1 + \hat{C}_1 = \hat{p}_2 + \hat{C}_2,$$

$$\hat{p}_1^* + \hat{C}_1^* = \hat{p}_2^* \hat{C}_2^*.$$

Therefore, noting from equations 7.3 that $\hat{p}_1 - \hat{p}_2 = \hat{p}_1^* - \hat{p}_2^*$, we have

$$\hat{C}_1 - \hat{C}_2 = \hat{C}_1^* - \hat{C}_2^* = \hat{p}_2 - \hat{p}_1. \tag{7.6}$$

Equation 7.6 implies that the elasticities of substitution in consumption between the two commodities are equal to unity in both countries. If we introduce the equilibrium conditions for commodity markets,

$$X_1 = C_1 + C_1^*, \tag{7.7a}$$

$$X_2^* = C_2 + C_2^*, \tag{7.7b}$$

equation 7.6 implies

$$\hat{X}_1 - \hat{X}_2^* = \hat{p}_2 - \hat{p}_1. \tag{7.8}$$

The assumption of a unitary elasticity of substitution in consumption is rather restrictive, so we will relax this assumption and discuss the case of a nonunitary elasticity of substitution later in this chapter. Suppose that the elasticity of substitution of consumption between good 1 and good 2 is σ, where $0 < \sigma < +\infty$, and that it is identical for both countries. Then by the same procedure used to derive equation 7.8, we can obtain

$$\hat{X}_1 - \hat{X}_2^* = \sigma(\hat{p}_2 = \hat{p}_1) \tag{7.8*}$$

instead of equation 7.8[3]

If the elasticity of substitution is not equal to unity, the price-index equations 7.5 are no longer exactly true and should be interpreted as linearized approximations of the true price indices that are locally valid in the neighborhood of the equilibrium.

It is assumed that the only financial assets in the world are the monies of the two countries. We thus neglect the effect of bonds and the effect of capital movements. This assumption may be somewhat stringent, but it will help to obtain a clear picture of differences in the monetary mechanism between the fixed and flexible exchange rate regimes.

Total expenditures are given by

$$p_1 C_1 + p_2 C_2 = vM, \tag{7.9a}$$

$$p_1^* C_1^* + p_2^* C_2^* = vM^*, \tag{7.9b}$$

where M and M^* are the stocks of money outstanding in the two countries and v is the consumption velocity of money (assumed to be constant).

Equations 7.9 can be regarded as the expression for money hoarding behavior as well. This formulation is consistent with the analysis of Dornbusch and Mussa (1975), who derive a hoarding function based on a constant expenditure velocity rather than a constant income velocity using an optimization approach. In general v is an increasing function of the expected rate of inflation,[4] so that

$$v = v(\pi),$$

$$v^* = v^*(\pi^*).$$

Accordingly, v and v^* may be different when π and π^* are different. In order to simplify the algebra, we will assume for the time being that $v (= v^*)$ is constant through time. In section 4 we introduce consumption velocities that depend on the expected rates of inflation using the following particular form:

$$v = ae^{\varepsilon\pi}, \tag{7.9a*}$$

$$v^* = ae^{\varepsilon\pi^*}. \tag{7.9b*}$$

The dynamic nature of the model is generated mainly by the short-run and long-run Phillips curve relationships. As the short-run Phillips curve, we will assume the following relationships:

$$\hat{w} = \phi(X_1) + \lambda\pi, \tag{7.10a}$$

$$\hat{w}^* = \phi(X_2^*) + \lambda\pi^*, \tag{7.10b}$$

$$0 \leq \lambda \leq 1$$

where λ is the parameter indicating the degree of money illusion and π the expected inflation rate. In the absence of money illusion, λ is equal to unity. Note that short-run Phillips curve relations are defined between output and the rate of wage increase and not between unemployment and the rate of wage increase. However, since output and employment are uniquely related by equations 7.1, we are justified in defining the Phillips curve relationship in terms of output and the rate of wage increase. Naturally, $\phi'(X_1) > 0$ and $\phi'(X_2^*) > 0$, and both derivatives approach infinity when X_1 and X_2^* approach the full-employment output levels.

We will adopt an adaptive formulation of the formation of price expectations π and π^*:

$$\dot{\pi} = \gamma(\hat{p} - \pi), \tag{7.11a}$$

$$\dot{\pi}^* = \gamma(\hat{p}^* - \pi^*), \tag{7.11b}$$

$$\gamma > 0$$

where $\hat{p}$ and $\hat{p}^*$ are as defined in equations 7.5.

Under a system of flexible exchange rates, the exchange rate is determined in such a way that the balance of payments is equated to zero. Since the balance of payments equals the difference between income and expenditure in the absence of capital movements, we always have

$$p_1 X_1 = p_1 C_1 + p_2 C_2, \tag{7.12a}$$

$$p_2^* X_2^* = p_1^* C_1^* + p_2^* C_2^*. \tag{7.12b}$$

Accordingly, under flexible exchange rates, we obtain from equations 7.9

$$p_1 X_1 = vM, \tag{7.13a}$$

$$p_2^* X_2^* = vM^*. \tag{7.13b}$$

On the other hand, under fixed exchange rates equations 7.12 no longer hold. However, for the world as a whole, income does equal expenditure. Since we can assume that $p_1 = p_1^*$ and $p_2 = p_2^*$, we obtain the following by adding equations 7.12a and 7.12b:

$$p_1 X_1 + p_2 X_2^* = v(M + M^*). \tag{7.14}$$

We have now introduced all of the components of the model. Equations 7.1, 7.2, 7.3, and 7.13 or 7.14 can easily be linearized in terms of the rate of increase variables that are denoted by adding a caret on the variable names. Let us write the complete system in terms of the rate of increase variables. We could generalize the system by allowing different values of α, β, γ, and the function ϕ for each country, but we refrain from doing so because this would only complicate the notation without substantially altering the results.

Under a flexible exchange rate regime, we have

	Country 1	Country 2	
Short-run Phillips curves	$\hat{w} = \phi(X_1) + \lambda\pi$	$\hat{w}^* = \phi(X_2^*) + \lambda\pi^*$	(7.10)
Adaptive expectations	$\dot{\pi} = \gamma(\hat{p} - \pi)$	$\dot{\pi}^* = \gamma(\hat{p}^* - \pi^*)$	(7.11)
Price index	$\hat{p} = \alpha\hat{p}_1 + (1-\alpha)\hat{p}_2$	$\hat{p}^* = \alpha\hat{p}_1^* + (1-\alpha)\hat{p}_2^*$	(7.5)
Demand for labor (from 7.1 and 7.2)	$\hat{w} = \hat{p}_1 - \dfrac{1-\beta}{\beta}\hat{X}$	$\hat{w}^* = \hat{p}_2^* - \dfrac{1-\beta}{\beta}\hat{X}^*$	(7.15)
Hoarding and expenditures (from 7.13)	$\hat{M} = \hat{p}_1 + \hat{X}_1$	$\hat{M}^* = \hat{p}_2^* + \hat{X}_2^*$	(7.16)
Exchange rate (from 7.3)	$\hat{p}_1 = \hat{q} + \hat{p}_1^*$	$\hat{p}_2 = \hat{q} + \hat{p}_2^*$	(7.18)

Commodity	$$\hat{X}_1 - \hat{X}_2^* = \hat{p}_2 - \hat{p}_1$$	(7.8)
market		

or

$$\hat{X}_1 - \hat{X}_2^* = \sigma(\hat{p}_2 - \hat{p}_1)$$ (7.8*)

There are thirteen equations in the system. There are twelve endogenous variables: $\hat{w}$, $\hat{w}^*$; π, π^*; $\hat{p}_1$, $\hat{p}_2$; $\hat{p}_1^*$, $\hat{p}_2^*$; $\hat{p}$, $\hat{p}^*$; and X_1, X_2^*. Under a flexible exchange rate regime, $\hat{q}$ is also an endogenous variable, and the system is complete with respect to the given values of $\hat{M}$ and $\hat{M}^*$. There are four differential equations with respect to π, π^* and X_1, X_2^*. (The other variables are involved only as rates of increase, so that they can be regarded as regular variables.) Accordingly, we need four initial conditions for X_1, X_2^* and π, π^* in order to describe the full workings of the system.

Under fixed exchange rates, q is kept constant. Thus, we can set $q = 1$, and accordingly $p_1 = p_2^*$, $p_2 = p_2^*$, and $p = p^*$. Therefore, it is also natural to assume that $\pi = \pi^*$ always holds. For the hoarding-expenditure relationship, we have from equation 7.14

$$\alpha(\hat{p}_1 + \hat{X}_1) + (1 - \alpha)(\hat{p}_2 + \hat{X}_2^*) = \frac{\dot{M} + \dot{M}^*}{M + M^*}.$$ (7.14')

Under a fixed exchange rate regime we have the following system of equations. (Primes added to the equation numbers denote the case of fixed exchange rates.)

	Country 1	Country 2	
Short-run Phillips curves	$\hat{w} = \phi(X_1) + \lambda\pi$	$\hat{w}^* = \phi(X_2^*) + \lambda\pi^*$	(7.10')
Adaptive expectations	$\dot{\pi} = \gamma(\hat{p} - \pi)$		(7.11')
Price index	$\hat{p} = \alpha\hat{p}_1 + (1 - \alpha)\hat{p}_2$		(7.5')
Demand for labor	$\hat{w} = \hat{p}_1 - \dfrac{1 - \beta}{\beta}\hat{X}_1$	$\hat{w}^* = \hat{p}_2 - \dfrac{1 - \beta}{\beta}\hat{X}_2^*$	(7.15')
Hoarding and expenditures	$\alpha(\hat{p}_1 + \hat{X}_1) + (1 - \alpha)(\hat{p}_2 + \hat{X}_2^*) = \dfrac{\dot{M} + \dot{M}^*}{M + M^*}$		(7.14')

Commodity $\hat{X}_1 - \hat{X}_2^* = \hat{p}_2 - \hat{p}_1$ (7.8*')
market

or

$$\hat{X}_1 - \hat{X}_2^* = \sigma(\hat{p}_2 - \hat{p}_1)$$ (7.8*')

There are eight equations in the system and eight endogenous variables: $\hat{w}$, $\hat{w}^*$; π, $\hat{p}_1$, $\hat{p}_2$, $\hat{p}$; and X_1, X_2.

Even under fixed exchange rates, the growth rate of the total world money supply is an exogenous variable, so we can solve the system for a given value of $(\dot{M} + \dot{M}^*)/(M + M^*)$. Under fixed exchange rates, we have three differential equations with respect to π, X_1, and X_2^*.

In the next two sections, we compare the two regimes under the assumption of unitary elasticity of substitution between consumption goods, 7.8 or 7.8'. In section 4, the effect of a nonunitary elasticity of substitution (7.8*) will be studied along with the effect of a variable consumption velocity of money.

Flexible Exchange Rates

Under a flexible exchange rate regime countries can decide on their rates of monetary expansion $\dot{M}$ and $\dot{M}^*$. Let us denote the exogenous rates of monetary expansion as

$\hat{M} = \theta$ (7.19a)

$\hat{M}^* = \theta^*$.   (7.19b)

Then from equations 7.16, 7.8, and 7.5 we obtain

$\hat{p}_1 = \theta - \hat{X}_1, \quad \hat{p}_1^* = \theta^* - \hat{X}_1,$ (7.20)

$\hat{p}_2 = \theta - \hat{X}_2^*, \quad \hat{p}_2^* = \theta^* - \hat{X}_2^*,$ (7.21)

and

$\hat{p} = \theta - \{\alpha\hat{X}_1 + (1 - \alpha)\hat{X}_2^*\}, \quad \hat{p}^* = \theta^* - \{\alpha\hat{X}_1 + (1 - \alpha)\hat{X}_2^*\}.$ (7.22)

From 7.18 and 7.20 (or 7.21), we have the following relationship, which determines the movement of the exchange rate under this system:

$\hat{q} = \theta - \theta^*,$ (7.23)

Thus, under flexible exchange rates and under the assumption of a unitary elasticity of substitution in consumption (that is, equation 7.8), the rate of depreciation in the exchange rate is equal to the difference between the growth rate of the money supply of the home country and that of the foreign country.

By substituting 7.15, 7.20, 7.21, and 7.22 into 7.10 and 7.11, we can obtain the basic system of differential equations for this two-country world under flexible exchange rates:

$$\hat{X}_1 = \beta(\theta - \phi(X_1) - \lambda\pi),$$

$$\dot{\pi} = \gamma\{\theta - [\alpha\hat{X}_1 + (1 - \alpha)\hat{X}_2^*] - \pi\},$$

$$\hat{X}_2^* = \beta(\theta - \phi(X_2^*) - \lambda\pi^*,$$

$$\dot{\pi}^* = \gamma\{\theta^* - [\alpha\hat{X}_1 + (1 - \alpha)\hat{X}_2^*] - \pi^*\}.$$

By transforming the output variables according to $x_1 \equiv \log X_1$ and $x_2^* \equiv \log X_2^*$ and by defining a new function $\psi(x) \equiv \phi(e^x)$ with property $\psi'(x) > 0$, we can obtain the following approximately linear system:

$$\dot{x}_1 = \beta(\theta - \psi(x_1) - \lambda\pi), \tag{7.24}$$

$$\dot{\pi} = \gamma\{\theta - [\alpha\dot{x}_1 + (1 - \alpha)\dot{x}_2^*] - \pi\}, \tag{7.25}$$

$$\dot{x}_2^* = \beta(\theta^* - \psi(\dot{x}_2^*) - \lambda\pi^*), \tag{7.26}$$

$$\dot{\pi}^* = \gamma\{\theta^* - [\alpha\dot{x}_1 + (1 - \alpha)\dot{x}_2^*] - \pi^*\}. \tag{7.27}$$

If $\alpha = 1$ or $\alpha = 0$, then the above system can be transformed into a recursive system. However, by the hypothesis that the two economies trade with one another, $0 < \alpha < 1$, and hence they are interrelated by the terms $(1 - \alpha)\dot{x}_2^*$ in equation 7.25 and $\alpha\dot{x}_1$ in 7.27.

Let us now study the property of the equilibrium solutions of the system. Setting all the time derivatives equal to zero and denoting equilibrium values by $\bar{x}_1$, $\bar{\pi}$, and so forth, we have the following pairs of equilibrium conditions for each country:

$$\psi(\bar{x}_1) = \theta - \lambda\bar{\pi} = (1 - \lambda)\theta, \tag{7.28}$$

$$\bar{\pi} = \theta \tag{7.29}$$

and

$$\psi(\bar{x}_2^*) = \theta^* - \lambda\bar{\pi}^* = (1 - \lambda)\theta^*, \tag{7.30}$$

$$\bar{\pi}^* = \theta^*. \tag{7.31}$$

We note from equations 7.29 and 7.31 that, under flexible exchange rates,

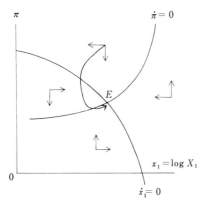

Figure 7.1

the equilibrium rate of expected inflation, which is at the same time equal to the equilibrium rate of actual inflation, coincides with the rate of monetary expansion in each country. Similarly, one country can decide on the level of its equilibrium output independently of the monetary policy of the other country. If money illusion is absent ($\lambda = 1$), the long-run Phillips curve is vertical, and each country cannot choose an output level other than the level corresponding to the natural rate of unemployment, which is defined by $\psi(\bar{x}_1) = 0$ and $\psi(\bar{x}_2^*) = 0$. Thus, under flexible exchange rates, each country can pursue an independent monetary policy as far as the target of the equilibrium rate of inflation, or possibly the equilibrium level of employment, is concerned if some degree of money illusion is present ($\lambda < 1$).

   If we consider the process of adjustment to equilibrium, however, economic fluctuations in the two countries are no longer mutually independent even under flexible exchange rates.

   Now let us examine the stability properties of the system. Suppose that we can neglect the interdependence term, so that $(1 - \alpha)\dot{x}_2^* = 0$ in equation 7.25 and $\alpha\dot{x}_1 = 0$ in equation 7.27. Then we can show that both separate systems—7.24 with 7.25 and 7.26 with 7.27—are stable by evaluating the trace and the determinant of the Jacobian matrix of these subsystems.[5] If we do not neglect these interdependence terms, the stability of the system of four differential equations is no longer obvious. Two stable systems can be unstable if they are interrelated. We shall show, however, in the chapter appendix that the combined system of four equations is locally stable for the relevant values of the parameters.[6]

   To study the process of adjustment to equilibrium, we can appeal to phase diagrams. Suppose that the value of $\dot{x}_2^*$ is given exogenously. Then we can

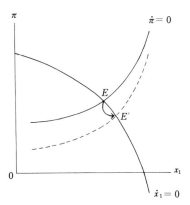

Figure 7.2

draw a phase diagram for x_1 and π as in figure 7.1. (Similarly, if the value of $\dot{x}_1$ is given, we can draw a phase diagram for x_2^* and π^*.) In figure 7.1 the $\dot{x}_1 = 0$ locus is drawn as a downward-sloping curve, which is an upside-down version of the short-run Phillips curve, since the locus is described by $\pi = (\theta - \psi(x_1))/\lambda$; the $\dot{\pi} = 0$ locus for a given value of $\dot{x}_2^*$ is drawn as an upward-sloping curve, which is also a transposed picture of the short-run Phillips curve, since the locus is described by

$$\pi = \frac{(1 - \alpha\beta)\theta + \alpha\beta\psi(x_1) - (1 - \alpha)\dot{x}_2^*}{1 - \alpha\beta\lambda}.$$

The dynamic adjustment paths of x_1 and π are depicted by arrows.

Let us now consider the effects of changes in the exogenous parameters. An increase in the rate of domestic money supply will shift both curves upward. In the absence of money illusion ($\lambda = 1$), in particular, an increase in the rate of domestic money supply will shift both curves upward by the same amount so that the new equilibrium will be directly above the old equilibrium, leaving the equilibrium level of production unchanged. During the transition to the new equilibrium, employment and the expected rate of inflation will approach the new equilibrium in a counterclockwise direction, as a result of which there will be a temporary boom in the economy.

An increase in foreign production (an increase in $\dot{x}_2^*$) will shift the $\dot{\pi} = 0$ locus downward. This situation is shown in figure 7.2. The new equilibrium is shown by E', and the economy will approach the new equilibrium along the path indicated by the arrow. The channel of interdependence can be explained as follows: An increase in the production of commodity 2 in the foreign country will lead to an improvement in the terms of trade of the home

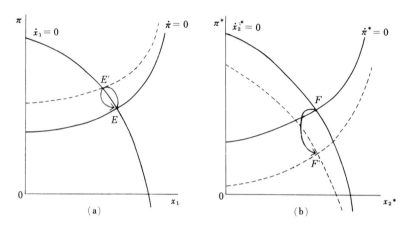

Figure 7.3

country. Then, since the price index that reflects the living standard has declined, the home country can enjoy a higher level of employment. This channel through the adjustment process is operative even under flexible exchange rates.

Let us study this channel of interdependence more closely by examining the effect of a monetary contraction in the other country and the effect of a sudden productivity decline in the other country.

In figure 7.3a, the phase diagram for country 1 is drawn under the assumption that $\dot{x}_2^* = 0$; in figure 7.3b the phase diagram for country 2 is drawn under the assumption that $\dot{x}_1 = 0$. Suppose that both economies are initially in equilibrium at E and F. Suppose that the monetary authority of country 2 then adopts a contractionary monetary policy and reduces its rate of monetary expansion. Then the new equilibrium for country 2 under the assumption that $\dot{x}_1 = 0$ will be F', which is located below F in the absence of money illusion, as indicated in the figure, and to the southwest of F in the presence of money illusion. Accordingly, x_2^* and π^* will start moving along the path indicated by the arrow in figure 7.3b, meaning that country 2 suffers from a temporary recession. For country 1, $\dot{x}_2^*$ will become negative temporarily, and the $\dot{\pi} = 0$ locus will shift upward as indicated by the dotted curve in figure 7.3a. Therefore the initial impact of a contractionary monetary policy undertaken by country 2 will be temporary stagflation in country 1. Eventually, country 2 will settle down to point F', and $\dot{x}_2^*$ will become zero again. When this occurs, the $\dot{\pi} = 0$ locus will return to its initial position, and country 1's initial equilibrium E will be restored.[7]

Next let us consider the case in which, for some reason (say, a drought in

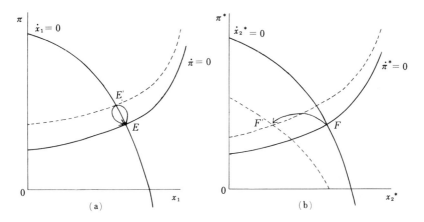

Figure 7.4

agriculture or an energy crisis), the productivity of country 2 declines. Suppose that there is a reduction in the value of β in country 2 but that country 1's β remains constant. If the Phillips curve in terms of unemployment remains the same, the Phillips curve in terms of the level of product will shrink to the left because there is a relationship such that $x_2^* \equiv \log X_2^* = \beta \log N^*$. Therefore, the effect of a productivity decline in country 2 can be depicted in figure 7.4b as the mutual shift of both curves to the left. Then, since $\dot{x}_2^*$ temporarily becomes negative, the $\dot{\pi} = 0$ locus will again shift upward temporarily in figure 7.4a. In this way, a productivity decline in the other country will cause temporary stagflation in the home country.

In short, under flexible exchange rates, a recession triggered by monetary or real causes in the foreign country will tend to be transmitted to the home country as temporary stagflation.

Fixed Exchange Rates

Under fixed exchange rates, the rate of increase in the money supply of each country is no longer a policy variable because attempts to increase the domestic money supply are partly offset by a deficit in the balance of payments. As we saw in chapter 5, under fixed exchange rates the stock of money supply is backed either by domestic credit creation or by international reserves. That is,

$$M = D + R,\tag{7.32a}$$

$$M^* = D^* + R^*,\tag{7.32b}$$

where D and D^* are the amounts of domestic credit creation, and R and R^* are the amounts of foreign reserves. The monetary authorities can control the values of D and D^*, but they cannot control the values of R and R^*. Therefore M and M^* are endogenously determined. Assuming that q is identically equal to unity, we have an additional equation that indicates the constancy of total international reserves:

$$R + R^* = \bar{R}. \tag{7.33}$$

Let us define the policy variables under fixed exchange rates as

$$\theta = \frac{\dot{D}}{M} = \frac{\dot{D}}{D + R},$$

$$\theta^* = \frac{\dot{D}^*}{M^*} = \frac{\dot{D}^*}{D^* + R^*}.$$

Note that θ and θ^* are no longer the rates of increase in the actual money supply but rather the rates of increase in domestic credit creation relative to the outstanding money supply.[8] By virtue of equation 7.33,

$$\dot{R} + \dot{R}^* = 0.$$

Therefore, the rate of increase in the total world money stock can be expressed as

$$\frac{\dot{M} + \dot{M}^*}{M + M^*} = \frac{\dot{D} + \dot{R} + \dot{D}^* + \dot{R}^*}{M + M^*}$$

$$= \frac{\dot{D} + \dot{D}^*}{M + M^*}$$

$$= \frac{M}{M + M^*}\theta + \frac{M^*}{M + M^*}\theta^*$$

$$= \omega\theta + (1 - \omega)\theta^*, \tag{7.34}$$

where ω is the ratio of the money stock in country 1 to the total world money stock; that is, $\omega \equiv M/(M + M^*)$.[9]

Therefore, from equation 7.14' we obtain for a fixed exchange rate regime

$$\alpha(\hat{p}_1 + \hat{X}_1) + (1 - \alpha)(\hat{p}_2 + \hat{X}_2^*) = \omega\theta + (1 - \omega)\theta^* \equiv \bar{\theta}, \tag{7.35}$$

where $\bar{\theta}$ is the average rate of money supply growth in the world.

Under the assumption of a unitary elasticity of substitution in consumption, we have equation 7.8', so that

$$\hat{p}_1 + \hat{X}_1 = \hat{p}_2 + \hat{X}_2^* = \bar{\theta}. \tag{7.36}$$

Substituting equation 7.36 into equations 7.10', 7.15', 7.5', and 7.11', we obtain the basic system of differential equations for the three variables X_1, X_2^*, and π (the stability of this system is proved in the appendix):

$$\hat{X}_1 = \beta(\bar{\theta} - \phi(X_1) - \lambda\pi),$$

$$\hat{X}_2^* = \beta(\bar{\theta} - \phi(X_2^*) - \lambda\pi),$$

$$\dot{\pi} = \gamma\{\bar{\theta} - [\alpha\hat{X}_1 + (1 - \alpha)\hat{X}_2^*] - \pi\},$$

or, rewritten in terms of $x_1 \equiv \log X_1$, $x_2^* \equiv \log X_2^*$, and π,

$$\dot{x}_1 = \beta(\bar{\theta} - \psi(x_1) - \lambda\pi, \tag{7.37}$$

$$\dot{x}_2^* = \beta(\bar{\theta} - \psi(x_2^*) - \lambda\pi), \tag{7.38}$$

$$\dot{\pi} = \gamma\{\bar{\theta} - [\alpha\dot{x}_1 + (1 - \alpha)\dot{x}_2] - \pi\}. \tag{7.39}$$

By comparing the system of equations 7.37–7.39 for fixed exchange rates with the system of equations 7.24–7.27 for flexible exchange rates, one can clearly see the contrast. The linkages through the terms of trade ($\alpha\dot{x}_1$ and $(1 - \alpha)\dot{x}_2^*$ in equation 7.39) are still present under fixed exchange rates. Moreover, a new linkage through monetary interdependence (expressed by $\bar{\theta}$) appears under fixed exchange rates. Thus, monetary autonomy is not realized under fixed exchange rates. In particular, if a country is small relative to the other—for example, $\omega < 1 - \omega$—then the impact of its own monetary policy on itself is limited. In short, under fixed exchange rates, the channel of monetary interdependence through the balance of payments operates in addition to the channel through the terms of trade and the wage-price spiral, while under flexible rates only the second channel operates.

In order to illustrate the difference in interdependence between the two regimes, let us consider the effects of monetary contraction in country 2 under fixed exchange rates. In figure 7.5 the initial equilibria are again depicted as E and F. Note that E and F are at the same level of π because rates of inflation are identical in both countries under fixed exchange rates. Now suppose that the monetary authority of country 2 reduces its rate of credit expansion by θ^*. The result will naturally be a downward shift in both curves in figure 7.5b, and the new equilibrium will be F'. F' will be located to the southeast of F in the presence of some money illusion, but the intensity of the shift will be weaker than under flexible exchange rates because the down-

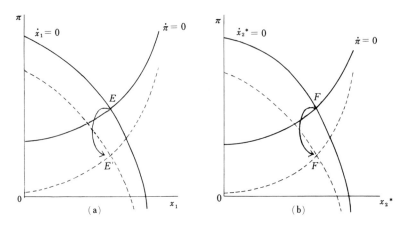

Figure 7.5

ward shift in the $\dot{x}_2^* = 0$ locus will be equal not to $\Delta\theta^*$ but to $(1 - \omega)\,\Delta\theta^*$. On the other hand, the effects of the monetary contraction will spill over to country 1, where both curves will shift by precisely the same amount as in country 2, so that the new equilibrium in country 1 becomes E'. The adjustment paths in both countries will then start to move counterclockwise, as indicated in figure 7.5. Initially both $\dot{x}_1$ and $\dot{x}_2^*$ will become negative and will cause a temporary upward shift in the $\dot{\pi} = 0$ loci in both 7.5a and 7.5b. Eventually, however, the $\dot{\pi} = 0$ loci will move back down again in such a way that they pass through E' and F'. In contrast to the case of flexible exchange rates, in which a recession is transmitted as temporary stagflation, a recession is transmitted as a recession under fixed exchange rates.[10]

Some Generalizations of the Model

In this section we relax some of the restrictive assumptions concerning consumption and hoarding behavior.

Nonunitary Elasticity of Substitution in Consumption

First consider the effect of a nonunitary elasticity of substitution in consumption.

Flexible Exchange Rates
Suppose $\sigma \neq 1$ in equation 7.8*. Then, under flexible exchange rates, we obtain instead of equations 7.20–7.22

$$\hat{p}_1 = \theta - \hat{X}_1, \quad \hat{p}_1^* = \theta^* - (1 + \delta)\hat{X}_1 + \delta\hat{X}_2^*, \tag{7.20*}$$

$$\hat{p}_2 = \theta + \delta\hat{X}_1 - (1 + \delta)\hat{X}_2^*, \quad \hat{p}_2^* = \theta^* - \hat{X}_2^*, \tag{7.21*}$$

and

$$\hat{p} = \theta - \{\alpha - (1 - \alpha)\delta\}\hat{X}_1 - (1 - \alpha)(1 + \delta)\hat{X}_2^*,$$
$$\hat{p}^* = \theta^* - \alpha(1 + \delta)\hat{X}_1 - \{-\alpha\delta + (1 - \alpha)\}\hat{X}_2^*, \tag{7.22*}$$

where δ is defined as the exponential parameter of the constant-elasticity-of-substitution (CES) utility function such that

$$\delta = \frac{1}{\sigma} - 1, \qquad -1 < \delta < +\infty$$

($\delta = 0$ if the elasticity of substitution is unity), and α is the share of expenditure on commodity 1 in the neighborhood of the equilibrium. Or, by defining[11]

$$a = \alpha - (1 - \alpha)\delta, \quad b = (1 - \alpha)(1 + \delta),$$
$$a^* = \alpha(1 + \delta), \quad b^* = -\alpha\delta + (1 - \alpha), \tag{7.40}$$

equation 7.22* can be written as

$$\hat{p} = \theta - a\dot{x}_1 - b\dot{x}_2^*, \quad \hat{p}^* = \theta^* - a^*\dot{x}_1 - b^*\dot{x}_2^*.$$

Therefore, if the elasticity of substitution in consumption is not unity but equal to δ in both countries, the basic system of differential equations is

$$\dot{x}_1 = \beta(\theta - \psi(x_1) - \lambda\pi), \tag{7.24}$$

$$\dot{\pi} = \gamma(\theta - a\dot{x}_1 - b\dot{x}_2^* - \pi), \tag{7.25*}$$

$$\dot{x}_2^* = \beta(\theta^* - \psi(x_2^*) - \lambda\pi^*), \tag{7.26}$$

$$\dot{\pi}^* = \gamma(\theta^* - a^*\dot{x}_1 - b^*\dot{x}_2^* - \pi^*), \tag{7.27*}$$

where a, b, a^*, and b^* are as defined by equation 7.40.

In this more general case, however, the simple relationship that describes the path of the exchange rate—equation 7.23—does not hold except in equilibrium. From equation 7.18 or 7.20* we obtain

$$\hat{q} = (\theta - \theta^*) + \delta(\hat{X}_1 - \hat{X}_2^*). \tag{7.23*}$$

If the elasticity of substitution is much less than unity, then δ will take a large value. In that case, movements in $\hat{q}$ will depend crucially on the relative movements in output fluctuations in the two countries except in equilibrium when $\dot{x}_1 = \dot{x}_2^* = 0$.

Comparing the basic system of differential equations with that of section 2, we can see that the equilibrium values are not affected by the relaxation of the unitary-elasticity assumption. The stability of the system with a nonunitary elasticity in consumption is proved in the chapter appendix. However, the intensity of interdependence through $b\dot{x}_2^*$ in equation 7.25* and $a^*\dot{x}_1$ in equation 7.27* is stronger for the world economy in the case of a smaller value of the elasticity of substitution in consumption σ. When σ is equal to unity, $b = 1 - \alpha$ and $a^* = \alpha$. But when σ is much smaller than unity, the values of b and a^* can become very large. In fact, they approach infinity as the elasticity of substitution σ approaches zero ($\delta \to \infty$). In such a case the upward shifts in the $\dot{\pi} = 0$ and $\dot{\pi}^* = 0$ loci are very large.

This implies that, in an economy where substitution in consumption is difficult, a decline in the output of import goods in the foreign country will impose strong stagflationary pressures on the home country.

Fixed Exchange Rates
Under fixed exchange rates, we can obtain the following equations by solving equations 7.8*' and 7.35 simultaneously in terms of $\hat{p}_1$ and $\hat{p}_2$:

$$\hat{p}_1 = \bar{\theta} - \{1 + (1 - \alpha)\delta\}\hat{X}_1 + (1 - \alpha)\delta\hat{X}_2^*,$$
$$\hat{p}_2 = \bar{\theta} + \alpha\delta\hat{X}_1 - (1 + \alpha\delta)\hat{X}_2^*, \tag{7.41}$$

where δ is defined as $\delta = 1/\sigma - 1$.

Therefore, from equations 7.10', 7.11', and 7.15', we have the following system of differential equations in terms of x_1, x_2^*, and π:

$$\dot{x}_1 = \frac{\beta}{1 + \beta(1 - \alpha)\delta}\{\bar{\theta} - \psi(x_1) + (1 - \alpha)\delta\dot{x}_2^* - \lambda\pi\}, \tag{7.37*}$$

$$\dot{x}_2^* = \frac{\beta}{1 + \beta\alpha\delta}\{\bar{\theta} - \psi(x_2^*) + \alpha\delta\dot{x}_1 - \lambda\pi\}, \tag{7.38*}$$

$$\dot{\pi} = \gamma\{\bar{\theta} - \alpha\dot{x}_1 - (1 - \alpha)\dot{x}_2^* - \pi\}. \tag{7.39*}$$

I do not intend to perform a detailed analysis of this general formulation, although I will prove its stability in the chapter appendix. It will suffice to point out that, when σ is small and δ is large, the dominant linkage between the two countries is through the output equations 7.37* and 7.38* rather than through the price equation 7.39* under fixed exchange rates. The difference between the two regimes can be most clearly understood by comparing the

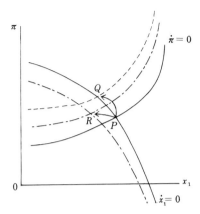

Figure 7.6

effects of a real reduction in $\dot{x}_2^*$ on country 1 under the two regimes. Suppose $\dot{x}_2^* < 0$ and δ is large. Then, under flexible exchange rates, the $\dot{\pi} = 0$ locus will shift sharply upward, as shown in equation 7.25*. Under fixed exchange rates, the $\dot{x}_1 = 0$ locus will shift sharply downward, while the $\dot{\pi} = 0$ locus will shift upward only slightly. Since the $\dot{\pi} = 0$ locus is much flatter than the $\dot{x}_1 = 0$ locus, we obtain the results shown in figure 7.6. Under flexible exchange rates, the intersection point of the two curves shifts temporarily to Q; under fixed exchange rates, the intersection point shifts temporarily to R. In fact we can prove that the abscissa of Q is equal to that of R and that the distance between Q and R increases with δ.[12] Thus, real output fluctuations in the foreign country are likely to be transmitted as output fluctuations under fixed exchange rates and as price-cum-output fluctuations under flexible exchange rates. This difference probably stems from the buffer mechanism of international reserves under fixed exchange rates, the mechanism Hicks (1974) named the "fix-price economy."

Variable Consumption Velocities of Money

Finally, we will relax the assumption that the consumption velocity is constant. If we use the particular forms of v and v^* in equation 7.9*, then equation 7.16 becomes

$$\theta + \varepsilon\dot{\pi} = \hat{M} + \varepsilon\dot{\pi} = \hat{p}_1 + \hat{X}_1, \tag{7.16a*}$$

$$\theta^* + \varepsilon\dot{\pi}^* = \hat{M}^* + \varepsilon\dot{\pi}^* = p_2^* + \hat{X}_2^*. \tag{7.16b*}$$

Also, equation 7.14′ becomes

$$\alpha(\hat{p}_1 + \hat{X}_1) + (1 - \alpha)(\hat{p}_2 + \hat{X}_2^*) = \frac{\dot{M} + \dot{M}^*}{M + M^*} + \varepsilon\dot{\pi}, \tag{7.14*′}$$

or, in place of equation 7.35, we have

$$\alpha(\hat{p}_1 + \hat{X}_1) + (1 - \alpha)(\hat{p}_2 + \hat{X}_2^*) = \bar{\theta} + \varepsilon\dot{\pi}. \tag{7.35*}$$

Therefore, if we replace θ, θ^*, and $\bar{\theta}$ by $(\theta + \varepsilon\dot{\pi})$, $(\theta^* + \varepsilon\dot{\pi}^*)$, and $(\bar{\theta} + \varepsilon\dot{\pi})$, we can then obtain the generalized system for flexible and fixed exchange rates and proceed with the analysis in almost the same way as above except for the following considerations. First, in order for the system to be stable, $\gamma\varepsilon$ must not exceed unity. If $\gamma\varepsilon$ exceeds unity, even the truncated system of one country—for example, the system for country 1 with a given value of $\dot{x}_2^*$— can be unstable. Second, the introduction of $\varepsilon\dot{\pi}$ or $\varepsilon\dot{\pi}^*$ brings in linkages in the output equations even under flexible exchange rates. However, since the effect on the price equation $\dot{\pi} = 0$ $(\dot{\pi}^* = 0)$ of $\dot{x}_2^*$ $(\dot{x}_1)$ is much stronger than its effect on the output equation $\dot{x}_1 = 0$ $(\dot{x}_2^* = 0)$, the qualitative nature of the adjustment processes derived will remain unchanged.

Summary and Concluding Remarks

The results concerning the differences in monetary mechanisms between the two regimes can be summarized as follows:

1. The channel of monetary interdependence through disequilibria in the balance of payments works under the fixed exchange rate regime but is blocked under the flexible exchange rate regime. In this sense, monetary authorities regain their independence under flexible exchange rates.

2. The channel of interdependence through the terms of trade and the wage-price spiral, however, works not only under the fixed exchange rate regime but also under the flexible exchange rate regime. This causes the transmission of business cycles from one country to another.

3. Under fixed exchange rates, both channels operate. A recession initiated by a monetary contraction in one country may be transmitted to the other as a recession.

4. Under flexible exchange rates, only the second channel operates. Accordingly, a recession caused by monetary or real causes in one country is likely to be transmitted to the other as a temporary stagflation.

5. Under flexible exchange rates, the rate of change in the exchange rate is

determined by the difference in the rate of increase of the money supply that exists between the two countries after the equilibrium levels of employment have been attained. Moreover, the same conclusion holds even before the equilibrium levels of employment have been attained if the elasticity of substitution in consumption equals unity.

6. The second channel through the terms of trade and the wage-price spiral becomes significant when the elasticity of substitution between the two consumption goods is much less than unity. In that case, however, the effect through the terms of trade and the wage-price spiral is reflected more in output variations under fixed exchange rates and in price-cum-output variations under flexible exchange rates. This difference probably stems from the buffer mechanism of international reserves under fixed exchange rates.

The strategic structure of monetary interdependence under a fixed exchange rate regime is that of a cooperative game in which the noncooperative behavior of participating countries will lead to a prisoner's dilemma situation. Under a flexible exchange rate regime, on the other hand, each country can choose its desired combination of employment and the rate of inflation as far as the equilibrium values of employment and the rate of inflation are concerned. We have seen, however, that the two economies are interrelated during the process of adjustment, even under flexible exchange rates, through the terms of trade and the wage-price spiral. An expansion of output in a foreign country will exert a favorable though temporary impact on both employment and the price level of the home country through an improvement in the terms of trade. This may be one of the reasons why some countries in the world apparently try to persuade other countries to take the initiative in adopting expansionary policies instead of initiating expansionary policies themselves.

Appendix: Stability of the Two-Country Model (General Case)

This appendix examines the stability of the two-country system under the general assumption that the elasticity of substitution in consumption need not be unity. The case with unitary elasticity of substitution—the case with $\delta = 0$, $a = a^* = \alpha$, and $b = b^* = 1 - \alpha$—is a special case of the following analysis.

Flexible Exchange Rates

The characteristic equation of the system of equations 7.24, 7.25*, 7.26, and 7.27* can be written

$$\begin{vmatrix} -\beta\bar{c} - z & -\beta\lambda & 0 & 0 \\ -\gamma az & -\gamma - z & -\gamma bz & 0 \\ 0 & 0 & -\beta\bar{c}^* - z & -\beta\lambda \\ -\gamma a^* z & 0 & -\gamma b^* z & -\gamma - z \end{vmatrix} = 0,$$

where $c \equiv \psi'(x_1)$ and $c^* \equiv \psi'(x_2^*)$; that is,

$$\{z^2 + [\beta\bar{c} + \gamma(1 + a\beta\lambda)]z - \beta\gamma\bar{c}\}\{z^2 + [\beta^*\bar{c} + \gamma(1 - b^*\beta\lambda)]z + \beta\gamma\bar{c}^*\}$$

$$- \gamma^2\beta^2 a^* b\lambda^2 z^2 = 0. \tag{7.A1}$$

The system is locally stable if all the roots of equation 7.42 have negative real parts. We may appeal directly to the Routh-Hurwitz conditions, but it is easier to make use of Rouché's theorem (see Ahlfors 1966 and Yoshida 1965), which states: "Suppose that $f(z)$ and $h(z)$ are analytic and satisfy the inequality $|f(z)| > |h(z)|$ on a closed contour C (i.e., C is homologous to zero). Then $f(z)$ and $f(z) + (z)$ have the same number of roots enclosed by C." Let

$$f(z) \equiv \{z^2 + [\beta\bar{c} + \gamma(1 - a\beta\lambda)]z + \beta\gamma c\}$$

$$\times \{z^2 + [\beta\bar{c}^* + \gamma(1 - b^*\beta\lambda)]z + \beta\gamma b^*\}$$

and

$$h(z) \equiv -\gamma^2\beta^2 a^* b\lambda^2 z^2.$$

It is easy to see that $f(z)$ does not have any root within a limitlessly large semicircle to the right of the origin and the imaginary axis. On the other hand, if $|z|$ is large enough, $|f(z)| > |h(z)|$. On the imaginary axis $z = yi$, where i indicates the imaginary unit,

$$|f(z)| = \{[\beta\bar{c} + \gamma(1 - a)]^2 y^2 + (\beta\gamma\bar{c} - y^2)^2\}^{1/2}$$

$$\times \{[\beta\bar{c}^* + \gamma(1 - b^*\beta\lambda)]^2 y^2 + (\beta\gamma\bar{c}^* - y^2)\}^{1/2}$$

$$> y^2[\beta\bar{c} + \gamma(1 - a\beta\lambda)][\beta\bar{c}^* + \gamma(1 - b^*\beta\lambda)]$$

and

$$|h(z)| = y^2\gamma^2\beta^2 a^* b\lambda^2.$$

However,

$$\gamma^2(1 - a\beta\lambda)(1 - b^*\beta\lambda) - \gamma^2\beta^2 a^* b\lambda^2 = \gamma^2(1 - \beta\lambda)(1 - \beta\lambda\delta) > 0,$$

because, from the definition of a, b, a^*, and b^* in equation 7.40,

$$a + b^* = 1 - \delta,$$

$$ab^* - a^*b = -\delta,$$

and, by hypothesis, $\beta < 1$ and $\lambda > 1$. Therefore, $|f(z)| > |h(z)|$ on the imaginary axis.

Accordingly, on the limitlessly large semicircle described above, the condition for Rouché's theorem is satisfied. Therefore, all the roots of $f(z) + h(z) = 0$ have negative real parts, and the system is locally stable.

Fixed Exchange Rates

The characteristic equation of the system of equations 7.37*, 7.38*, 7.39* can be written as

$$\begin{vmatrix} -\beta_1\bar{c} - z & \beta_1(1 - \alpha)\delta z & -\beta_1\lambda \\ \beta_2\alpha\delta z & -\beta_2\bar{c}^* - z & -\beta_2\lambda \\ -\gamma\alpha z & -\gamma(1 - \alpha)z & -\gamma - z \end{vmatrix} = 0,$$

where

$$\beta_1 + \beta/\{1 + \beta(1 - \alpha)\delta\},$$

$$\beta_2 = \beta/\{1 + \beta\alpha\delta\},$$

or as

$$A_0 z^3 + A_1 z^2 + A_2 z + A_3 = 0,$$

where

$$A_0 = 1 - \beta_1\beta_2\alpha(1 - \alpha)\delta^2,$$

$$A_1 = \gamma\{1 - \beta_1\beta_2\alpha(1 - \alpha)\delta^2\} - \lambda\gamma\{\beta_1\alpha + \beta_2(1 - \alpha) + 2\beta_1\beta_2\alpha(1 - \alpha)\delta\}$$
$$+ [\beta_1\bar{c} + \beta_2\bar{c}^*],$$

$$A_2 = \gamma\{\beta_1\bar{c}[1 - \lambda(1 - \alpha)] + \beta_2\bar{c}^*(1 - \lambda\alpha)\},$$

$$A_3 = \dot{\gamma}\beta_1\beta_2\bar{c}\,\bar{c}^*.$$

It is easy to see from the definition of β_1 and β_2 that

$$A_0 = 1 - \beta_1\beta_2\alpha(1 - \alpha)\delta^2 > 0.$$

It is obvious that $A_2 > 0$ and $A_3 > 0$. Moreover, since

$$1 - \beta_1\beta_2\alpha(1-\alpha)\delta^2 - \lambda\{\beta_1\alpha + \beta_2(1-\alpha) + 2\beta_1\beta_2\alpha(1-\alpha)\delta\}$$

$$\geqq \frac{1 + \beta\delta - \beta - \beta^2\delta}{(1 + \beta(1-\alpha)\delta)(1+\beta\alpha\delta)}$$

$$= \frac{(1-\beta)(1+\beta\delta)}{(1+\beta(1-\alpha)\delta)(1+\beta\delta\alpha)} = 0, \tag{†}$$

we can also conclude that $A_1 > 0$.

Therefore, to check the Routh-Hurwitz conditions we have to prove that

$$A_1 A_2 > A_0 A_3.$$

By virtue of equation †, we have

$$A_1 > [\beta_1\bar{c} + \beta_2\bar{c}^*].$$

Therefore,

$$A_1 A_2 \geqq [\beta_1\bar{c} + \beta_2\bar{c}^*]\gamma\{\beta_1\bar{c}[1 - \lambda(1-\alpha)] + \beta_2\bar{c}^*(1-\lambda\alpha)\}$$

$$\geqq [\beta_1\bar{c} + \beta_2\bar{c}^*]^2\gamma$$

$$\geqq \beta_1\beta_2\bar{c}\,\bar{c}^*\gamma$$

$$= A_3$$

$$\geqq A_0 A_3.$$

This establishes the local stability of the system.

8

Monetary Interdependence under a Managed Float System

One of the reasons why experience with flexible exchange rates has not been as successful as expected may be that the flexible exchange rate regime is not in fact operating in as pure a form as the logic of the system requires. Actually, the determination of the exchange rate is not left completely in the hands of market forces but is influenced by government intervention. Thus, we are living in a world of "managed" or "controlled" floating.

In order to evaluate the recent performance of the world economy, we need a theoretical framework for analyzing the system of managed floating. Thus far the analysis of managed floating has been primitive. I hope that this chapter will serve as a step toward clarifying the nature of interdependence among monetary policies and the strategic structure of the game under managed floating.

Monetary authorities often claim that their interventions in foreign exchange markets are only of a smoothing character and not meant to influence trends in exchange rates; however, from the fact that some countries have accumulated or decumulated a substantial amount of reserves even after the collapse of the Smithsonian agreement, one can deduce that interventions have been used not only to smooth movements of exchange rates but also to influence exchange rate movements.

Under complete or "clean" floating, exchange rates are determined by market forces. Accordingly, the level or trend of exchange rates should not be included in the list of policy goals. Nor should the breakdown of the balance of payments into the current and capital accounts be a concern of policy authorities. In actual practice, however, there are pressures from exporters, import competitors, and others for the government to include the current account and the level of the exchange rate as policy targets. This creates interesting but difficult problems relating to conflicting exchange rate policy targets among national economies.

Mussa (1976) analyzes the issue of policy conflicts and policy coordination under managed floating. Policy conflicts arose during the 1930s, when everyone wanted to devalue relative to everyone else. Mussa argues, however, that under a system of controlled floating such policy conflicts are not inevitable, because the system has more freedom than a system of fixed exchange rates. Although a conflict arises under fixed exchange rates whenever one government wants to expand and another government wants to contract, this conflict is easily resolved under controlled floating. Policy conflicts under controlled floating arise only when two countries want to expand output or reduce inflation simultaneously and each wants to pursue this objective using their mutual exchange rate. The need for policy coordination arises in such a situation. Mussa then argues that, as is clearly indicated by the monetary approach to the balance of payments, the required type of coordination is among monetary policies, similar to the monetary coordination suggested by McKinnon (1974).

A Framework for Analyzing the Managed Float

Let us consider a world where national economies are sufficiently integrated that their price levels exhibit a relationship predicted by purchasing power parity theory. In this section we return to the framework of chapter 5 and concentrate on the long-run growth path of such a world economy, assuming that the real rates of growth of each country are exogenously given.

Suppose that there exist n countries in the world under a managed float regime. As in chapter 5, let us denote the money stock outstanding in the ith country by M_i. Let us take the currency of the first country, say dollars, as the numéraire, and let R_i be the reserves of the ith country, measured in terms of the currency of the first country. Let the exchange rate of country i (the value of a dollar in terms of the home currency) be q_i. Naturally, $q_1 = 1$ by definition.[1] Since an increase in the money stock is backed either by an increase in international reserves R_i or an increase in domestic credit D_i, one may write

$$\dot{M}_i = q_i \dot{R}_i + \dot{D}_i, \tag{8.1}$$

where a dot indicates a time derivative.[2]

Define the total reserves in the world as R, where

$$R = \sum_{i=1}^{n} R_i. \tag{8.2}$$

As in chapter 5, R_i consists of gold, SDRs and foreign exchange. If country 1 (say the United States) is the reserve-currency country, then R_i for country 2 to n may include liquid liabilities of the U.S. monetary system, so that R_1 may become negative. The purchasing power parity relationship requires

$$p_i = q_i p_1, \qquad i = 2, \ldots, n. \tag{8.3}$$

The demand for real money balances is assumed to be a function of real income Q_i. In the real world the demand for money may depend on the interest rate and other factors, but in order to focus on the long-run behavior of the system, where the rate of interest can be regarded as constant, we have made various simplifying assumptions.

There are two alternative ways to formulate the monetary approach to the balance of payments. One is to use a discrete-time model and to allow lags in the process of balance of payments adjustment. The other is to appeal to a continuous-time model and to describe the dynamic process as a moving equilibrium. In this chapter we will adopt the second approach, as we did in chapter 5.

If we denote the income elasticity of the demand for money by η_i and the percentage rate of change of a variable by a caret, then logarithmic differentiation of equation 5.2 yields

$$\hat{M}_i - \hat{p}_i = \eta_i \hat{Q}_i, \tag{8.4}$$

or, in view of equation 8.1,

$$\frac{\dot{D}_i + q_i \dot{R}_i}{M_i} = \hat{p}_i + \eta_i \hat{Q}_i. \tag{8.5}$$

Equation 8.5 differs from equation 5.3 in that the $q_i (i = 2, \ldots, n)$ are no longer fixed at unity. We see from this equation that the money supply can be increased either through pure domestic credit creation, $\dot{D}_i$, or through a surplus in the balance of payments, $q_i \dot{R}_i$.

The simplest way of interpreting this equation is to assume that the government does not sterilize the inflow or outflow of reserves. However, even when the government engages in sterilizing operations, equation 8.5 follows if we define the policy variable, $\dot{D}_i$, to be inclusive of sterilizing operations.[3]

Define the relative balance of payments normalized by the money supply as

$$z_i = \frac{\dot{R}_i}{M_i / q_i}.$$

Then equation 8.5 can be rewritten as

$$\theta_i + z_i = \hat{p}_i, \tag{8.6}$$

where

$$\theta_i \equiv \frac{\dot{D}_i}{M_i} - \eta_i \hat{Q}_i.$$

From the purchasing-power-parity relationship 8.3, we obtain

$$\hat{p}_i = \hat{q}_i + \hat{p}_i. \tag{8.7}$$

Thus, we have the following relationship among excess money creation, the balance of payments, and the price level of country 1:

$$\theta_i + z_i = \hat{p}_1 + \hat{q}_i. \tag{8.8}$$

Define the relative magnitude of the amount of outstanding money as ω_i, such that

$$\omega_i = \frac{\bar{M_i/q_i}}{\sum\limits_{k=1}^{n} (M_k/q_k)}.$$

After multiplying equation 8.8 by ω_i and then summing over $i = 1, \ldots, n$, we obtain

$$\sum_{i=1}^{n} \omega_i \theta_i + \sum_{i=1}^{n} \omega_i z_i = \sum_{i=1}^{n} \omega_i \hat{q}_i + \hat{p}_1. \tag{8.9}$$

However,

$$\sum_{i=1}^{n} \omega_i z_i = \frac{\sum\limits_{i=1}^{n} \left(\dfrac{M_i}{q_i} \cdot \dfrac{q_i \dot{R}_i}{M_i} \right)}{\sum\limits_{k=1}^{n} \left(\dfrac{M_k}{q_k} \right)} = \frac{\sum\limits_{i=1}^{n} \dot{R}_i}{\sum\limits_{k=1}^{n} (M_k/q_k)} = \frac{\dot{R}}{\sum\limits_{k=1}^{n} (M_k/q_k)} \equiv G_R. \tag{8.10}$$

Thus, the weighted sum of the normalized balance of payments is equal to the exogenous increase in total international reserves normalized by the total world money stock in term of dollars. This normalized increase in total international reserves is denoted by G_R.

The following mechanism is working behind equation 8.5. National policy authorities have two policy instruments: increasing domestic credit creation $\dot{D}_i$ and manipulating the exchange rate $\hat{q}_i$ by intervening in the foreign exchange market. Intervention in the foreign exchange market may change the balance of payments, but it is assumed either that governments do not sterilize the effect of balance of payments disequilibria on the domestic monetary base or that any attempt at sterilization is included in the definition of $\dot{D}_i$.

From now on we will treat excess money creation θ_i $(i = 1, 2, \ldots, n)$ and the rate of change in the exchange rate $\hat{q}_i$ $(i = 2, \ldots, n)$ as policy variables. To some readers it may seem more natural to consider excess money creation θ_i and the (relative) amount of government intervention z_i as policy variables. Suppose for a moment that the θ_i's and z_i's are policy instruments. Since

$$\sum_{i=1}^{n} \omega_i z_i = G_R$$

holds as an identity, only $(n - 1)$ of the z_i's are independent. (This is an expression of the redundancy problem under a managed float system.) Therefore, one must treat one of z_i's as being passively determined.

Suppose that z_1 is passively determined in this way:

$$z_1 = \frac{1}{\omega_1}\left(G_R - \sum_{i=2}^{n} \omega_i z_i\right).$$

Then, from equation 8.8,

$$\hat{q}_j = (\theta_j + z_j) - (\theta_1 + z_1)$$

$$= -G_R/\omega_i + (\theta_j - \theta_1) + (1 - \omega_j/\omega_1)z_j + \sum_{i \neq 1, j} (\omega_i/\omega_1)z_i, \qquad (8.8a)$$

$$j = 2, \ldots, n.$$

Thus, given the θ_i's $(i \neq j)$ and z_i's $(i \neq 1, j)$, the jth country can decide on its rate of depreciation. Therefore, a one-to-one correspondence exists between the case where the θ_i's $(i = 1, \ldots, n)$ and z_i's $(i = 2, \ldots, n)$ are strategies and the case where the θ_i's $(i = 1, \ldots, n)$ and $\hat{q}$'s $(i = 2, \ldots, n)$ are strategies. Since both cases are equivalent, we will use the latter formulation in which the rate of excess money creation and changes in exchange rates are treated as policy instruments.[4]

From equation 8.9 we obtain

$$\hat{p}_1 = G_R + \sum_{i=1}^{n} \omega_i(\theta_i - \hat{q}_i) \qquad (8.11)$$

for country 1 and

$$\hat{p}_j = G_R + \sum_{i=1}^{n} \omega_i(\theta_i - \hat{q}_i) + \hat{q}_j \qquad (8.12)$$

for the jth country. These are essentially a generalization of Johnson's (1972a) formula, though the expression is much simpler because of changes in the definitions of the variables. Since $\hat{q}_1$, the numéraire, has been set equal to unity throughout, $\hat{q}_1 = 0$. Accordingly, the weighted average can be rewritten as

$$\sum_{i=1}^{n} \omega_i(\theta_i - \hat{q}_i) = \omega_1 \theta_1 + \sum_{i=2}^{n} \omega_i(\theta_i - \hat{q}_i).$$

Thus, in a world where national economics are linked closely enough to realize the relationship of purchasing power parity, the price level of the numéraire country will be determined by the sum of the relative increase in (outside) international money and the weighted average of excess money creation minus the rate of depreciation in the exchange rate relative to the numéraire currency. Equation 8.12 indicates that price changes in other countries are determined by the sum of price inflation in the numéraire country and the rate of depreciation in their exchange rate.

The monetary structure of the managed float system is described by equations 8.11 and 8.12. Under fixed exchange rates one can speak of the world price level, which is determined by the weighted average of excess money creation. Under flexible exchange rates each country can choose its own price level, which is determined mainly by its own money supply. Under managed floating each country is still able to choose its own price level, which is determined, on one hand, by the weighted average of rates of excess money creation minus rates of depreciation and, on the other, by its own rate of depreciation.

As was correctly pointed out by Johnson (1972a), devaluation is equivalent to domestic credit contraction in its effect on the balance of payments. The same statement can also be applied to the price level of countries in the rest of the world. With respect to the price level of the devaluing country, however, devaluation has a positive effect that is similar to domestic credit expansion mitigated by the factor $(1 - \omega_i)/\omega_i$.

Devaluation denotes a change in the relative value of domestic and foreign money. Accordingly, for other countries, devaluation exerts an effect that is equivalent to a decrease in the foreign money supply. For the home country, devaluation is equivalent to an increase in the amount of money stock in the rest of the world.

Under fixed rates, the effect of credit contraction in one country is diluted or leaked to the rest of the world through balance of payments adjustments. Under managed floating, the depreciation of its currency by one country negatively affects the rest of the world while bringing about domestic expansion. Because of this asymmetry, manipulation of exchange rates is a very powerful policy instrument.

It would be instructive to compute the average world price level weighted by the monetary weights ω_i. Let us multiply equation 8.12 by ω_j, for $j = 1,$ ..., n, noting that equation 8.11 can be interpreted as a special case of 8.12 with $\hat{q}_1 = 0$, and sum. We then obtain the simple relationship

$$\sum_{j=1}^{n} \omega_j \hat{p}_j = G_R + \sum_{j=1}^{n} \omega_j \theta_j. \tag{8.13}$$

Thus, we can state the following: Suppose that the world price level is defined as the weighted average of national price levels, the weights being the relative monetary magnitudes. Then the world price level is determined by the weighted average of excess money creation and the relative growth of outside international reserves. An attempt to manipulate exchange rates will result in opposite effects on the home country and on the rest of the world, and, since the opposing effects will cancel each other out, the net effect on the world price level will be nil.

International Conflicts of Monetary Policies concerning Desired Levels of Exchange Rates

So far the question of which country can decide exchange rates remains unanswered. An exchange rate is itself the relative price of currencies. For example, q_j is the relative price of the numéraire currency in terms of the currency of the jth country. Because a change in the exchange rate is a powerful weapon, it matters greatly which country has control over a particular exchange rate. In order to answer this question, we shall study more carefully the interdependent nature of monetary policies and the determination of exchange rates in a simplified model of the world economy consisting of two countries.

Suppose there are only two countries in the world, the United States and Europe. In addition, suppose that the supply of outside international money is held constant, so that $G_R = 0$. Then our basic relationship, equations 8.11 and 8.12, will be reduced to

$$\omega_1 \theta_1 + \omega_2 \theta_2 = \hat{p}_1 + \omega_2 \hat{q}_2, \tag{8.14}$$

$$\omega_1 \theta_1 + \omega_2 \theta_2 = \hat{p}_2 - \omega_1 \hat{q}_2. \tag{8.15}$$

The balances of payments of the two countries are expressed by

$$z_1 = \omega_2 \{ -\theta_1 + (\theta_2 - \hat{q}_2) \} \tag{8.16}$$

and

$$z_2 = \omega_1\{\theta_1 - (\theta_2 - \hat{q}_2)\}. \tag{8.17}$$

It is easy to verify the relationship

$$\omega_1 z_1 + \omega_2 z_2 [= G_R] = 0.$$

The structure of this interplay of monetary policies cum exchange rate policies is seen most clearly by considering the system of equations 8.14 and 8.15 in the context of the policy assignment problem formulated by Mundell (1962).

Suppose a_1 is the most desired rate of inflation for country 1 and a_2 is that for country 2. To achieve these targets, there are three policy instruments: θ_1, θ_2, and $\hat{q}_2$. In order to achieve both targets at the same time, the policy instruments must satisfy

$$\omega_1 \theta_1 + \omega_2 \theta_2 = a_1 + \omega_2 \hat{q}_2 \tag{8.18}$$

and

$$\omega_1 \theta_1 + \omega_2 \theta_2 = a_2 - \omega_1 \hat{q}_2. \tag{8.19}$$

Even though two policy instruments θ_1 and θ_2 may seem to be sufficient to achieve both goals a_1 and a_2, given an arbitrary value of $\hat{q}_2$, it is not so. The simultaneous equation system is degenerate and has solutions if and only if $\hat{q}_2$ satisfies

$$a_1 + \omega_2 \hat{q}_2 = a_2 - \omega_1 \hat{q}_2,$$

that is,

$$\hat{q}_2 = a_2 - a_1. \tag{8.20}$$

If condition 8.20 is satisfied, any combination of θ_1 and θ_2 with a varying parameter k, such that

$$\theta_1 = a_1 + \omega_2 k, \tag{8.21}$$

$$\theta_2 = a_2 - \omega_1 k \tag{8.22}$$

will satisfy the system of equations 8.18 and 8.19.

With this preparation we can now readily analyze the characteristics of alternative exchange rate regimes. Under flexible rates, q_2 moves so as to equate both z_1 and z_2 to zero in equations 8.16 and 8.17, so $\hat{p}_1 = \theta_1$ and $\hat{p}_2 = \theta_2$. Therefore there is no interdependence or conflict between monetary policies in the long run since each country can set θ equal to a_i.

Under fixed exchange rates, $\hat{q}_2$ is set equal to zero by definition. Accordingly, equations 8.18 and 8.19 cannot be satisfied simultaneously unless a_1 happens to equal a_2. If there is a discrepancy in the preferences of the two countries concerning the desired rate of inflation or the desired level of the balance of payments, then a gamelike situation will emerge.

Under managed floating—a mixture of the above two systems—price levels can be chosen independently, provided that $\hat{q}_2$ is chosen to be equal to the difference between the desired inflation rate of one country and that of the other. Thus, by coordinating monetary policies and manipulating exchange rate policies so as to satisfy equations 8.21 and 8.22, both countries can achieve the first best situation, a Paretian combination of price changes. This is possible if the balance of payments is in equilibrium—that is, when the system is operated as if it were a genuine float.

But this is not a necessary condition for the system to work. Even though θ_1 and θ_2 are set according to equations 8.21 and 8.22 with a nonvanishing k, the policy targets are satisfied as long as $\hat{q}_2 = a_2 - a_1$. In this case international reserves of the country with a rate of monetary expansion smaller than the value of a_i will continue to accumulate indefinitely.

Suppose, however, that each country is not indifferent about the rate of depreciation $\hat{q}_2$. It is possible that a country will want a certain rate of currency depreciation for various reasons, for example, due to the lobbying of export producers and import competitors.[5] Both countries are free to choose their own rates of monetary expansion, but if they do not agree with each other on the appropriate change in the exchange rate, then a conflict situation will emerge. First, if they differ on the desired rate of depreciation of the currency of country 2 (appreciation of the currency of country 1), conflict will occur. Second, even if they agree on the desired value of $\hat{q}_2$, if it does not coincide with $a_2 - a_1$, problems will arise.

The structure of possible conflict under managed floating can be illustrated by a Cournot diagram, because equation 8.18 and 8.19 can be interpreted, respectively, as the reaction curves of country 1 and country 2. In figure 8.1 the rates of excess money creation, which are strategies in this game, are depicted on the axes. The reaction curves of country 1 and country 2 are drawn as lines AA and BB. Let us assume, for simplicity, that $a_1 = a_2 = a > 0$ but that the rate of currency depreciation desired by country 2 is $b_2 > 0$. Then, given the rate of currency depreciation b_2, the reaction curve of country 1 will be located above that of country 2. Since both lines are parallel, there will be no equilibrium point. The path indicating the process of policy reactions will be driven down as shown by the arrows in the figure. Unless $\hat{q}_2$ is taken as the appropriate value ($= a_2 - a_1 = 0$ in this particular

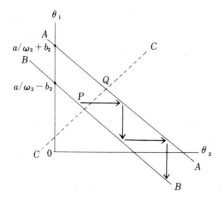

Figure 8.1

example), the process of policy retaliation may lead to a combination of accelerated monetary expansion by one country and accelerated contraction by the other.

Realistically, however, the current operation of the world monetary regime is not represented by the unconstrained choice of monetary policies and exchange rate changes. The reserve-currency country usually does not intervene in the foreign exchange market, but non-reserve-currency countries select combinations of monetary and exchange rate policies under contraints on their balance of payments. In the two-country model this can be formulated as follows: The right to determine $\hat{q}_2$ is left to the monetary authorities of country 2, which is, in turn, restricted by the balance of payments constraint

$$z_2 = \omega_1[\theta_1 - (\theta_2 - \hat{q}_2)] \geqq 0. \tag{8.23}$$

Therefore, country 2 can operate only under the dotted line CC, which has a $45°$ angle. If the balance of payments must be in strict equilibrium, country 2 should be on line CC. In other words, CC becomes the virtual reaction curve of country 2. In this case Q is the only solution. However, if both countries learn that $\hat{q}_2$ must be set equal to $(a_2 - a_1)$ for the simultaneous achievement of price targets, they may agree on the value of $\hat{q}_2 = a_2 - a_1$ and return to complete floating.

In reality, relationship 8.23 is not a strict equality but allows inequality. Therefore, the entire region below the dotted curve CC is feasible for country 2 and, of course, for country 1. Therefore, in this more realistic setting there is still the danger of unstable policy interactions as long as the balance of payments surplus does not necessarily induce the non-reserve-currency country to expand its money supply or appreciate its currency (J. M. Henderson 1975).

The well-known redundancy problem reemerges in a new context. In a world of managed floating, the redundancy problem generally takes the form that there are only $(n - 1)$ relative prices—exchange rates—to be determined but that there are n policy authorities. One solution is for the reserve-currency country (for example, country 1) to refrain from intervening in the foreign exchange market and for all other countries to intervene in terms of dollars. That would solve the redundancy problem but would put non-reserve-currency countries in an advantageous strategic position when there is a conflict about the proper rate of exchange rate depreciation (Cooper 1972).

One the other hand, if every country intervenes in the foreign exchange markets and tries to influence exchange rates, the policy outcome will be indeterminate because an attempt by one central bank to depreciate its own currency by buying other currencies will be counteracted by the attempt by other central banks to buy that currency. The structure of the conflict in such a case would be zero-sum, and some type of international agreement would be necessary to induce exchange rates to settle down to stable values.

Of course, if there were a numéraire that is not a national currency, this redundancy problem would formally vanish. Suppose that the value of every currency is measured by a currency unit, say SDRs, and that any country can intervene in the foreign exchange markets by selling or buying SDRs. Then every country can set the nominal value of its own currency in terms of SDRs. However, difficulties still remain because it is not the nominal value of a currency in terms of some numéraire but the value of a currency relative to that of other currencies that matters to policy authorities.

This analysis of interdependence depends on various simplifying assumptions. In the next section we examine the workings of the managed float system in a model that allows both employment and the price level to vary.

Transmission of Economic Fluctuations under Managed Floating

So far the real side of the economy—in particular real national income—has been assumed to be exogenously given. However, mere monetary effects are of little interest to economists unless they have some bearing on the real side of the economy. We now consider the process of the transmission of business cycles under managed floating.

Consider a world consisting of two countries where a Phillips curve relationship generates output fluctuations in each. In this section we abstract from secular growth factors in order to present a simplified picture of the transmission of short-run output fluctuations. In each country the demand for real money balances is assumed to be proportional to real permanent income. Real permanent income is again assumed to be constant.

Let the short-run Phillips curve relationships in the two countries be expressed as

$$\hat{w}_i = \psi(X_i) + \pi_i, \psi'(X_i) > 0, \qquad i = 1, 2, \tag{8.24}$$

where $\hat{w}_i$, X_i, and π_i are, respectively, the money wage rate, output, and the expected rate of inflation in the ith country. The expected rate of inflation is formed by an adaptive process,

$$\dot{\pi}_i = \gamma(\hat{p}_i - \pi_i), \qquad i = 1, 2. \tag{8.25}$$

The demands for labor and output are determined by marginal productivity conditions and by the production function $F(N)$:

$$w_i/p_i = F'(N_i), X_i = F(N_i), \qquad i = 1, 2. \tag{8.26}$$

Since the demand for real money balances is assumed to be proportional to constant permanent income, we have

$$\hat{p}_i = \hat{M}_i, \qquad i = 1, 2. \tag{8.27}$$

The purchasing-power-parity relationship requires

$$q_2 p_1 = p_2,$$

or

$$\hat{p}_1 + \hat{q}_2 = \hat{p}_2. \tag{8.28}$$

Thus we have, from equations 8.27 and 8.28,

$$\hat{M}_1 + \hat{q}_2 = \hat{M}_2. \tag{8.29}$$

On the other hand, as explained in section 1,

$$\omega_1 \hat{M}_1 + \omega_2 \hat{M}_2 = G_R + \omega_1 \theta_1 + \omega_2 \theta_2, \tag{8.30}$$

where ω_i is the relative monetary weight of country i and θ_i equals $\dot{D}_i/M_i$. Setting $G_R = 0$ for simplicity, we obtain

$$\hat{p}_1 = \hat{M}_1 = \omega_1 \theta_1 + \omega_2(\theta_2 - \hat{q}_2),$$

$$\hat{p}_2 = \hat{M}_2 = \omega_1(\theta_1 + \hat{q}_2) + \omega_2 \theta_2.$$

Thus, if we specify production functions of the Cobb-Douglas type with

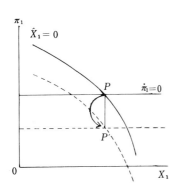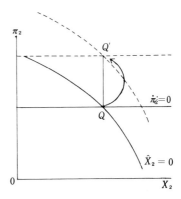

Figure 8.2

exponent β, i.e., $F(N) = N^\beta$, we can derive the following pairs of differential equations:

$$\hat{X}_1 = \bar{\beta}\{\omega_1\theta_1 + \omega_2(\theta_2 - \hat{q}_2) - \psi(X_1) - \pi_1\},$$

$$\dot{\pi}_1 = \gamma\{\omega_1\theta_1 + \omega_2(\theta_2 - \hat{q}_2) - \pi_1\},$$
$$\tag{8.31}$$

$$\hat{X}_2 = \bar{\beta}\{\omega_1(\theta_1 + \hat{q}_2) + \omega_2\theta_2 - \psi(X_2) - \pi_2\},$$

$$\dot{\pi}_2 = \gamma\{\omega_1(\theta_1 + \hat{q}_2) + \omega_2\theta_2 - \pi_2\},$$
$$\tag{8.32}$$

where

$$\bar{\beta} \equiv \beta/(1 - \beta).$$

The interdependence of the two economies can be illustrated by the phase diagrams in figure 8.2. The solid curves in figure 8.2 indicate the loci of $\hat{X}_i = 0$ and $\dot{\pi}_i = 0$. The $\hat{X}_i = 0$ locus is drawn as an upside-down image of the Phillips curve; the $\dot{\pi}_i = 0$ locus is drawn as a horizontal line, the height of which can be defined as the monetary factor:

$$\omega_1\theta_1 + \omega_2(\theta_2 - \hat{q}_2) \quad \text{for country 1,}$$

$$\omega_1(\theta_1 + \hat{q}_2) + \omega_2\theta_2 \quad \text{for country 2.}$$

Under flexible exchange rates, each country can choose its own money supply so that only its rate of monetary expansion comes into the picture. In other words, there is a self-correcting mechanism in the exchange rate market that ensures that $q_2 = \theta_2 - \theta_1$ so that the above monetary factor always equals θ_i for all countries i. Therefore, each country can independently decide the levels of the equilibrium values of P and Q. Suppose that country 2 expands its money supply. Then equilibrium shifts from Q to Q', and, under the assumption of adaptive expectations, country 2 can enjoy short-term prosperity, as indicated by movement in a counterclockwise direction. This expansion is not transmitted to country 1 except for the terms-of-trade effect discussed in chapter 7.

On the other hand, $\hat{q}_2$ is always equal to zero under fixed exchange rates, so that each country cannot choose an independent economic policy. The two equilibrium points P and Q must always lie on the same horizontal level. Monetary expansion in one country is necessarily leaked to the other; a temporary boom in one country is transmitted to the other as a boom.

In a world of managed floating, monetary factors can diverge from one another by an amount equal to $\hat{q}_2$. The salient feature of this regime is that, in spite of the interdependence between monetary factors, each country can choose different monetary factors by changing its own rate of monetary expansion, and, if the country holds the initiative in determining the exchange rate, by changing the rate of currency depreciation as well. The effect of exchange rate depreciation on the two countries is in opposite directions.

Suppose that country 2 starts depreciating its currency by intervening in the foreign exchange market so that $\hat{q}_2$ becomes positive. The monetary factor for country 2 increases, while the monetary factor for country 1 decreases. The equilibrium in country 2 shifts upward to Q', while that in country 1 shifts downward to P'. Thus, the economy in country 2 experiences prosperity, depicted by a counterclockwise movement from Q to Q', while the economy in country 1 experiences a recession, moving from P to P'. The horizontal gap PP' equals $\omega_2 \hat{q}_2$, and the horizontal gap $Q'Q$ equals $\omega_1 \hat{q}_2$. Therefore, both gaps add up to the value of $\hat{q}_2$. The smaller is the scale ω_2 of country 2, the larger is the relative weight of QQ' to PP'.

The depreciation of country 2's currency may cause a chain reaction due to the monetary interdependence between the two countries. If country 1 waits long enough, the economy will eventually reach the solution P that is less inflationary. But if country 1 is impatient, it may appeal to expansionary monetary policy to push P' up slightly. This monetary policy will increase Q' a little further, and the effect on the world as a whole will be more inflationary as compared with the initial situation.

By itself, the depreciation of the currency of country 2 has no substantial effect on the average world price level, because inflationary effects in country 2 are offset by deflationary effects in country 1. If country 1 cannot endure the deflationary pressures caused by the depreciation of currency 2, however, the induced monetary expansion in country 1 may leave some long-run effects on the average rate of world inflation. It is worth noting that this effect, due to interdependence, does not operate if country 2 initially appeals to monetary policies rather than to a depreciation of its currency.

Fluctuations in output in this model occur because the expected rate of inflation, which is formed adaptively, lags behind the actual rate of inflation in both countries. If expectations are formed rationally, then the paths on average would be vertical movements directly from Q to Q' and directly from P to P'. Again, monetary factors would lose their systematic influence on real phenomena. The working of the world economy returns to those models that assume flexible exchange rates or perfect price flexibility. However, one must notice that the information requirement for rational expectations in a regime of managed floating is much larger than that in a closed model and even larger than that in a regime of complete floating. Not only are individuals required to forecast correctly the rates of monetary expansion of both countries—this in itself is a rather strong assumption in the light of the actual experiences of the world economy—but they are also required to forecast future changes in exchange rates correctly.

The above analysis reveals the policy implications of intervention in the foreign exchange market. Currency depreciation by one country affects that country in the same way as a monetary expansion in the rest of the world, and it affects the rest of the world in the same way as a monetary contraction in the home country.

9   Conclusion

I have attempted to answer the following two questions: (1) How does the choice of an international monetary regime affect the nature of policy interdependence and the distribution of economic welfare among countries? (2) Knowing the answer to the first question, what kind of international monetary regime is likely to be realized? In order to answer these questions, I have appealed to the tools of public economics, the theory of public choice, oligopoly theory, and game theory.

Changing the international monetary system, whether by reforming the existing regime or by adopting a new regime, requires a consensus among nations. Whether such a consensus can be reached depends on whether the proposed changes are seen as conferring economic gains on each nation. Political leadership also may play a role during the process of institutional development, that of orchestrating the realization of potential gains. Finally, reform of the international monetary system is more likely to occur during periods of international economic crisis when the deteriorating performance of the existing system makes formerly unattractive reform proposals more attractive.

When compared with the fixed exchange rate system, the system of flexible exchange rates has the major advantage of conferring greater autonomy on nations in the conduct of their monetary policies and thus in deciding their own price levels, but it also entails the cost of exchange risk resulting from exchange rate fluctuations. Even under a flexible exchange rate system, however, economic fluctuations may be transmitted internationally in the short run through changes in the terms of trade; moreover, because the buffer function of international reserves is no longer operative, recession in one country may lead to stagflation in other countries. Under a managed float system, intervention in the foreign exchange market by governments may cause monetary effects and, in some cases, beggar-thy-neighbor effects.

This book can provide only incomplete answers to the questions raised, primarily because of the inadequacy of my analysis but also because of the complexity of the problem posed. Any analysis involving two or more countries is necessarily quite complex; thus, in order to focus on international interdependence, I have limited my examination to the simplest models of the domestic economy. It is difficult to extend more sophisticated macroeconomic models of a closed or small economy to the case of two or more countries, and the marginal productivity in terms of economic implications is usually low.

During the 1970s, when the papers that form the basis for this book were being written, macroeconomics was undergoing fundamental changes in many aspects. In this book I have made extensive use of the short-run and long-run Phillips curves connected through adaptive inflationary expectations; such a formulation of the mechanism of economic fluctuations may be criticized on two grounds.

The first criticism is based on the rational expectations hypothesis, which claims that forming expectations adaptively is not necessarily consistent with rationality as it implies that people's expectations always lag behind reality. However, the adaptive expectations formulation can be defended on the ground that it is a good approximation of the real world, where information is imperfect and economic agents can obtain information only through a learning process. Moreover, if wage and other contracts can be revised only with a time lag, the qualitative properties of my models are unaltered even if we assume that expectations are rationally formed.

The second criticism concerns the use of the Phillips curve. It is argued that the Phillips curve is merely a reduced form relationship between the wage rate and unemployment, which should be studied in a framework that takes explicit account of disequilibrium in the goods and labor markets. The application of disequilibrium theory to international economics is undoubtedly desirable, and I leave it as a topic for further research.

Third, the discipline of international monetary economics has made considerable progress during the last ten years, partly in response to the adoption of a flexible exchange rate system. Such topics as the relationship between the stocks of assets in various currencies and exchange-rate changes, the law of one price regarding tradable goods, the flow-adjustment process in the goods market that lies behind the long-run purchasing-power relation, and the interactions between stock equilibrium and flow equilibrium have attracted much attention recently. However, the interest rate parity relationship cannot be examined using the models of this book, because they do not take explicit account of bonds. In order to achieve a better understanding of the interdependence among nations, we need a framework that explicitly incorporates bonds and nontraded goods. Much work remains to be done in this direction.

Fourth, the recent rapid development of game theory has contributed to a better understanding of the structure of cooperative solutions. Some readers may have the impression that my application of oligopoly theory to the comparison between the cooperative and noncooperative solutions is somewhat obsolete. As communication among nations through international conferences and other diplomatic channels becomes more frequent, a comparison of different cooperative solutions may be more relevant in many situations. Extensions in this direction are desirable.

As national economies become more and more interdependent, a better understanding of the nature of rule formation in the international economy and of the interdependence of economic policies among nations under given rules is urgently needed. Many problems in international monetary economics, as well as in international economics in general, are characterized by conflicts among a relatively small number of dominant countries. Public economics and game theory provide tools for understanding the structure of conflicts of interest in such situations. I hope that this book has aroused interest in the topic of interdependence among nations on issues relating to international economics. Further research in this direction, through clarifying the cost-benefit structure of international conflicts, may contribute to reducing international tensions and to preventing the occurrence of crises in international economic relations, as well as in international relations in general.

Postscript

More than three years have passed since the publication of the original (Japanese) version of this book. After I finished my manuscript, in the spring of 1980, substantial developments were occurring in the study of policy interdependence in the world economy. It would take another book to incorporate all the recent developments in the literature concerning international policy interdependence and to add my independent analyses of them. Therefore, I do not dare try to summarize recent developments in the theory of international policy interdependence; I would rather refer the reader to the balanced survey article by Richard N. Cooper (1984), who has been a forerunner in this field and a sympathetic critic of my work. It seems appropriate, however, that I comment on recent developments.

When I was working on several of the articles that form the basis of this book I often felt astray from the main current of economic thinking, because only a very few people showed interest in them. Recently, however, the game-theoretic or oligopoly-theoretic analysis of international policy interdependence has started to attract the attention of many scholars in international economics. When I attended an NBER conference in Cambridge, Massachusetts, in the summer of 1983, I was pleasantly surprised to find a substantial number of works in progress on the topic of policy interdependence. The world I analyzed was more often the world under fixed exchange rates, where the price level or the rate of inflation is more or less common to each country and can be regarded as a kind of public good. Recent works have mostly concentrated on the working of international policy interdependence under flexible exchange rates, where the linkage of interdependence is more subtle. Moreover, recent economists were working on more complex models with more sophisticated methodologies, such as differential games. I felt like a country boy who had played around with a desk calculator on a certain problem and suddenly found out that city children were using high-speed electronic computers to solve the same problems, and even more complex ones.

I would like to make several observations on the recent developments in the study of policy interdependence and coordination.

Under fixed exchange rates, the structure of policy interdependence was quite simple: The price level was related to the weighted average of the rates of monetary expansion, while the balance of payments was related to the difference between this average and the rate of monetary expansion of the particular country, and there was an embedded tendency for the price levels of various countries to converge to a common level translated by the exchange rates. Thus, the analogy of public goods or bads carried through as emphasized in this book. The nature of interdependence was further explored by Johansen (1982), who took account of the fact that monetary expansion may lead to a situation where the economy hits its capacity limit. The energetic work of Bryant (1980) brought the question of policy interdependence to the attention of economists. (See also Jones 1982.)

The adoption of flexible exchange rates essentially blocked the parallel movements of price levels, so the nature of monetary interdependence became more subtle. The strength of monetary interdependence under flexible exchange rates is, so to speak, of the second degree if the strength of the linkage of the price levels under fixed exchange rates is of the first degree. [McKinnon (1984) claims, however, that national price levels are better explained by a weighted average of the strength of monetary policies of major countries than solely by the strength of their own monetary policies. If his claim is true, it implies that the externalities among price levels under fixed exchange rates still exist under flexible exchange rates.] Moreover, the direction of spillover effects of monetary policy is not certain. Positive spillover effects are naturally working through the effect of the aggregate demand multiplier as well as through the terms-of-trade effect, which is also discussed in chapter 7 of this book. However, negative spillover effects are working through the rate of interest and capital mobility, analyzed by Mundell (1968) and Fleming (1962). Canzoneri and Gray (1985) clarified the nature of interdependence under these positive and negative spillover effects, incorporating energy shocks in the picture as well. There are several works along this line.

In a world of flexible exchange rates, the price level and the inflation rate of a single country are primarily, if not perfectly, determined by the strength of the country's monetary expansion. However, the levels of economic activities of a single country depend not only on the country's monetary policy but also on the monetary policies taken by other countries. The direction of the influence of the monetary policies of other countries may be positive or negative, depending on the nature of the interdependence. If positive spillover effects are dominant, one can easily see that noncooperative behavior will lead to a situation where each country pursues a less expansionary policy than is required to attain a cooperative situation. On the other hand, if the negative spillover effects are stronger, the noncooperative situation will be such that every country pursues a more expansionary policy than is required to attain a cooperative situation (Canzoneri and Gray 1985, Corden 1983, de Macedo 1983).

The static feature of the money-policy game was extended by several authors to a dynamic context. Aoki (1981) developed analytical techniques that made the analysis of the two-country model much easier. Sachs (1983) and Miller and Salmon (1983) elaborated the structure of the policy game using the technique of differential games. Most of their results, as well as the result of a simple attempt in the appendix to chapter 5 of this book, seem to suggest that the strategic structure obtained in the static models still holds in the stationary state of a dynamic game. In addition, of course, the dynamic path toward a stationary equilibrium can be traced clearly by the technique of differential games. In order to enrich the content of the dynamic analysis of policy games, however, we may have to introduce more structured concepts recently developed by game theorists. For example, the nature of reputation-making by governments should be studied with reference to various new concepts such as subgame perfectness or sequential equilibrium.

The next way to extend this kind of analysis is to introduce strategic structures between the government and private agents within a country. In other words, the strategic structure of the domestic economy should be considered simultaneously with the structure of the international sphere. In this respect, Rogoff's (1983) modification of the usual conclusion of externality by introducing wage negotiations between the government and private agents suggests a new direction in this kind of development.

One serious drawback of my book is that the argument has little empirical content. It is one thing to say that there is a difference between noncooperative and cooperative equilibria; it is quite another to say that the gain from cooperation is substantial. Oudiz and Sachs (1984) made a substantial breakthrough into this difficult impasse. They argued quite convincingly that even though the gain from this kind of macroeconomic cooperation exists, the magnitude of cooperation may not be so great, except for the case when the United States really cooperates with other countries despite the fact that she gains little from such cooperation. This result is quite reasonable in the theoretical context of the analysis of the effect of relative sizes. This has an interesting implication for the current American policy of international "benign neglect" (Feldstein 1983). Above all, Oudiz and Sachs contributed much to the discussion of policy coordination under empirical scrutiny.

Finally, I would like to address the points that many critics have raised about the series of analyses in which game theory or public economics is used to study the strategic structure of international interdependence.

The first type of criticism starts from the remark that people do talk at economic summits and administrative negotiations. Thus, critics claim that emphasis on noncooperative solutions or equilibria is not so relevant. [Incidentally, the economic function of summitry is interestingly described by de Menil (1983).] This remark may be valid indeed. However, since in the usual situations there are several or infinite combinations of cooperative situations, the position of a noncooperative solution has an important effect on the choice among the points on the contract curve. The location of the Nash equilibrium, for example, would decide which point on the contract curve is more likely to be attained by cooperation. At least in this world of imperfect information and the difficulty of perfect cooperation, one should study the strategic structure of the relationship between noncooperative and cooperative situations. Even if it is easy to cooperate perfectly, this question still remains: Which point among cooperative solutions will be realized?

Another group of critics attacks my approach from the opposite ground. Every government is under various political constraints. Accordingly, there is hardly any mechanism (or political feasibility) of realizing the fruit of economic cooperation. Each country has its national sovereignty over its economic policy. Therefore, they argue, it is natural for a country to assign all national economic policies to its own national policy objectives. From this viewpoint there is little reward from talking about ideal combinations or assignments of economic policies among countries (Komiya 1978; see also Feldstein 1983).

As I explained in chapter 4, the assignment approach must be supplemented by optimization and by a strategic approach. Moreover, I do not think that the meaning of the whole exercise is just to persuade policymakers of the need for cooperation. Indeed, government policy authorities are constrained by domestic constraints and tend to pursue national benefits. However, the world system can be regarded as better designed if nationalistic, noncooperative policies tend to produce an outcome that is close to the cooperative solution. The purpose of studying international system design is to conceive an economic system that is "incentive compatible" (Hurwicz 1972) in the sense that policy making following nationalistic incentives does not result in situations where the benefit of the world as a whole is seriously undermined. From this standpoint, more attention should be paid to the first major topic of this book. The question was under what circumstances national governments are more eager to agree on a system of rules, given the benefit-cost structure of various international regimes. Therefore, one should ask not only how one can design a system of rules under which national economic policies are incentive compatible but also how the rules can be designed in such a way that national governments are willing to participate in a new regime.

In the field of political science there have also occurred various theoretical developments, which I, as an economist, have been able to follow only partially. The works of Koehane (1984) and others (see Krasner 1983) contain useful applications of economists' ways of thinking to political science and ask how the structure of incentives for the design of an international regime can be improved. There still seems to remain much uncultivated soil between political science and economics regarding the question of what kinds of international regimes are likely to be adopted in the light of benefit-cost structures. A similar question can be asked not only with regard to monetary regime (as discussed in this book) but also with regard to trade rules such as the GATT or even informal voluntary export constraints.

In short, this book contains materials that some readers may find a little old-fashioned. However, there are many issues that can be developed still further on the basis of some of the ideas suggested in it.

Bibliography for Postscript

Aoki, Masanao. 1981. *Dynamic Analysis of Open Economies*. New York: Academic.

Bryant, Ralph C. 1980. *Money and Monetary Policy in Interdependent Nations*. Washington, D.C.: Brookings Institution.

Buiter, W. H., and R. C. Marston, eds. 1985. *International Economic Policy Coordination*. Cambridge University Press.

Canzoneri, M., and J. A. Gray. 1985. "Two Essays on Monetary Policy in an Interdependent World." *International Economic Review* (forthcoming).

Cooper, Richard N. 1984. "Economic Interdependence and Coordination of Economic Policies." In R. Jones and P. B. Kenen, eds., *Handbook of International Economics*. Amsterdam: North-Holland.

Corden, W. M. 1983. Macroeconomic Policy Interaction Under Flexible Exchange Rates: A Two-Country Model. Australian National University, Canberra.

de Macedo, Jorge Braga. 1983. Policy Interdependence Under Flexible Exchange Rates: A 2-country Model. Paper presented at NBER Conference on the International Coordination of Economic Policy, Cambridge, Mass.

de Menil, George. 1983. *Economic Summitry*. New York: Council on Foreign Relations.

Feldstein, Martin S. 1983. "The World Economy Today." *Economist*, June 11.

Fleming, J. Marcus. 1962. "Domestic Financial Policies Under Fixed and Flexible Exchange Rates." *International Monetary Fund Staff Papers* 9, no. 3: 369–379.

Hurwicz, Leonid. 1972. "On Informationally Decentralized Systems." In C. B. McGuire and R. Randner, eds., *Decision and Organization*. Amsterdam: North-Holland.

Johansen, Leif. 1982. "A Note on the Possibility of an International Equilibrium with Low Levels of Activity." *Journal of International Economics* 13, no. 3/4: 257–266.

Jones, Michael. 1982. "Automatic Output Stability and the Exchange Arrangement: A Multi-Country Analysis." *Review of Economic Studies* 49: 91–107.

Koehane, Robert O. 1984. *After Hegemony: Cooperation and Discord in the World Political Economy*. Princeton University Press.

Komiya, Ryutaro. 1978. "Is International Co-ordination of National Economic Policies Necessary?" In P. Oppenheimer, ed., *Issues in International Economics*. Oriel.

Krasner, Stephen D., ed. 1983. *International Regimes*. Ithaca, N.Y.: Cornell University Press.

McKinnon, Ronald. 1984. "An International Standard for Monetary Stabilization." *Policy Analyses in International Economics*, no. 8. Washington, D.C.: Institute for International Economics.

Miller, Marcus H., and M. Salmon. 1985. "Policy Coordination and Dynamic Games." In W. H. Buiter and R. C. Marston, eds., *International Economic Policy Co-ordination*. Cambridge University Press.

Mundell, Robert A. 1968. *International Economics*. New York: Macmillan.

Oudiz, G., and J. Sachs. 1984. "Macroeconomic Policy Coordination among the Industrial Economies." Brookings Papers on Economic Activity.

Rogoff, Kenneth. 1983. "Productive and Counterproductive Cooperative Monetary Policies." International Finance Discussion Paper no. 233, Federal Reserve System.

Sachs, Jeffrey. 1983. "International Policy Coordination in a Dynamic Macro-economic Model." NBER Discussion Paper no. 1166.

Notes

Chapter 1

1. Notable exceptions are Kindleberger (1970) and Aubrey (1969). The latter emphasizes political aspects more than my book does and concludes that the position of the United States in international politics determines the nature of its balance of payments. See also Strange 1976, Cohen 1977, and note 2 in chapter 3.

2. I do not think that game theory can solve all problems in social science. Moreover, the concepts and methods of game theory used in this book are rudimentary and informal. I would therefore like to leave it to readers to decide to what extent the game theoretic approach used in this book is effective. However, I believe that in order to tackle the problem of mutual dependence among agents, it is necessary to try approaches free from the confines of traditional price theory. This book represents one such attempt.

Chapter 2

I am much indebted to Ryuichiro Tachi for helpful comments on the organization of this chapter.

1. Japan's attitude toward international monetary reform may have to change. It should abandon its traditional attitude of merely following the world, or following the United States, passively. Instead it should take an active role in improving the international monetary system, while keeping its own economic interests, as well as the common interests of the world economy, in mind.

2. For detailed discussions of the seigniorage problem see Grubel and Johnson (in Mundell and Swoboda 1968), Corden 1972, chap. 6, and McKinnon 1974. I thank my referee for helpful comments on this point.

3. Recent developments in multistage game theory, including the topics around the "chain store paradox," indicate that the story can become quite involved.

4. Since the IMF charter does not provide an exact definition of fundamental disequilibrium, the rule is incomplete; the interpretation of this phrase has created much confusion.

Chapter 3

I am indebted to Charles P. Kindleberger for his constructive suggestions through-out this study. I am also grateful to Robert Z. Aliber, John Greenwood, Eiichi Hizen, Takashi Inoguchi, Kanji Ishii, Kinhide Mushakoji, Naoshi Sekiguchi, and Hiroshi Shimbo for helpful comments.

1. Here I am using the term *monetary union* or *integration* in a quite general sense to include loose associations of national economies in which the member countries are connected by fixed exchange rates with or without coordination of monetary policies, as well as perfectly integrated national economies using a common currency.

2. Among these few exceptions are Nye (1973), Johnson (1972b), Cooper (1972), and Aliber (1973).

3. Cooper (1974) also gives a discussion of the political economy aspects of economic integration in general.

4. For a discussion of the benefits and costs of monetary integration, see Aliber 1972. See also Corden 1972 concerning the costs and Ingram 1973 concerning the benefits.

5. The probability of becoming the pivotal vote of a decision as measured by the Shapley value or by the power index will definitely increase. For a discussion of the Shapley value and the related power index, see Riker and Ordeshook 1973, chap. 6.

6. The increased satisfaction of political leaders or central bankers does not neces-sarily mean the increased satisfaction of consumers.

7. If the world is on a fixed exchange rate system, the formation of a monetary union will increase the bargaining power of member countries in the game consisting of the interplay of monetary policies. See chapter 5.

8. Early writers emphasized this benefit of monetary integration. See Guggenheim 1973.

9. These spillover effects are closely associated with the functions of money as a unit of account and a medium of exchange. In addition, the formation of a monetary union broadens the options available to developing countries when they are choosing their own exchange rate systems. In addition to pegging their exchange rates to some international currency or allowing them to float, developing countries also have the option of pegging their exchange rates to the currency of the monetary union.

10. Buchanan (1964, p. 2) limits the scope of his analysis to a purely economic conflict. It is possible, however, to apply the analogy to politico-economic conflicts.

11. The spillover effect on nonmembers is an exception.

12. A similar approach is taken in Krämer 1971.

13. For a discussion of hansatsu, its economic roles, and its relation to privately issued notes, see Shimbo 1972.

14. Saitō (1939) provides an excellent study of the Latin Monetary Union.

Chapter 4

I am indebted to Akihiro Amano, Richard N. Cooper, Jurg Niehans, and Eisuke Sakakibara for helpful criticisms and suggestions concerning this chapter.

1. See, for example, Leijonhufvud 1968, Negishi 1979, and Uzawa 1978–1979. The analysis of international interdependence in an explicit disequilibrium framework constitutes a major topic for further research.

2. More precisely, S should denote saving plus net interest income on international lendings, but for simplicity, the latter is ignored here.

3. That is, R or R^* can even become negative as a result of an expansion in D or D^*.

4. In order to understand more fully the character of the Cournot and Stackelberg solutions, we need to know whether the outcomes generated by the process of policy interplays would converge ultimately to these solutions along a stable time path. We also need to know the speed of this process relative to the speed of adjustment assumed in the Keynesian model.

Chapter 5

I am indebted to Hiroshi Atsumi, Jacob Frenkel, Harry G. Johnson, Jorge Marquez, Michihiro Ohyama, Yūsuke Onitsuka, and Takashi Takayama for helpful comments.

1. It may be possible to extend the results to a more realistic situation in which a national price level can deviate from the world price level by appealing to the traded-nontraded good model developed by Dornbusch (1973b).

2. For discussions of the optimal rate of inflation, see Bailey 1956, Phelps 1965, and M. Friedman 1969. In the actual world wage and price rigidity would make further reductions in the rate of inflation below a certain level undesirable for a monetary authority. Such situations may not be fully consistent with the analysis below where the real rates of growth of nations are exogenously given; however, the strategic structure of the interplay of monetary policies would remain almost the same under such situations.

3. For the reserve country, I do not exclude the possibility that R_i may become negative. For example if the amount of dollars held by foreign monetary authorities exceeds the reserve assets held by the United States, then R_i for the United States will be negative. We assume for simplicity that the private sector does not hold any foreign currency even though allowing for this possibility does not change subsequent results.

4. For our purposes we do not need to deal explicitly with the sterilization question because the strategic variable $\dot{D}/M$ is monetary expansion in excess of monetary expansion due to a balance of payments surplus. If a country sterilizes its surplus, we can merely treat $\dot{D}/M$ as being negative. If, however, sterilization policy is undertaken independently of the strategically determined changes in the money supply according to some rule, such as requiring that a certain percentage of the balance of payments be sterilized (that is, defining θ_i as a fixed proportion of z_i), then the analysis would have to be modified. In that case excess sterilization is inherently unstable, as shown by De Grauwe (1975, 1977).

5. See Johnson 1972a. Here we follow Johnson in assuming that the ω_i's are fixed. For simplicity we will confine ourselves to the continuous version of the monetary approach with smooth adjustment in the money market. For a different approach, see Dornbusch 1973a and Komiya 1974.

6. Mathematically the Pareto-optimal configuration is obtained by varying β_k within the interior of the $(n - 1)$ dimensional simplex.

7. In this particular sense the Pareto-optimal configuration reflects the aggregation of the preferences of the monetary authorities. In fact in the special case of quadratic utility functions analyzed in the next section, the Pareto-optimal rate of inflation is the weighted average of the desired rates of inflation, the weights being the relative importance of each country.

8. This new weight $\bar{\omega}_i$ is monotonically related to ω_i, with the larger country being represented more than proportionately in the new weight. It is worth noting that $\bar{\omega}$ becomes smaller if a country is divided into smaller countries in the general case of $n > 2$.

9. If the non-reserve-currency countries wish to keep the ratio of international reserves to the outstanding domestic money supply constant, then $\dot{R}_i/R_i = \pi + \eta_i \dot{Q}_i/Q_i$.

10. Even in the short run capital losses may have to be taken into account if we adopt the perfect foresight assumption. But since b_i itself is changing, we do not incorporate it formally into the model.

Chapter 6

I am much indebted to Rudiger Dornbusch, Ryutaro Komiya, Kiyohiko Nishimura, and Michihiro Ohyama for their helpful comments.

1. More generally a constant may be multiplied to the exponential form, but goods can be measured in normalized units so that the multiplicative constant will be unity.

2. For a discussion of the rational expectations hypothesis and its economic implications, see Nagatani 1975 and Mutoh and Shizuki 1980.

3. Here it is implicitly assumed that, when deciding how much labor to supply, the labor side is concerned solely with the real wage rate measured in terms of the general price level and that a continuous deterioration in the terms of trade does not

affect labor supply directly, even though it implies that the purchasing power of the country is declining. If this assumption does not hold, my conclusion has to be modified. In Japan it is often said that during the first oil crisis, the firm stand taken by labor concerning the real wage rate raised the natural rate of unemployment, while during the second oil crisis, self-restraint on the labor side over wage increases minimized the need to adjust the employment level. Thus in these cases, the specification of labor supply is of crucial importance. Also it can be easily shown that labor supply is independent of the terms of trade if labor has a Cobb-Douglas type utility function that incorporates leisure and good 2 as its components.

4. The Jacobian of the system is written

$$\begin{pmatrix} -\psi'/(1 - \beta_1) & -\lambda/(1 - \beta_1) \\ 0 & -\gamma \end{pmatrix}$$

Accordingly its trace is negative, and its determinant positive.

5. The Jacobian of the system is written

$$J = \begin{pmatrix} -(1 - \gamma\varepsilon)\psi'/\Delta & -\{\lambda(1 - \gamma\varepsilon) + \gamma\varepsilon\}/\Delta \\ \gamma\beta\psi'/\Delta & -\gamma(1 - \beta\lambda)/\Delta \end{pmatrix}$$

If $1 - \gamma\varepsilon > 0$, then $\Delta = 1 - \gamma\varepsilon(1 - \beta) > 0$, and

Trace $[J] = \{-(1 - \gamma\varepsilon)\psi' - \gamma(1 - \beta\lambda)\}/\Delta < 0$,

det. $[J] = \gamma\psi'\{(1 - \gamma\varepsilon)(1 - \beta\lambda) + \beta[\lambda(1 - \gamma\varepsilon) + \gamma\varepsilon]\}/\Delta^2 > 0$.

Therefore, the system is locally stable, and by Olech's Theorem (Olech 1963), it is globally stable as well. Suppose, however, that $1 - \gamma\varepsilon < 0$. Then the trace of the Jacobian could easily be positive for a large value of ψ'.

6. From equations 6.26″ and 6.25″, we find that $\dot{\pi} = 0$ shifts by $\alpha_2/(1 - \beta\lambda)$ and that $\dot{y} = 0$ shifts by $\alpha_2/(1 - \beta\lambda)$. Furthermore, in the case of (6.25″), $\dot{y} = 0$ shifts by $\varepsilon\gamma\alpha_2/[\lambda(1 - \gamma\varepsilon) + \gamma\varepsilon]$.

We can also see that

$$\frac{\alpha_2}{1 - \beta\lambda} - \frac{\varepsilon\gamma\alpha_2}{[\lambda(1 - \gamma\varepsilon) + \gamma\varepsilon]} = \frac{\lambda\alpha_2(1 - \gamma\varepsilon) + \beta\lambda\varepsilon\gamma\alpha_2}{(1 - \beta\lambda)[\lambda(1 - \gamma\varepsilon) + \gamma\varepsilon]} > 0,$$

noting that $0 < \beta < 1$ and $0 \leqq \lambda \leqq 1$.

Chapter 7

This chapter is based to a large extent on "International Transmission of Stagflation under Fixed and Flexible Exchange Rates," *Journal of Political Economy* 86 (1978), which I wrote jointly with Makoto Sakurai, to whom I would like to express my gratitude. I would also like to thank Kazumasa Iwata, Michio Morishima, Kazuo Sato, Kazuo Ueda and Hirofumi Uzawa for their valuable comments and criticisms.

1. For a Keynesian analysis of the diffusion of inflation, see Uzawa 1971.

2. From now on most equations will be presented in pairs. Equations 7.1a and 7.1b, for example, will be referred to collectively as 7.1.

3. More precisely we can derive (7.8a) from a flow utility function of the CES type defined on consumption flows:

$$u = [\bar{\alpha} C_1^{-\delta} + (1 - \bar{\alpha}) C_2^{-\delta}]^{-1/\delta},$$

where $\delta = 1/\sigma - 1$.

4. Suppose that a representative individual maximizes $\int_0^\infty U(u, M/p) e^{-\rho t} dt$, given M_0 and subject to $p_1 C_1 + p_2 C_2 + \dot{M} = Y + T$, where $u = u(C_1, C_2)$ is a flow utility index defined on consumption flows, Y and T are nominal earned income and nominal transfers, and ρ is the rate of time preference. Then as we saw in the appendix to chapter 6, solving this optimization problem yields the expenditure function $C = vm$, where the consumption velocity v is an increasing function of $\rho + \pi$.

5. The stability condition of the linearized system is that the trace of the Jacobian be negative and the determinant be positive.

6. In the two-variable case local stability implies global stability by Rouché's theorem. In the case of more than two variables, however, the proof of global stability becomes difficult and the Liapunov function cannot be derived. Thus an analysis based on the following diagrams is incomplete because in such nonlinear systems we cannot exclude the possibility that exogenous disturbances will give rise to limit cycles or unstable paths. However, an intuitive explanation in terms of these phase diagrams is very helpful in achieving an understanding of the economic meaning of the interdependence of economic fluctuations under the two different systems.

7. The initial movement in $\dot{x}_1$ induces an additional upward shift in the $\dot{\pi}^* = 0$ locus and so forth. The stability analysis in the appendix to this chapter shows that both paths eventually return to the new equilibrium. $\dot{x}_2^*$ becomes positive before it settles at F so that the $\dot{\pi} = 0$ locus shifts below its initial position; however, this tendency is counterbalanced by the reciprocal effect of $\dot{x}_1$ on the other country.

8. The notation of sections 2 and 3 is consistent because under flexible exchange rates $R = R^* = 0$, $\dot{D} = \dot{M}$, and $\dot{D}^* = \dot{M}^*$.

9. ω is variable unless $\theta = \theta^*$. However, equation 7.34 holds approximately if $(\theta - \theta^*)$ is small in absolute value. We will therefore use equation 7.14' as an approximation even when $\theta \neq \theta^*$.

10. I did not give an explicit expression for the balance of payments between the two countries because the balance of payments depends not only on the growth rates of money supply but also on the actual levels of the money stock (Dornbusch 1973). Only when we can regard as constant the income velocity of money rather than the consumption velocity can we obtain explicit formulas for the balance of payments in terms of θ and θ^*. See chapters 5 and 8.

11. $a < 1$, $b^* < 1$, and $b > 0$, $a^* > 0$.

12. Under both regimes, the effect of $\dot{x}_2^*$ on the (temporary) equilibrium value of x_1 is expressed as

$$\frac{d\bar{x}_1}{d\dot{x}_2^*} = (1 + \delta)(1 - \alpha)\lambda/(\psi(x_1)).$$

On the other hand, the effect of $\dot{x}_2^*$ on the (temporary) equilibrium value of π is expressed as

$$\frac{d\bar{\pi}}{d\dot{x}_2^*} = (1 + \delta)(1 - \alpha)$$

under flexible exchange rates and as

$$\frac{d\bar{\pi}}{d\dot{x}_2^*} = 1 - \alpha$$

under fixed exchange rates.

Thus, the distance between Q and r is equal to $\delta(1 - \alpha)$, which is an increasing function of δ.

Chapter 8

I would like to thank Ryutaro Komiya and Takahiko Mutoh for their helpful comments.

1. Since the dollar is used as the numéraire, to be consistent, the exchange rate of country i's currency should be expressed in dollars per unit of country i's currency. However, I shall adhere to the common practice of defining q in terms of units of the home currency per dollar.

2. The balance sheet of the monetary sector may appear to be $M_i = q_i R_i + D_i$. But this is false because, under a managed float regime, one must treat capital gains or losses due to depreciation or appreciation of currency properly. Rigorously, the balance sheet must be expressed as $K_i + M_i = q_i R_i + D_i$, where K_i is the net worth of the monetary sector. Taking the time derivative, one obtains $\dot{K}_i + \dot{M}_i = \dot{q}_i R_i + q_i \dot{R}_i + \dot{D}_i$. In most countries, however, capital gains (or losses) due to changes in exchange rates are credited (or debited) as the change in the net worth of the monetary sector. Therefore $\dot{K}_i = \dot{q}_i R_i$, so that equation 8.1 holds. In other words capital gains or losses due to exchange rate fluctuations are not automatically reflected as an increase in the money supply.

3. However, if sterilization policy takes the form of relating D_i to R_i by some rule, then the analysis that follows must be modified. In a model similar to the one formulated here, De Grauwe (1975) shows that if monetary policy follows the rule $\dot{D}_i = \bar{D}_i - \gamma \dot{R}_i$ ($0 < \gamma < 1$), then the world economy would become unstable when the degree of sterilization (that is, the value of γ) is high.

4. If equation 8.8a is viewed as a linear transformation from z_i ($i = 2, \ldots, n$) to $\hat{q}_i$ ($i = 2, \ldots, n$), the transformation matrix is nonsingular and there is a one-to-one correspondence between the two.

5. The motives for choosing particular values of $\hat{q}_2$ are not endogenously derived from the model in the previous section. In the following discussion of short-run effects, such motives become more comprehensible.

Bibliography

In Japanese

Hamada, K. 1968, "Seichō-Seisaku to Kokusai-Kinyū (Growth policy and international finance)." In Z. Tsukui and Y. Murakami, eds., *Keizai-Seichō-Riron no Tenbō* (A survey of the theory of economic growth). Tokyo: Iwanami Shoten.

Hamada, K. 1971. "Kokusai-Tsūka-Seido no Sentaku to sono Rigai-Kankei (The choice of international monetary regimes and conflicts of national interest)." *Kikan Gendai Keizai*, no. 1.

Hamada K. 1981. "Kokusai-Kinyū no Seiji-Keizai-Gaku (The political economy of international monetary interdependence)." *Kinyū-Gakkai-Hōkoku* 51. Tokyo: Tōyōkeizai-Shinpōsha.

Mutoh, T., and T. Shizuki. 1980. *Gōriteki-Kitai to Manetarizumu* (Rational expectations and monetarism). Tokyo: Nihon Keizai Shinbunsha.

Nagatani, K. 1975. *Kahei-Keizai no Riron* (The theory of monetary economics). Tokyo: Sōbunsha.

Ōishi, S. 1974. *Ōoka Echizen no Kami Tadasuke* (The lord of Ōoka Echizen). Tokyo: Iwanami Shoten.

Okuguchi, K. 1971. *Kasen no Riron* (The theory of oligopoly). Tokyo: Sōbunsha.

Ono, Y. 1980. *Kasen-Shijō-Kōzō no Riron* (The theory of oligopolistic market structure). Tokyo University Press.

Ōwase, T. 1970. *Kasen-Keizai-Riron no Kōzō* (The structure of the economic theory of oligopoly). Tokyo: Shinhyōron.

Saitō, R. 1939. *Kokusai-Kahei-Seido no Kenkyū* (Studies of the international monetary system). Tokyo: Nihon-Hyōronsha.

Sakudō, Y. 1958. *Kinsei Nihon Kaheishi* (Monetary history of modern Japan). Tokyo: Atene Shinsho, Kōbundō.

Shimbo, H. 1972. "Hansatsu ni tsuite no Ichikōsatsu—Tokugawa-Jidai no Shinyō-Seido to no Kanren ni oite (A study on paper money in the Tokugawa Era)." *Annals of Economic Studies*, no. 19.

Suzuki, M. 1959. *Gēmu no Riron* (Game theory). Tokyo: Keisō Shobō.

Suzuki, M., ed. 1970. *Kyōsō-Shakai no Gēmu no Riron* (The game theory of a competitive society). Tokyo: Keisō Shobō.

Suzuki, M. 1981. *Gēmu no Riron no Kiso* (Foundations of game theory). Tokyo: Kyōritsu Shuppan.

Uzawa, H. 1978–1979. "Fukinkō Dōgaku Josetsu" (An introduction to disequilibrium dynamics), I–IV." *Kikan Gendai Keizai.*

Yamaguchi, K. 1966. *Hansatsu-Shi Kenkyū Josetsu* (Towards the history of local currency). Tokyo: Bank of Japan.

Yoshida, Y. 1965. *Kansūron* (Complex analysis). 2d ed. Tokyo: Iwanami Zensho.

In English

Ahlfors, L. V. 1966. *Complex Analysis.* 2d ed. New York: McGraw-Hill.

Aliber, R. Z. 1972. "Uncertainty, Currency Areas and the Exchange Rate System." *Economica* (November).

Aliber, R. Z. 1973. "National Preferences and the Scope for International Monetary Reform." Essays in International Finance, no. 101. Princeton: Princeton University Press.

Aliber, R. Z., ed. 1974. *National Monetary Policies and the International Financial System.* University of Chicago Press.

Aliber, R. Z., ed. 1977a. *The Political Economy of Monetary Reform.* London: Macmillan.

Aliber, R. Z. 1977b. "Monetary Rules and Monetary Reform." In Aliber 1977a.

Aubrey, H. G. 1969. "Behind the Veil of International Money." Essays in International Finance, no. 71. Princeton University Press.

Aumann, R. J. 1964, "Markets with a Continuum of Traders." *Econometrica* 32: 39–50.

Bacharach, M. 1976. *Economics and the Theory of Games.* London: Macmillan.

Bailey, M. J. 1956. "The Welfare Cost of Inflationary Finance." *Journal of Political Economy* 64: 93–110.

Bergsten, C. F., and L. B. Krause, eds. 1975. *World Politics and International Economics.* Washington, D.C.: Brookings Institution.

Berkovitz, L. 1971. "Lectures on Differential Games." In H. W. Kuhn and G. P. Szego, eds., *Differential Games and Related Topics*, Amsterdam: North-Holland.

Bertrand, J. 1883, "Review of 'Théorie mathématique de la richesse sociale and Recherches sur les Principes mathématiques de la théorie des richesses.'" *Journal des Savants*, pp. 499–508.

Brito, D. L., and J. D. Richardson. 1975. "Some Disequilibrium Dynamics of Exchange Rate Changes." *Journal of International Economics* 5: 1–13.

Brunner, K., and A. H. Meltzer, 1971. "The Use of Money: Money in the Theory of an Exchange Economy." *American Economic Review* 61.

Buchanan, J. M. 1964. "An Economic Theory of Clubs." *Economica* 32.

Buchanan, J. M. 1971. "Toward Analysis of Closed Behavioral Systems." In J. M. Buchanan and R. D. Tollison, eds., *Theory of Public Choice*. Ann Arbor: University of Michigan Press.

Clough, S. B. 1964. *The Economic History of Modern Italy*. New York: Columbia University Press.

Cohen, B. J. 1977. *Organizing the World's Money, The Political Economy of International Monetary Relations*. New York: Macmillan.

Cooper, R. N. 1968. *The Economics of Interdependence*. New York: McGraw-Hill.

Cooper, R. N. 1969. "Macroeconomic Policy Adjustment in Interdependent Economies." *Quarterly Journal of Economics* 83 (February).

Cooper, R. N. 1971. "Currency Devaluation in Developing Countries." Essays in International Finance, no. 86. Princeton University Press.

Cooper, R. N. 1972. "Eurodollars, Reserve Dollars, and Asymmetries in the International Monetary System." *Journal of International Economics* 2: 325–344.

Cooper, R. N. 1974. "Worldwide vs. Regional Integration: Is there an Optimal Size of the Integrated Area?" Paper presented at the Fourth World Congress of International Economic Association, August.

Cooper, R. N. 1975. "Prolegomena to the Choice of an International Monetary System." In Bergsten and Krause 1975.

Corden, W. M. 1972. "Monetary Integration." Essays in International Finance, no. 93. Princeton University Press.

Cournot, A. 1838. *Researches sur les principes mathématiques de la théorie des richesses*. Paris: Hachette.

De Grauwe, P. 1975. "The Interaction of Monetary Policies in a Group of European Countries." *Journal of International Economics* 5.

De Grauwe, P. 1977. "Monetary Interdependence among Major European Countries." In Aliber 1977a.

Dornbusch, R. 1973a. "Currency Depreciation, Hoarding, and Relative Prices." *Journal of Political Economy* 81: 893–915.

Dornbusch, R. 1973b. "Devaluation, Money, and Nontraded Goods." *American Economic Review* 63: 871–880.

Dornbusch, R., and M. Mussa. 1975. "Consumption, Real Balances and the Hoarding Function." *International Economic Review* 16: 415–421.

Dornbusch, R., and P. Krugman. 1976. "Flexible Rates in the Short-Run." Brookings Papers on Economic Activity, vol. 3. Washington, D.C.: Brookings Institution.

Edgeworth, F. 1881. *Mathematical Psychics.* London: Kegan Paul.

Ellis, H. S. 1934. *German Monetary Theory, 1905–1933.* Cambridge, Mass.: Harvard University Press.

Ethier, W. 1976. "Exchange Depreciation in the Adjustment Process." *Economic Record* 52: 443–451.

Fellner, W. 1949. *Competition among the Few.* New York: Knopf.

Fleming, J. M. 1962. "Domestic Financial Policies under Fixed and under Floating Exchange Rates." *IMF Staff Papers* 9 (November): 369–379.

Fleming, J. M. 1971. "On Exchange Rate Unification." *Economic Journal* 81 (September).

Frenkel, J. A., and H. G. Johnson, eds. 1976. *The Monetary Approach to the Balance of Payments.* London: George Allen and Unwin.

Friedman, B. M. 1979. "Optimal Expectations and the Extreme Information Assumptions of 'Rational Expectations' Macromodels." *Journal of Monetary Economics* 5: 23–41.

Friedman, J. W. 1977. *Oligopoly and the Theory of Games.* Amsterdam: North-Holland.

Friedman, M. 1968. "The Role of Monetary Policy." *American Economic Review* 58: 1–15.

Friedman, M. 1969. *The Optimum Quantity of Money.* Chicago: Adline.

Frohlich, N., J. A. Oppenheimer, and O. R. Young. 1971. *Political Leadership and Collective Goods.* Princeton University Press.

Gordon, R. J. 1977. "Interrelations between Domestic and International Theories of Inflation." In Aliber 1977a.

Gorman, W. M. 1958. "Tariffs, Retaliation and the Elasticity of Demand for Imports." *Review of Economic Studies* 25 (June).

Guggenheim, T. 1973. "Some Early Views on Monetary Integration." In Johnson and Swoboda 1973.

Hamada, K. 1966. "Strategic Aspects of the Taxation of Foreign Investment Income." *Quarterly Journal of Economics* 80 (August): 361–375.

Hamada, K. 1974. "Alternative Exchange Rate Systems and the Interdependence of Monetary Policies." In Aliber 1974.

Hamada, K. 1976. "A Strategic Analysis of Monetary Interdependence." *Journal of Political Economy* (August): 677–700.

Hamada, K. 1976. "The Terms of Trade and Imported Stagflation under Alternative Exchange Rate Regimes: A Small Country Case." Mimeographed.

Hamada, K. 1977. "On the Political Economy of Monetary Integration: A Public Economics Approach." In Aliber 1977a.

Hamada, K. 1979. "Macroeconomic Strategy and Coordination under Alternative Exchange Rates." In R. Dornbusch and J. Frenkel, eds., *International Economic Policy*. Baltimore: Johns Hopkins University Press.

Hamada, K. 1979. "A Game-Theoretic Approach to International Monetary Confrontations." In S. J. Brams, A. Schotter, and G. Schwödiauer, eds., *Applied Game Theory*. Vienna: Institute for Advanced Studies.

Hamada, K. 1979. "On the Coordination of Monetary Policies in a Monetary Union." Paper presented at the Colloquium on New Economic Approaches to the Study of International Integration, European University Institute.

Hamada, K., and K. Ueda. 1977. "Random Walks and the Theory of the Optimal International Reserves." *Economic Journal* 87 (December).

Hamada, K., and M. Sakurai. 1978. "International Transmission of Stagflation under Fixed and Flexible Exchange Rates." *Journal of Political Economy*

Helliwell, J., and R. McRae. 1977. "The Interdependence of Monetary, Debt and Fiscal Policies in an International Setting." In Aliber 1977a.

Henderson, W. O. 1939. *The Zollverein*. Cambridge University Press.

Henderson, J. M. 1975. "Asymmetry in Quasi-Fixed Exchange-Rate System." *Journal of International Economics* 5 (May): 167–187.

Hicks, J. R. 1974. *The Crisis in Keynesian Economics*. Oxford: Basil Blackwell.

Ingram, J. C. 1973. "The Case for European Monetary Integration." Essays in International Finance, no. 98. Princeton University Press.

Johnson, H. G. 1953. "Optimum Tariffs and Retaliation." *Review of Economic Studies* 21.

Johnson, H. G. 1972a. "The Monetary Approach to Balance-of-Payments Theory." *Journal of Financial and Quantitative Analysis* (March): 1555–1572.

Johnson, H. G. 1972b. "Political Economy Aspects of International Monetary Reform." *Journal of International Economics* 2.

Johnson, H. G., and A. K. Swoboda, eds. 1973. *The Economics of Common Currencies*. London: George Allen & Unwin.

Keynes, J. M. 1936. *The General Theory of Money, Interest and Employment*. London: Macmillan.

Keynes, J. M. 1947. "The International Monetary Fund." In S. E. Harris, ed., *The New Economics: Keynes' Influence on Theory and Public Policy*. London: Dennis Dobson.

Kindleberger, C. P. 1970. *Power and Money*. New York: Basic Books.

Komiya, R. 1966. "Monetary Assumptions, Currency Depreciation, and the Balance of Trade." *Economic Studies Quarterly* 17: 9–23.

Komiya, R. 1969. "Economic Growth and the Balance of Payments: A Monetary Approach." *Journal of Political Economy* 77.

Krämer, H. R. 1971. "Experience with Historical Monetary Unions." In H. Giersch, ed., *Integration durch Währungsunion*. Mohr, Tübingen: Institute für Weltwirtschaft an der Universität Kiel.

Kruger, A. O. 1977. "Current Account Targets and Managed Floating." In Aliber 1977a.

Kuga, K. 1973. "Tariff Retaliation and Policy Equilibrium." *Journal of International Economics* (November).

Laffer, A. B. 1973. "Two Arguments for Fixed Rates." In Johnson and Swoboda 1973.

Laursen, S., and S. A. Metzler. 1950. "Flexible Exchange Rates and the Theory of Employment." *Review of Economics and Statistics* 32 (November): 281–299.

Leijonhufvud, A. 1968. *On Keynesian Economics and the Economics of Keynes.* New York: Oxford University Press.

Lucas, R. E. 1972. "Expectations and the Neutrality of Money." *Journal of Economic Theory* 4 (April).

Luce, D., and H. Raiffa. 1957. *Games and Decisions.* New York: John Wiley.

McKinnon, R. I. 1963. "Optimum Currency Areas." *American Economic Review* 53: 712–724.

McKinnon, R. I. 1974. "A Tripartite Agreement or a Limping Dollar Standard?" Essays in International Finance, no. 106. Princeton University Press.

Meade, J. E. 1951. *The Theory of International Economic Policy.* Vol. 1: *The Balance of Payments.* London: Oxford University Press.

Mundell, R. A. 1961. "Optimum Currency Areas." *American Economic Review* 51: 657–664.

Mundell, R. A. 1962. "The Appropriate Use of Monetary and Fiscal Policy under Fixed Exchange Rates." *IMF Staff Papers* 9 (March).

Mundell, R. A. 1963. "Capital Mobility and Stabilisation Policy under Fixed and Flexible Exchange Rates." *Canadian Journal of Economics and Political Science* 29 (November): 475–485.

Mundell, R. E. 1968. *International Economics.* New York: Macmillan.

Mundell, R. E. 1971. *Monetary Theory: Inflation, Interest, Growth in the World Economy.* Pacific Palisades, Calif.: Goodyear.

Mundell, R. E. 1973. "Uncommon Arguments for Common Currencies." In Johnson and Swoboda 1973.

Mundell, R. E., and A. K. Swoboda, eds. 1968. *Monetary Problems of the International Economy.* University of Chicago Press.

Mussa, M. 1976. "The Exchange Rates, the Balance of Payments and Monetary and Fiscal Policy under a Regime of Controlled Floating." *Scandinavian Journal of Economics* 17: 229–249.

Neumann, J. von, and O. Morgenstern. 1944. *Theory of Games and Economic Behaviour*. Princeton University Press.

Negishi, T. 1972. *General Equilibrium Theory and International Trade*. Amsterdam: North-Holland.

Negishi, T. 1979. *Microeconomic Foundations of Keynesian Macroeconomics*. Amsterdam: North-Holland.

Niehans, J. 1968. "Monetary and Fiscal Policies in Open Economies under Fixed Exchange Rates: An Optimizing Approach." *Journal of Political Economy* 76 (July–August): 893–943.

Nielsen, A. 1933. "Monetary Union." *Encyclopedia of Social Science*, vol. 10. New York: Macmillan.

Nye, J. S. 1973. "The Political Context." In L. B. Krause and W. S. Salant, eds., *European Monetary Unification and its Meaning to the United States*. Washington, D.C.: Brookings Institution.

Ohyama, M. 1976. "Macro- and Micro-economic Theories: A Synthesis." Paper presented at the TCER Conference in Zushi, Japan.

Olech, C. 1963. "On the Global Stability of an Autonomous System on the Plane." In J. P. Lassalle and J. B. Diaz, eds., *Contribution to Differential Equations*, Vol. I. New York: Wiley.

Olson, M., Jr. 1965. *The Logic of Collective Action: Public Goods and Theory of Groups*. Harvard Economic Studies, vol. 124. Cambridge: Harvard University Press.

Olson, M., Jr., and R. Zeckhauser. 1966. "An Economic Theory of Alliances." *Review of Economics and Statistics* 43.

Parkin, N. 1977. "World Inflation, International Relative Price and Monetary Equilibrium under Fixed Exchange Rates." In Aliber 1977a.

Phelps, E. S. 1965. "Anticipated Inflation and Economic Welfare." *Journal of Political Economy* 73: 1–13.

Phelps, E. S. 1967. "Phillips Curves, Expectations of Inflation and Optimal Unemployment over Time." *Economica* 34 (August): 254–281.

Riker, W. H., and P. C. Ordeshook. 1973. *An Introduction to Positive Political Theory*. Englewood Cliffs, N. J.: Prentice-Hall.

Russett, B. M., ed. 1968. *Economic Theory of International Politics*. Chicago: Markham.

Sargent, T. J., and N. Wallace. 1975. "Rational Expectations, the Optimal Monetary Instrument and the Optimal Money Supply Rule." *Journal of Political Economy* 83 (April).

Samuelson, P. A. 1947. *Foundations of Economic Analysis*. Cambridge: Harvard University Press.

Samuelson, P. A. 1967. *Economics: An Introductory Analysis.* 7th ed. New York: McGraw-Hill.

Scarf, H. 1967, "The Core of an *N* Person Game." *Econometrica* 35: 50–69.

Scitovsky, T. 1941. "A Reconsideration of the Theory of Tariffs." *Review of Economic Studies* 9 (Summer).

Shinkai, Y. 1975. "A Model of Imported Inflation." *Journal of Political Economy* 83.

Simaan, M., and T. Takayama. 1974. "Dynamic Duopoly Game: Differential Game Theoretic Approach." Faculty Working Paper 155. Urbana-Champaign: University of Illinois.

Stackelberg, H. von. 1934. *Marktform und Gleichgewicht.* Vienna: Springer.

Stolper, G. 1967. *The German Economy: 1870 to the Present.* Translated by T. Stolper. New York. Harcourt, Brace & World.

Strange, S. 1976. "International Monetary Relations." In A. Shonfield, ed., *International Economic Relations of the Western World, 1959–1971,* vol. 2. London: Oxford.

Swoboda, A. K, and R. Dornbusch. 1973. "Adjustment, Policy, and Monetary Equilibrium in a Two-Country Model." In M. B. Connolly and A. K. Swoboda, eds. *International Trade and Money.* London: George Allen and Unwin.

Telser, L. G. 1972. *Competition, Collusion, and Game Theory.* Chicago: Aldine-Atherton.

Tinbergen, J. 1952. *On the Theory of Economic Policy.* Amsterdam: North-Holland.

Tsiang, S. C. 1975. "The Dynamics of International Capital Flows and Internal and External Balance." *Quarterly Journal of Economics* 89: 195–214.

Uzawa, H. 1971. "Diffusion of Inflationary Processes in a Dynamic Model of International Trade." *Economic Studies Quarterly* 22: 14–37.

Wagner, R. E. 1966. "Pressure Groups and Political Entrepreneurs: A Review Article." *Papers on Non-Market Decision Making* 1.

Willis, H. P. 1901. *A History of the Latin Monetary Union: A Study of International Monetary Action.* University of Chicago Press.

Yeager, L. B. 1968. *The International Monetary Mechanism.* New York: Holt, Rinehart and Winston.

Index